PORNOGRAPHY and the Criminal Justice System

PORNOGRAPHY
and the
Criminal Justice System

Carmen M. Cusack

CRC Press
Taylor & Francis Group
Boca Raton London New York

CRC Press is an imprint of the
Taylor & Francis Group, an **informa** business

CRC Press
Taylor & Francis Group
6000 Broken Sound Parkway NW, Suite 300
Boca Raton, FL 33487-2742

Printed on acid-free paper
Version Date: 20141002

International Standard Book Number-13: 978-1-4822-6001-4 (Paperback)

Visit the Taylor & Francis Web site at
http://www.taylorandfrancis.com

and the CRC Press Web site at
http://www.crcpress.com

Contents

Acknowledgments

Thanks to friends, family, colleagues, and CRC Press/Taylor & Francis Group for their support. Special thanks to Ralphe Cusack, Yeller Cusack, Whisper Cusack, and MEW, PC, and BC.

Introduction

Pornography and the Criminal Justice System explains and analyzes how the criminal justice system treats pornography. This book examines a variety of gray areas, especially the difficult task of defining "pornography." *Pornography and the Criminal Justice System* discusses why some erotic depictions are celebrated, but some are defined as a "crime." Several chapters discuss contemporary legal standards for proving pornography crimes and potential legal defenses for pornography offenses. *Pornography and the Criminal Justice System* introduces readers to investigation, evidence collection, witness testimony, expert testimony, interagency collaboration, and other aspects of policing and prosecuting pornography. Readers will learn about important cases, laws, and trends in society, on the Internet, and in the legal system.

Readers will also learn various arguments favoring and opposing decriminalization of all pornography, including hard-core pornography, synthetic pornography, and child pornography. Some arguments in favor of decriminalization include free speech and contemporary tolerance for nontraditional sexuality; arguments against decriminalization include maintenance of traditional morality and relationships between sex crimes and pornography. Political, religious, cultural, and historical perspectives are analyzed. Historical and current interpretations of First Amendment protections of free speech are discussed in detail. Arguments that traditional morality suppresses political minorities, for example, homosexuals and females, support decriminalization policies. Decriminalization analyses differentiate between victimless pornography production and harmful pornography production. No definitive research explains causal relationships between viewing pornography and harmful behavior.

Pornography and the Criminal Justice System discusses abundant research demonstrating patterns, correlations, disorder comorbidity, connections to human trafficking, and other findings about relationships between pornography, mental disorders, and crime. This book discusses therapeutic treatment for pornography addiction, pedophilia, and other disorders, as well as incarceration, chemical castration, sex offense registries, and other criminal justice responses to sex crime.

Pornography and the Criminal Justice System presents data about which population demographics are more likely to commit particular pornography offenses and why some of these proclivities may be generalizable to all populations who participate in online file sharing communities. International and foreign laws, policies, attitudes, and definitions of pornography are cited and compared to those of the United States. International and comparative research elucidates online pornography communities and data routing, U.S. policy rationales, U.S. federal offenses, global contexts for commercial sex industries, international interagency collaboration, and diverse approaches to pornography in criminal justice systems.

About the Author

Carmen M. Cusack *holds a BA cum laude* from Florida International University (FIU), a JD from FIU, and a PhD in Criminal Justice specializing in Behavioral Science from Nova Southeastern University. She has taught criminal justice at universities throughout Florida and Alaska. Her forthcoming publication is entitled *Animals and Criminal Justice* (Transaction Publishers, 2015). She is the editor of *Journal of Law and Social Deviance* and serves as an editor for *The Qualitative Report* and *Journal of Men's Studies.* She has published several research articles relevant to *Pornography and the Criminal Justice System.* Dr. Cusack once worked in the commercial pornography industry.

1 Philosophical and Jurisprudential Underpinnings

Overview

This chapter discusses links between philosophy, morality, law, and pornography and how society protects or criminalizes speech based on morality. Though some philosophies formidably argue about pornography, normative views tend to govern the criminal justice system's treatment of speech and pornographic depictions. Regulation of morality vacillates in context, but traditional understandings of morality are often inextricable from society's perceptions of normality. In the United States, First Amendment free speech rights prevent federal and state governments from criminalizing depictions of sex organs, sexual behavior, and sexuality. However, First Amendment free speech rights are not limitless. Some forms of speech are so offensive or harmful that society and the government are unwilling to protect them, which means that they may be banned. Various kinds of speech may be defined and treated differently under the law based on how offensive mainstream society perceives certain speech to be. Erotica, pornography, obscenity, child pornography, hard-core pornography, and other depictions are discussed in this chapter as speech. Producing, displaying, transmitting, selling, and possessing sexual depictions involve different speech acts. Sometimes various speech acts are treated more harshly than others, but at other times, various speech acts receive similar treatment under the law. Some laws criminalize certain offensive or harmful speech directly, but other laws weigh different factors. Factors may include subject matter, time and place, and audience. Law also controls which drawings, sounds, photos, videos, sculptures, or any other kinds of depictions may be produced and shared in public or private.

Nudity, Morality, and Pornography

Society's opinions about nudity shift depending on the time, place, person, and purpose of nudity (Leff, 1995; *Piarowski v. Illinois Community College District 515*, 1985). In context, a naked human form may represent or communicate nature, sex, defeat, confidence, aggression, insanity, purity, spirituality, immaturity, vulgarity, immorality, or other qualities. A viewer's perception of nudity may differ from a nude individual's intentions or perceptions of nudity.

For the most part, morality has been the basis for regulating public displays of nudity in the United States. Traditional Anglo Protestant moral standards shape secular laws. Though, as religious influence has waned over the past two centuries, standards have become more liberal. Now, most states only criminalize exposure of genitals and secondary genitals (e.g., buttocks and breasts). Proscriptions against exposure of genitals can be justified, to an extent, under health codes because bare genitals and buttocks can transmit diseases. However, public nudity is generally criminalized under morality statutes, that is, indecency laws. Exhibition of female breasts is criminalized in many jurisdictions (Cusack, 2012). A few jurisdictions require full coverage of breasts, whereas others require only partial coverage or pasties. Over the years, varying exceptions have been made for breast-feeding. In some states, nursing women must make attempts to cover themselves, whereas in other states, women can openly bare their breasts. Some states only permit mothers to nurse their infants, while some states allow any woman to feed toddlers or unspecified-aged children. Jurisdictional variations reflect localities' opinions about babies and breast-feeding, female sexuality, modesty, and justification of public nudity. Some jurisdictions have eliminated disparate nudity laws for women only after being successfully challenged on constitutional grounds. Some jurisdictions have never enacted disparate nudity laws, but these jurisdictions are the minority.

Nudity laws require bare minimum coverage, but norms also dictate modesty. Some people publicly uncover as much skin as legally possible, while many are guided by cultural norms. Secular norms may call for coverage of the torso and possibly the legs or arms depending on the person and the occasion. Yet, some non-Protestant religious norms may call for increased modesty. For example, some Muslims or Jews may cover their heads or hair, grow beards or wear veils, and cover their arms, legs, and necks. One rationale for dressing very modestly is that modest dress helps to control lust. Theoretically, following these dress codes reduces opportunities for immodest displays and incitement of lust in viewers. Some members of the Church of Latter-Day Saints may wear undergarments that act like coveralls. Reminiscent of undergarments from centuries past, their garments remind adherents to remain pure, and they also provide parameters that outer clothing must cover. Clothing that covers the undergarments, that is, thighs and upper portion of the arms, is considered to be modest.

Sensitivities may range broadly toward nudity and depictions of nudity. Localities may treat nudity, modesty, and pornography distinctly and may be influenced by particular norms, values, or religious traditions. These norms will set boundaries for public and private depictions and displays of nudity. Though pornography is normally viewed in private, at stores it is sold in public. Many pornography vendors will censor magazines depicting nudity on covers, yet art vendors dealing nude depictions may not. Certain nude sculptures, paintings, and photos may be considered to be art in the city of New York, but the same depictions may be considered to be smut in the Bible Belt. Conservative localities may view liberal jurisdictions' treatment of traditional morality as a form of social decay. Liberal jurisdictions may view conservative localities as living in the past rather than preserving moral constancy, tradition, and integrity.

At times, courts have sided with both liberal and conservative views of morality and nudity. In *Four Star Publications*, the court wrote, "The morals of America are besieged today by an unprincipled force which will spare no home or community in its quest for illicit profits" (*Four Star Publications, Inc. v. Erbe*, 1960). The court denounced obscene literature depicting adults in "films, decks of playing cards, photographs, 'comic' books, salacious magazines, paperbacked books and other pornographic products" (*Four Star Publications, Inc. v. Erbe*, 1960). The court vocalized its perception of society's sadness that malt shops, candy stores, drugstores, and other wholesome establishments began carrying material featuring nudity and sex acts. *Four Star Publications* described how previously "only the bawdiest of gathering places" made pornographic depictions available, but debasement of adults and teens has entered the mainstream. Suggesting that future generations will continue to let go of traditional morality, the court articulated how skepticism has infiltrated youths' views of morality. "While they are impressionable, American youths are remarkably wise in recognizing pseudo-piety in adults and the sham of a society which condones declining morality" (*Four Star Publications, Inc. v. Erbe*, 1960).

Courts have long linked crime and immorality (*Four Star Publications, Inc. v. Erbe*, 1960). Much like conservative Islamic or Jewish views that displaying flesh invites lust, the court in *Four Star Publications* asserted a relationship between obscenity and increased rape and sex crimes. This relationship continues to be researched, and it is discussed in Chapter 6. While a significant amount of literature demonstrates correlations between violent sex crimes and pornography, inverse correlations also exist. Typically, obscenity correlates with crime in studies. Yet, interpretation of *obscenity* varies between researchers and lawmakers, even when they use standard terms, for example, *hard-core pornography* and *sexually violent films.*

In *Lawrence v. Texas*, the U.S. Supreme Court held that the right to privacy guaranteed that adults could have nonharmful, consensual sex in private (*Lawrence v. Texas*, 2003). This meant that same-sex couples could no longer be prosecuted for engaging in private, consensual sodomy. *Lawrence*'s holding also meant that consensually produced depictions of sodomy between adults in private no longer evidenced the crime of sodomy. Nevertheless, *obscenity* is not exclusively defined by whether pornography depicts legal activities. Thus, depictions of legal sodomy may constitute obscenity. Many people still believe that sodomy is immoral, so depictions of sodomy may be offensive to some communities.

Some courts have protected hard-core depictions relating to a right to privacy. Moral codes set forth by the federal government have been argued to burden Americans' constitutional rights to produce and distribute hard-core pornography. This analysis departs from the traditional analysis of obscenity, which essentially asks whether the depictions are too morbid, offensive, and valueless to enter public life. Chapter 3 discusses these standards in detail.

The court in *Extreme Associates* used an analysis that justifies viewers' privacy rights to watch hard-core pornography (*U.S. v. Extreme Associates, Inc.*, 2005). That court has protected extreme pornographic images of gang rape and murder (*U.S. v. Extreme Associates, Inc.*, 2005). It extended the right to privacy analysis to pornography production and distribution. Its application of privacy laws to public transmission of obscenity was groundbreaking. That court's holding could have significantly expanded legal analysis of obscenity laws, but it has not been precedent setting because that judgment was overturned and charges against the defendants were reinstated. Though the defendants pleaded in that case and, thus, were not convicted on appeal, other courts continue to follow more traditional analyses. Chapter 16 discusses more details about *U.S. v. Extreme Associates, Inc.* (2005).

Feminism and Pornography

In the late 1960s, second-wave feminists began confronting society's escalating acceptance of mainstream and hard-core pornography (Dworkin, 1999). Some radical feminists felt that pornography production constituted civil rights violations because women were forced to work under unequal and illegal conditions. Claiming that pornography was produced by pimps, Katharine MacKinnon and Andrea Dworkin pioneered novel arguments against pornography. Their arguments garnered attention from legislative bodies throughout the United States. Though Dworkin and MacKinnon testified before Congress, legislation that they drafted was overly inclusive of lawful commercial activities, like advertisements. Dworkin and MacKinnon were unable to precisely define *pornography*. This is no surprise, since courts routinely struggle to define *pornography* on a case-by-case basis. Thus, Dworkin and MacKinnon's bid for regulation of women's working conditions failed to heighten protections against sexism and gendered abuse.

Since the 1980s, radical feminist ideology has permeated mainstream ideas about pornography, yet it has also lost some steam. Some critics argue that the definition of *hard-core pornography* has been pushed to further extremes in recent years because society has more tolerance of deviant sex acts. Content that was once considered to be deviant has become more mainstream. For example, depictions of gay male sodomy have become more common in mainstream pornography since the 1960s. Another example is that facial ejaculation and oral insemination may be considered mainstream in some jurisdictions (Salmon & Diamond, 2012). Radical feminists have argued, and continue to argue, that these depictions validate male supremacy by focusing on male pleasure but not female pleasure. In the radical feminist purview, ejaculation-centered depictions explicitly degrade women (Moore & Weissbein, 2010).

Hard-core pornography has often been described as antiwoman, but some women defend actors and viewers who exercise sexual agency. Sex-positive philosophy claims that all consensual sexual encounters that (1) do not harm participants and (2) benefit and pleasure participants are positive and acceptable sex acts. Some feminists have adopted sex-positive attitudes, and proponents of sex-positive philosophies may espouse feminist philosophies. There is some overlap between sex-positive philosophy and feminism but not radical feminism. Sex-positive philosophy departs significantly from radical feminism. On the surface, sex-positive notions of pornography resonate more than radical feminism with U.S. Supreme Court holdings (*Lawrence v. Texas*, 2003). Sex-positive philosophies are often used to defend sadomasochistic sex and pornography. Yet, U.S. Supreme Court holdings exclude harmful sex acts from the right to privacy, and explicit depictions of sadomasochism are not protected speech (*Lawrence v. Texas*, 2003). Thus, violent sex acts can be illegal in private and can amount to obscenity (Cusack, 2013).

Following the prominence of radical feminism in the 1970s, sex-positive and sex-radical lesbians in the 1980s and 1990s developed copious pornographic texts to challenge lesbian radical feminist proscriptions against pornography (Beirne, 2007). They confronted radical feminist theories about relationships between pornography and patriarchy. This era pornographized feminism and female pleasure-oriented sex. Sex-radical lesbian pornography led to increased depictions of lesbian sexuality, more mainstream media portrayals of lesbianism, and increased representations of lesbians as being feminine. Radical feminists were challenged by philosophical questions about normative society's rejection of pleasure-centered, lesbian pornography. Radical feminism continued to oppose pornographication because men mainly consume pornography.

Radical feminists claim that all pornography oppresses women because it depicts a dominant partner (Deckha, 2007). Radical feminists' position is known as "dominance feminism" because they argue that dominance is a masculine quality that has traditionally been used to oppress women, even if dominant partners give sexual pleasure to women. Dominance feminists believe that sadomasochism and bondage promote dominance, and it is usually the female who is subordinated. However, even when weaker females are allowed to dominate, sadomasochism promotes patriarchal attitudes, which are responsible for female subordination by males privately and politically. Sex-positive philosophies condone all sexual activity, including hard-core depictions of domination, as long as sex acts are voluntary. Dominance feminism claims that tolerance for voluntary sadomasochism results from internalized patriarch attitudes. Dominance feminism argues that women who elect to engage in sadomasochism and claim that they desire pain participate in painful sex acts to validate or overcome feelings of worthlessness or weakness. These feelings relate to internalized patriarchal attitudes.

Radical feminism continues to claim that pornography correlates with violence, but these theories have increasingly been challenged by social and behavioral science in recent decades. At least one study reported no consistent relationship between crime rate fluctuations and ease of access to violent pornography (Ferguson & Hartley, 2009). Generally, violent crime has decreased worldwide since the early 1970s, and access to hard-core and mainstream pornography has increased. On the basis of data, researchers have considered the possibility of an inverse relationship, yet they could not establish causality. As of yet, there is no definitive proof that pornography use lowers aggression or violence, though a few studies have concluded as much. An abundance of research links viewing violent pornography with perpetration of violent crimes and sex crimes. This is discussed in Chapter 6. Controversy continues about whether violent pornography directly causes abuse and subordination of women and whether radical feminists are justified in their attempts to increase government intervention and regulation.

Normal Sexuality

Adult sexuality is not fully biological. Over an individual's lifetime, sexuality and sexual activities occur on a spectrum between normal and deviant (Caudill, 1991). The meaning of "normal" may vary between traditional and contemporary social contexts. Traditional and contemporary understandings of "normal" shape the law. What was once considered to be a sex crime may later become mainstream, or lawful activities may be criminalized after some time (Schmeiser, 2008). "Normal" may partially be defined by gender, age, culture, class, and other factors. For example, in some traditional Latin American cultures, a cotillion signifies that a woman has reached maturation at fifteen years of age, and she may marry a man of any age. However, in Protestant Anglo American culture, a sweet sixteen party holds no such contemporary parallel. Though many sixteen year olds in the United States legally may withdraw from high school, work, and drive, most may not consent to marry or have sexual relationships with adults of any age.

Traditional members of society tend to segregate sexuality into two groups (Sutherland, 2003). The first group is considered to be normal. It is composed of natural, good, sanctioned, and blessed experiences. In the United States, traditional sex acts, including heterosexuality, marriage, monogamy, procreation, intragenerational relationships, noncommercial sex, and nonpornographic experiences, have nearly ubiquitously been considered to be good. The second group deviates from normal parameters. It is out of bounds, bad, unnatural, wrong, and abnormal. Homosexual, extramarital, promiscuous, lustful, commercial, masturbatory, casual, intergenerational, pornographic, public, and sadomasochistic sex acts are grouped together and considered to be bad.

Pornography is considered to be deviant, though social norms influence legal parameters for viewing, producing, and transmitting pornography. A person in the United States who is thought to be "normal" in public may privately engage in deviant pornographic practices or harbor unexpected attitudes or beliefs deviating from norms regarding pornography (Breger, 2005). Use of obscenity, by its definition, is not normative, and deviant depictions are not guaranteed protection under the law. For example, racially charged pornography has been found to be obscene, and community standards may not tolerate explicit culturally nuanced depictions. Racial and cultural themes do not automatically qualify as having redeeming political value. This is discussed further in Chapter 3. However, some pornography is protected, even though it is not considered to be normal. It is safe to say that protected images include traditional, inexplicit, and conservative depictions of sex.

Because sexuality is socially constructed, racial, cultural, and religious values influence norms (Morrison, Ryan, Fox, McDermott, & Morrison, 2008). Traditional European-American Christian norms dictate that sexual behavior and erotic thoughts are bad or wrong unless they have been prequalified as "normal" or are procreative. People who subscribe to these beliefs are likely to be unreceptive to social cues about sexuality. They may engage in more sexual austerity and behavior that is restricted by tradition. People who tend to be receptive to social cues about sexuality are more likely to encounter erotic depictions and be exposed to sexuality in the course of nonsexual activity. They think along sexual lines that are normative to sexually active people, and they are more likely to engage in sexual behavior.

Conservative sexual norms may be imparted by tradition, religion, and authority. Frequency of attending religious services may inversely relate to number of sex partners and age at which people begin engaging in sexual intercourse (Morrison et al., 2008). Religion may also influence whether people believe that viewing pornography is immoral. In addition to religion and family, a number of sources can help youth to formulate sexuality.

Information obtained from doctors, teachers, or authority figures will influence development of sexual practices (Arvidson, 1999). Acquired perceptions about virginity, self-image, and other moralized or socially constructed ideas will influence the contexts in which people consider intercourse to be "normal" and whether they will engage in it.

In 1994, U.S. Surgeon General Dr. Joycelyn Elders was forced to resign after claiming that masturbation was a normal part of human sexuality and that teaching schoolchildren to masturbate could reduce HIV (Bancroft, 1995; Jehl, 1994). In recent years, masturbation has not shifted from "bad" sexuality to "good" within traditional morality. Extramarital, adulterous, and promiscuous fantasies are still considered to be bad, and nonmarital sexual contact is bad. Social norms tend to be threatened by deviance. Some members of the good and normal group threaten deviants with punishment and shame (Senjo, 2010). The lure of belonging to the majority contrasts with rejection and humiliation inflicted on nonconformists. Thus, cost-benefit analyses demonstrate how and why status quos are maintained.

Despite gender roles, men and women in the same age group and culture may tend to share similar beliefs about sexual norms. For example, Canadian researchers surveyed 104 undergraduate students about their perceptions of normal sexuality (Morrison et al., 2008). Respondents assessed their positive and negative attitudes toward sexuality, religiousness, and sexual experience. Researchers hypothesized that males would be more likely than females to perceive a greater number of sex practices to be normal. Research hypotheses indicated that males and females would report sexual double standards, calling for men to normalize more sexual practices than women. One reason is that men are, or are perceived to be, more sexual because of double standards, thus they may be more likely to find that a variety of sexual practices are normal. It was hypothesized that lower acceptance of various sexual practices would correlate with higher religiousness. Researchers found that the sex of parties depicted in hypothetical scenarios influenced male and female respondents' perceptions of norms. Perceived parameters of normal and abnormal behavior were consistent among respondents. Both men and women reported that men who are disinterested in sex are considered to be abnormal, but disinterested women are considered to be less abnormal. Men who submit to sexual dominance or fantasize about homosexual sex acts are perceived to be abnormal. Perhaps this is because "gay sexuality, according to [a] common understanding, is all-encompassing, obsessive, and completely divorced from love, long-term relationships, and family structure—the civilizing influences that keep 'normal' sexuality under control" (Fajer, 1992, p. 514). The study suggests that Canadian students share cultural norms and adopted gender roles evenly between genders (Morrison et al., 2008).

Communities may deeply share perceptions of sexual norms and prurience. American courts' findings of obscenity rely on community standards' definitions of *obscenity*. Applying Morrison et al.'s (2008) findings to prosecution of obscenity in local communities, criminal justice members and jurors may not be influenced by conventions within their own genders as much as expectations for actors' genders. Criminal justice system members may believe that scenes are excessively deviant depending on local standards for performers' genders, that is, transsexuals, men, women, heterosexuals, homosexuals, or bisexuals.

Cultural normalcy is relative. Brazilian researchers found that adolescent girls' attitudes toward female same-sex kissing are very accepting (Gross, 2007). This sample was younger than the Canadian sample, and conservative morality may develop with age. In the Brazilian study, 78% of respondents reported fantasies of same-sex kissing after seeing lesbians kissing in person at nightclubs. Perhaps attendance of teens at nightclubs indicates lower religiosity and, thus, increased likelihood for sexual deviance or experience. The effect of witnessing male same-sex encounters is unknown, and girls' opinions about male same-sex kissing are unknown. Approximately one-quarter of Brazilian female respondents reported that they fantasized about same-sex kissing after observing a depiction of a lesbian relationship on a prime-time soap opera. The potential applicability of these findings to relationships between sexuality and viewing pornography are evident.

Harm Principle

The Harm Principle states that impingements on freedom are valid only when they protect victims from harm; thus, the First Amendment would protect all nonharmful speech. Therefore, this principle may be used to support decriminalization of all nonharmful pornography production and transmission. Pornography would be considered to be victimless when it is voluntarily produced and transmitted. In some senses, relying on the Harm Principle to regulate pornography could increase protection for performers (Cusack, 2011). Current law does not adequately censor prurient depictions of forced sex acts if harm is not depicted. Most jurisdictions may likely protect genuine depictions of people being forced to perform if depictions are not sexually violent. Chapter 7 discusses how and why forced production is illegal. However, nonviolent depictions are typically uncensored. Thus, viewers and producers are not deterred because regulations do not affect supply and demand.

The Harm Principle is often discussed in the context of sex work, for example, legalization of voluntary and victimless prostitution (Simowitz, 2013). The argument is that if prostitution is voluntary, then it is harmless. Criminalizing prostitution lowers protections for sex workers who cannot rely on law enforcement for safety. Thus, certain harms may be inflamed by criminalization. This argument directly applies to production of pornography involving prostitutes. Sexually transmitted diseases (STDs) have been cited as an important reason for criminalizing sex work under the Harm Principle. However, STD prevention is not a rational reason for differentiating between obscenity and pornography. STD transmission rates are likely to be similar during production of obscenity and pornography. Furthermore, sharing pornographic materials does not perpetuate disease. Thus, this reasoning cannot be applied in favor of criminalization of obscenity.

A popular argument used to support criminalization is that obscenity should not be legalized because it harms society. Obscenity creates social harms evident in secondary effects. "Secondary effects" describes increased crime in neighborhoods offering adult entertainment. Chapter 13 also discusses secondary effects. Secondary effects would not necessarily be reduced if the Harm Principle guided pornography laws. However, displaying legal pornography also creates secondary effects. Studies do not sufficiently demonstrate that publicly displaying obscenity would worsen secondary effects.

Since the 1960s, it has been argued that obscenity is harmful because it correlates with sex crimes and violent crimes. Courts have acknowledged and questioned this assertion and supporting studies (*Mapp v. Ohio*, 1961). In addition to a well-developed body of theoretical literature that questions whether pornography correlates with sex crime or violence, one study found that immediately after pornography use, hostility or aggression may be lower (Mancini, Reckdenwald, & Beauregard, 2012). Researchers found that victims of sexual abuse were injured less when offenders had used pornography immediately before committing crimes. Viewers' use of pornography or obscenity may directly reduce harm.

Numerous factors may impact how viewing pornography or obscenity correlates with violent sex crimes. Some of these factors are (1) viewer's age, (2) relationship between the parties, (3) offender's past sexual trauma and accompanying coping skills, (4) sexual arousal to obscenity, and (5) severity of violence (Corley & Hook, 2012; Latzman, Viljoen, Scalora, & Ullman, 2011; Mancini et al., 2012; Surjadi, Bullens, van Horn, & Bogaerts, 2010). These factors may support the idea that if harm is created by viewing obscenity, then it is not predictable or directly related. Harm could relate to several factors, many of which the government cannot control, for example, offenders' ages or past trauma. Though the government could potentially reduce harms by criminalizing obscenity, the results of their efforts may be too uncertain to justify total bans on speech content. Policies intending to reduce violence or sex crimes should not criminalize harmless speech that does not cause crime. The Constitution requires speech restrictions to be narrowly tailored to proscribe the smallest amount of speech necessary to accomplish the government's goal. If reduction of violent crime and sex crime is the basis for outlawing obscenity, then actual harms should be better documented to help create narrowly tailored obscenity laws (*Paroline v. U.S.*, 2014).

Conclusion

Pornography is not a static term. Significant theoretical debate about the term has influenced social conscience and criminal justice policies. As society continues to rework its understanding of "normal" sexuality, nudity, sexual consent, and deviance, several criminal justice approaches may change, including (1) definitions of "obscenity," (2) responses to the term, and (3) legal treatment of erotic depictions.

References

Arvidson, C. R. (1999). The adolescent gynecologic exam. *Pediatric Nursing, 25*(1), 71–74.

Bancroft, J. (1995, July 8). The facts of life: The creation of sexual knowledge in Britain, 1650–1950. *British Medical Journal, 310*(6997), 137.

Beirne, R. (2007). Dirty lesbian pictures: Art and pornography in *The L Word. Critical Studies in Television, 2*(1), 90–101.

Breger, C. (2005). Feminine masculinities: Scientific and literary representations of "female inversion" at the turn of the twentieth century. *Journal of the History of Sexuality, 14*(1–2), 76–106.

Caudill, D. S. (1991). Freud and critical legal studies: Contours of a radical socio-legal psychoanalysis. *Indiana Law Journal, 66*(3), 651–697.

Corley, M. D., & Hook, J. N. (2012). Women, female sex and love addicts, and use of the Internet. *Sexual Addiction and Compulsivity, 19*, 53–76.

Cusack, C. M. (2011). Busting patriarchal booby traps: Why feminists fear minor distinctions in child porn cases, an analysis of social deviance with in gender, family, or the home (etudes 4). *Southern University Law Review, 39*, 43–70.

Cusack, C. M. (2012). Boob laws: An analysis of social deviance within gender, family, or the home (etudes 2). *Women's Rights Law Reporter, 33*, 197–217.

Cusack, C. M. (2013). Obscene squirting: If the government thinks it's urine, then they've got another thing coming. *Texas Journal of Women and the Law, 22*, 45–69.

Deckha, M. (2007). Pain, pleasure, and consenting women: Exploring feminist responses to s/m and its legal regulation in Canada through Jelinek's the piano teacher. *Harvard Journal of Law and Gender, 30*, 425–459.

Dworkin, A. (1999). *Pornography and grief, violence and its alternatives.* New York: St. Martin's Press.

Fajer, M. A. (1992). Can two real men eat quiche together? Storytelling, gender-role stereotypes, and legal protection for lesbians and gay men. *University of Miami Law Review, 46*, 511–655.

Ferguson, C. J., & Hartley, R. D. (2009). The pleasure is momentary … the expense damnable? The influence of pornography and rape and sexual assault. *Aggression and Violent Behavior, 14*(5), 323–329.

Four Star Publications, Inc. v. Erbe, 181 F. Supp. 483, 485 (S.D. Iowa 1960).

Gross, K. (2007). Girls view same-sex kissing as normal. *Youth Studies Australia, 26*(2), 9.

Jehl, D. (1994, December 10). Surgeon general forced to resign by White House. *New York Times*. Retrieved from http://www.nytimes.com/1994/12/10/us/surgeon-general-forced-to-resign-by-white-house.html

Latzman, N. E., Viljoen, J. L., Scalora, M. J., & Ullman, D. (2011). Sexual offending in adolescence: A comparison of sibling offenders and nonsibling offenders across domains of risk and treatment need. *Journal of Child Sexual Abuse, 20*(3), 245–263.

Lawrence v. Texas, 539 U.S. 558 (2003).

Leff, T. P. (1995). Implications of government funding to the arts in the aftermath of *Rust v. Sullivan. American University Law Review, 45*, 353.

Mancini, C., Reckdenwald, A., & Beauregard, E. (2012). Pornographic exposure over the life course and the severity of sexual offenses: Imitation and cathartic effects. *Journal of Criminal Justice, 40*(1), 21–30.

Mapp v. Ohio, 367 U.S. 643 (1961).

Moore, L. J., & Weissbein, J. (2010). Cocktail parties: Fetishizing semen in pornography beyond bukkake. In K. Boyle (Ed.), *Everyday pornography* (pp. 77–89). New York: Routledge/Taylor & Francis Group.

Morrison, T. G., Ryan, T. A., Fox, L., McDermott, D. T., & Morrison, M. A. (2008). Canadian university students' perceptions of the practices that constitute "normal" sexuality for men and women. *The Canadian Journal of Human Sexuality, 17*(4), 161–171.

Paroline v. U.S., 2014 U.S. LEXIS 2936 (2014).

Piarowski v. Illinois Community College District 515, 759 F.2d 625 (7th Cir. 1985).

Salmon, C., & Diamond, A. (2012). Evolutionary perspectives on the content analysis of heterosexual and homosexual pornography. *Journal of Social, Evolutionary, and Cultural Psychology, 6*(2), 193–202.

Schmeiser, S. R. (2008). The ungovernable citizen: Psychopathy, sexuality, and the rise of medico-legal reasoning. *Yale Journal of the Law and the Humanities, 20*(2), 163–240.

Senjo, S. R. (2010). Homophobia: An Australian history. *Electronic Journal of Human Sexuality, 13*.

Simowitz, A. D. (2013). How criminal law shapes institutional structures: A case study of American prostitution. *American Criminal Law Review, 50*(1), 417.

Surjadi, B., Bullens, R., van Horn, J., & Bogaerts, S. (2010). Internet offending: Sexual and non-sexual functions within a Dutch sample. *Journal of Sexual Aggression, 16*(1), 47–58.

Sutherland, K. (2003). From jailbird to jailbait: Age of consent laws and the construction of teenage sexualities. *William and Mary Journal of Women and the Law, 9*, 313–349.

U.S. v. Extreme Associates, Inc., 2005 WL 121749 (W.D.Pa. Jan 20, 2005) (NO. CRIM.03-0203); 431 F.3d 150 (3d Cir. 2005).

Pornography in the U.S. Criminal Justice System

2

Overview

Binding, bright line rules in the U.S. criminal justice system are the result of centuries of cases, codes, and legal debate. Generally, First Amendment rights are interpreted in case law and statutory schemes to protect compelling and important state interests while limiting infringements on speech as much as possible. Definitions of *pornography* are virtually irrelevant to the criminal justice system because pornography is protected speech. However, protection of pornography is not limitless. Protections have often been defined by prosecution of obscenity, which is unprotected speech. Legality of pornography may be determined on a case-by-case basis, or depictions may be classified per se as unprotected speech, that is, sadomasochism and excretory pornography.

Defining Pornography

When the First Amendment was amended to the Constitution in 1791, the framers did not likely contemplate that every type of pornographic depiction would be legalized or protected. "In light of this history, it is apparent that the unconditional phrasing of the First Amendment was not intended to protect every utterance" (*Four Star Publications, Inc. v. Erbe*, 1960). Pornography has traditionally been protected speech unless it is depraved. Courts use a test to determine whether allegedly obscene material is protected. In *Roth v. U.S.* (1957), the Court articulated the first part of the contemporary test used to distinguish between legal pornography and illegal pornography. The full test was first articulated in *Miller v. California* (1973), which is discussed in great detail in Chapter 3. The first part of the test, used in *Roth*, determines whether the dominant theme in a depiction appeals to prurient interests in a manner that is offensive to the average person in the local community (*Roth v. U.S.*, 1957). In addition to that question, *Miller* asks whether offensive works pruriently depicting sex possess redeeming value; value must be more than *de minimis*. That consideration was added in 1973. Nevertheless, constitutional questions raised by obscenity trials are valuable.

First Amendment case law demonstrates that obscenity does not inherently contain redeeming value.

The First Amendment is supposed to protect all speech that is not unprotected. Unprotected speech may be criminalized. However, some speech may be persecuted even though it ought to be protected under the Constitution. Cambria List is a collection of pornographic themes that some industry insiders and members of the criminal justice system believe may be susceptible to prosecution (Abowitz, 2013). Cambria List includes traditionally obscene depictions. For example, traditionally obscene depictions may include physical violence and sexual assault (Farley, 2006). However, Cambria List includes somewhat common themes. Pornography is rife with material included on the list, but these topics allegedly could offend an average member of a community, for example, government agents and jurors. The list includes interracial sex, homosexual sex, and transsexual sex (Abowitz, 2013). The government would not articulate bigotry as the reason for prosecution; however, under the *Miller* test, the reasons why depictions are offensive do not need to be specified. The government is not required to specify why depictions are offensive if it can prove that depictions violate the law.

The term *child pornography* mischaracterizes the word *pornography*. Child pornography is not pornography. Child pornography is a specific class of speech that per se is banned. Pornography may be held to be obscene, or it may be protected. Thus, child pornography is not pornography, and it would be better titled "child exploitation material" or "depictions of child sex abuse." Sometimes, synthetic images that depict child abuse or exploitation do not amount to the legal definition of child pornography, but they are still unprotected when they qualify as obscenity. A common example of this may be explicit cartoons. Cartoon depictions may qualify as pornography, obscenity, and material harmful to minors, but not child pornography. Protected, mainstream pornography may be charged as obscenity if it is shown to minors with the intent to corrupt minors. Child pornography is discussed in further detail in Chapter 3 and Chapter 5.

First Amendment

The First Amendment protects free speech. "Speech" includes gestures, performance, language, drawings, photographs, and all forms of intentional communication. Nonverbal speech is protected under the First Amendment if it intends to communicate a particularized message that is likely to be understood by the average member of the public (*U.S. v. O'Brien*, 1968). Within a single pornography video, for example, several speech interests are protected. Some of the speech interests involved may include the director's vision, the actors' performances, a distributor's promotion of the work, and, potentially, the viewer's endorsement of the work by receiving the work. As long as the speech act is lawful, then the government is not concerned about the content of the message. For example, if transmitting pornography is legal, then the government is not concerned about whether transmitting a depiction actually did or intended to endorse the film. However, if the government has a compelling interest in eliminating from society the offense and depravity created by a message, then speech will not be protected irrespective of whether transmitting a film symbolically communicates an endorsement (*Chaplinsky v. State of New Hampshire*, 1942).

Judicially made standards of review for free speech and *stare decisis* protect lawful pornography but not unlawful pornography, that is, obscenity and child pornography. The court's standard of review requires strict scrutiny of most laws that impinge on free speech, including obscenity laws and child pornography laws (Liu, 2007; *New York v. Ferber*, 1982). Strict scrutiny means that the government must prove a compelling interest is at stake and that laws restricting free speech are necessary to achieve that interest. However, the government must also show that laws are so narrowly tailored that they accomplish the government's interest without censoring more speech than necessary. For example, the government may require pornography actors to use condoms to prevent high incidence of HIV and sexually transmitted disease (STD) transmission on pornography sets. Though this requirement may censor speech, the government's interest in health is compelling. In light of the fact that regular testing among actors has not eliminated HIV transmission on film sets, it seems as if there may be no less restrictive means for significantly reducing incidents of HIV transmission. Health codes and filming requirements must impinge on speech. This is discussed further in Chapter 6.

Certain speech acts can be regulated to maintain order in society. Though content of protected speech may not be abridged, the government may regulate time, place, and manner in which public speech occurs. For example, the government may require pornographers to seek a permit to film an inexplicit depiction during daylight hours at a public park (*Ward v. Rock Against Racism*, 1989). As long as public activities do not break the law (e.g., decency laws), then the government will only regulate the time, place, and manner. These regulations sometimes receive lower scrutiny (i.e., intermediate scrutiny), because they do not attack content but regulate public behavior to maintain order. Civil disobedience that communicates opposition to censorship or the government is not protected by the First Amendment.

Right to privacy is separate from a right to free speech. Rights to privacy emanate from substantive due process under the Fourteenth or Fifth Amendments, whereas the First Amendment protects free speech rights.

However, right to privacy protects simple possession of obscenity (*Stanley v. Georgia*, 1969). This right should not be construed to extend to additional acts, for example, buying obscenity online, intending to distribute obscenity, producing obscenity, or possessing child pornography.

One underdeveloped area of the law is whether inviting members of the public to view obscenity in one's home is protected by right to privacy. Potentially, differences may exist between protected in-home private activities or unprotected in-home public activities. For example, viewing obscenity in a bedroom during sex may be protected even though obscenity is displayed to a third party. The right to privacy protects private sex acts (*Lawrence v. Texas*, 2003). That right does not extend to unlawful, nonconsensual, or harmful sex acts. Viewing obscenity in one's home is protected under the same right, but an amalgamation of these doctrines may or may not create a distinct right to display obscenity in one's home during sex. Right to privacy extends to third parties in places where third parties hold a reasonable expectation of privacy. If a third party is merely guest within a home, than the third party may not possess an expectation of privacy. *Stare decisis* has not guaranteed a right to view obscenity during sex in a place where one holds no reasonable expectation of privacy. Inviting members of the public into one's home lowers expectations of privacy in that area of the home. Holding a screening for an obscene film in a living room likely merits neither free speech protection nor substantive due process protection of privacy.

Black Letter Laws

"Black Letter law" describes law that currently governs. Law that has been overruled or is no longer applicable is not Black Letter law. The term is most frequently used to describe U.S. Supreme Court rulings that are directly on point. Black Letter law may not always seem to draw a bright line. Sometimes, we must piece together Black Letter law to fully understand how the government deals with legal issues.

Pornography is erotic material protected by the First Amendment. The law articulates definitional and practical differences between profanity, public indecency, obscenity, child pornography, and pornography. Each of those kinds of speech is regulated or criminalized. Context will often factor into whether speech is protected or unprotected under Black Letter law. Courts may consider degree of explicitness, privacy, and audience. Kinds of speech may overlap, and a single incident could potentially be analyzed using several binding cases. Lower courts must correctly decide which Black Letter laws should be applied, or their decisions may be overturned.

Adult pornography is legal, but child pornography is not. However, the First Amendment protects adults' rights to label themselves as "young" or "teens" in erotic depictions (*Ashcroft v. Free Speech Coalition*, 2002; *New York v. Ferber*, 1982). Black Letter free speech law, arising from a child pornography case, protects adult actors' right to simulate or suggest that they are minor actors. This is discussed further in Chapter 5. Yet, these same depictions may be prosecuted as obscenity. Any prurient material that violates community norms and lacks redeeming social value may be criminalized. There is no right for teens to pretend to be adults in pornography. Typically, pornographers and teens may be held liable for commercially producing pornography of minors. Pornographers may be strictly liable for falling below the standard of care required to verify actors' ages (Fla. Stat. § 847.011(c)(d), 2012). In some jurisdictions, a bona fide belief may serve as a defense to distribution. Minor actors in nonpornographic films cannot be sexually exploited during filming or be portrayed to have engaged in explicit sex acts, even if no such acts occurred during filming. Films explicitly depicting scenes in which minors appear to be engaged in sex are obscene. Adults may not transmit pornography to minors.

Protected speech may become indecent, profane, or obscene if it is accessible to minors or distributed to minors (*Ginsberg v. New York*, 1968). Minors do not have the same privacy rights or speech rights as adults. In most jurisdictions, minors may not view pornography. Though Black Letter law protects parents' fundamental right to raise their children, introducing children to erotica is likely proscribed and generally excluded from the right to raise one's children in some jurisdictions. Parents may provide minors with erotica but not obscenity. The government possesses power to protect traditional family values. This is discussed further in Chapter 1, Chapter 5, and Chapter 12.

The Federal Communications Commission (FCC) is charged with enforcing federal communication laws. Indecent programming and foul language are prohibited at certain times, but obscenity is always prohibited on television and radio. The FCC uses the *Miller* test to determine whether obscenity has been broadcasted (*Miller v. California*, 1973). Broadcasts depicting sexual or excretory organs or functions in a patently offensive manner are indecent. Indecency presents a lower level of offense than obscenity. Indecent material receives First Amendment protection, but is restricted between the hours of 6 a.m. and 10 p.m. Profane language is so offensive that it presents a public nuisance. It also is prohibited during the same time frame as indecency. FCC analyzes complaints about content in the context that the broadcast is presented (Communications Decency Act, 1996). Local franchising authorities (LFAs) work with the FCC to enforce cable television regulations at local, municipal, and county levels. Complaints to LFAs may result in local action or involvement with the FCC, but cable programming is not subject to the same content restrictions as broadcasts. FCC cannot restrict the content of nonobscene cable programming because it is nonbroadcast programming. Because the FCC is bound by the *Miller* test, it encourages the public to file complaints with cable companies to achieve nongovernmental censorship (*Miller v. California*, 1973). Complaints to cable companies can affect programming more directly than the FCC in many cases.

The film industry is regulated by the Motion Picture Association of America's (MPAA's) Classification and Rating Administration (CARA). CARA produces the widely recognized film ratings R, PG-13, PG, and G. Filmmakers voluntarily apply for ratings. Typically, major motion picture production companies participate, but independent or foreign filmmakers may not (Bristol, 2007). Films that are not submitted to CARA are labeled "unrated" (*Joseph Burstyn, Inc. v. Wilson*, 1952). X-rated films and NC-17 films with graphic sexual content may not be shown to minors in public. Ratings are enforced by the industry, not the government; however, CARA's rating assures the public that rated films do not contain illegal content (*Joseph Burstyn, Inc. v. Wilson*, 1952; *People v. Luera*, 2001). Some parents may choose to attend R-rated, violent, and sexual films with children (*Fowler v. Board of Education of Lincoln County*, 1987). Parents, children, and theaters may be held liable for legal breaches, that is, minors watching X-rated films. CARA's ratings are similar to the Recording Industry Association of America's (RIAA's) use of parental advisory labels (PALs). PALs notify parents that content is not suitable for minors. Labels act as disclaimers, and stores may deny minors access to materials bearing warning stickers. However, warning stickers do not alleviate any parties of culpability if they knowingly distribute obscenity to minors. Philosophically and perhaps jurisprudentially, little difference exists between explicit music and explicit films. Black Letter obscenity law may be used to prosecute any adult material, including music. However, music is rarely prosecuted. This subject is discussed further in Chapter 3.

Conclusion

Pornography is a term used generally to describe sexual depictions. Colloquially, the term may be used to describe obscenity, public indecency, profanity, and child pornography. However, legally, pornography, obscenity, profanity, and child pornography are distinguishable. The First Amendment often protects pornography and profanity, depending on specific factors (e.g., time, audience, and place). The government usually seeks to define what is criminal rather than what is legal to inclusively protect the majority of speech and society. Black Letter law restriction speech accommodates average local sensitivities to sexual depictions while protecting as much speech as possible. Careful constructions and narrow interpretations of laws help accomplish these goals. However, laws are also designed to preserve public morality and, sometimes, private morality. Privacy is constitutionally protected under the Fourteenth and Fifth Amendments' substantive due process. Under these amendments, privately viewing obscenity and simple possession have been protected by the U.S. Supreme Court.

References

§ 504 Communications Decency Act (1996).

Abowitz, R. (2013, April 21). Rob black, porn's dirty whistlebower, spills trade secrets. *The Daily Beast.* Retrieved from http://www.thedailybeast.com/articles/2013/04/21/rob-black-porn-s-dirty-whistlebower-spills-trade-secrets.html

Ashcroft v. Free Speech Coalition, 535 U.S. 234 (2002).

Bristol, J. E. (2007). Free expression in motion pictures: Childhood sexuality and a satisfied society. *Cardozo Arts and Entertainment Law Journal, 25*(1), 333–365.

Chaplinsky v. State of New Hampshire, 315 U.S. 568 (1942).

Farley, M. (2006). Prostitution, trafficking, and cultural amnesia: What we must not know in order to keep the business of sexual exploitation running smoothly. *Yale Journal of Law and Feminism, 18*, 109–144.

Fla. Stat. § 847.011(c)(d) (2012).

Four Star Publications, Inc. v. Erbe, 181 F. Supp. 483, 486 (S.D. Iowa 1960).

Fowler v. Board of Education of Lincoln County, Ky., 819 F.2d 657 (6th Cir. 1987).

Ginsberg v. New York, 390 U.S. 629 (1968).

Joseph Burstyn, Inc. v. Wilson, 343 U.S. 495 (1952).

Lawrence v. Texas, 539 U.S. 558 (2003).

Liu, S. (2007). Ashcroft, virtual child pornography and first amendment jurisprudence. *UC Davis Journal of Juvenile Law and Policy, 11*, 1.

Miller v. California, 413 U.S. 15 (1973).

New York v. Ferber, 458 U.S. 747 (1982).

People v. Luera, 86 Cal. App. 4th 513 (2001).

Roth v. U.S., 354 U.S. 476 (1957).

Stanley v. Georgia, 394 U.S. 557 (1969).

U.S. v. O'Brien, 391 U.S. 367 (1968).

Ward v. Rock Against Racism, 491 U.S. 781 (1989).

Obscenity

3

Overview

Sexual depictions have been socially accepted and rejected at different points throughout history. Historical or contemporary depictions may be labeled as deviant or normative depending on a viewer's perspective. Classification of obscenity is often dependent on localities' sensitivities. Criminalized depictions are not rendered obscene according to individual viewer's tastes; depictions ought to be evaluated according to community and national standards even when judges, prosecutors, and police independently make determinations. Some critics argue that standards for obscenity vary too widely and evaluations may be unfair.

Explicit Depictions in World History

Tolerance for erotic art has varied throughout history. Though it may seem as if society has become more tolerant of deviant sexuality and erotica, some ancient cultures valued hard-core depictions. In ancient Greece, Rome, and India, depictions were publicly displayed that could be considered criminally obscene in some U.S. jurisdictions.

In ancient Greece, maps of the world of Herodotus were symbolically colorful, depicting realms of men, monsters, and chimaeras (Lasker, 2002). Like these maps, Greek art sometimes portrayed sexuality as being mythical and mixed. Compared to their contemporaries, Greeks were more comfortable with nudity and sexuality. In comparison to the present-day Greek Orthodox state, ancient Greece could be perceived as more liberal in some senses. For example, ancient Greeks shocked other cultures by performing Olympic exercises while nude (Wolfson, 1994). Ancient Greeks may still seem liberal in retrospect. For example, in 2005, a Greek gallery owner was prosecuted for obscenity because he displayed a painting that depicted a penis next to a cross ("Greek 'Obscene Art' Trial Delayed," 2005).

Ancient Greek epicurean hedonism promulgated unrestrained pursuit of pleasure for men. In pursuit of pleasure, men may penetrate young boys, who would offer themselves to men. Mating rituals required boys to acquiesce to a man's sexual fury. However, if men did not persist, then relationships remained educational and platonic. Freeborn boys and men were equals even though men subordinated boys. Penetrated boys would eventually lead families, unlike women. Nevertheless, being penetrated was unprestigious. Lesbianism among woman was despised because it was perceived as requiring women to assume penetrative roles. Socially, females were far beneath males, and penetration was reserved for men. Female sexuality was portrayed as monstrous and as a function to be conquered, while male sexuality was portrayed as heroic. Philosophers and poets disguised their lovers, and young lovers carefully cloaked their desires. Publicly, homosexuality between men was condemned. It was treated like rape of women and children, which was illegal and carried a high fine.

Ancient Greek poetry and literary art was littered with erotic and explicit depictions (Robson, 2009). Some literature graphically described debasing women, humiliating competitors by sexually exploiting their female relatives or lovers, bestiality, sodomy, and rape (Greek Islands, n.d.). Some Greek theater and comedy was phallic, homoerotic, and perverse. Some pottery and other fine art included graphic depictions of alternative sexualities, sexual conquests, group sex, sodomy, cunnilingus, autoeroticism, and sex between humans, devils, gods, beasts, and mythical creatures. Some works were censored during this era, and some ancient Greek works could still be labeled "obscene" in some jurisdictions.

Ancient Romans also produced perverse and erotic art approximately 2,000 years ago. An example of Roman poetry continues to impose shock today (Higgins, 2009). Gaius Valerius Catullus produced obscene poetry describing forceful sodomy, graphic coital insertion, fellatio, and sex between minors, among other graphic, deviant, and aggressive themes. Thirty-two of Catullus's 113 poems are traditionally excluded from university studies and translated collections because of their explicit content.

In Pompeii, sexual images were displayed in public (Gye, 2013; "Pompeii," 2012). Sex and sexuality were considered to be normal ways of achieving and experiencing pleasure, and the god Eros was present in Roman society quite some time before the goddess of love. Public displays depicted traditional and outlying sexuality, for example, bestiality, transsexualism, or sex with mythical creatures. Depictions were likely displayed not to arouse the public, but to suggest to them that sex was positive, natural, and normal. Comedy and good fortune were expressed in pornographic depictions in Pompeii. Phalluses in full or partial states of turgidity and flaccidity were present throughout the town (Figure 3.1). However, the seeming omnipresence of erect phalluses may have sewn anxiety in some Roman men. After Pompeii was destroyed by a volcanic eruption, surviving art was locked behind a wall until the nineteenth century. During the height of the free love era in the twentieth century, Pompeian relics were available for public viewing, but

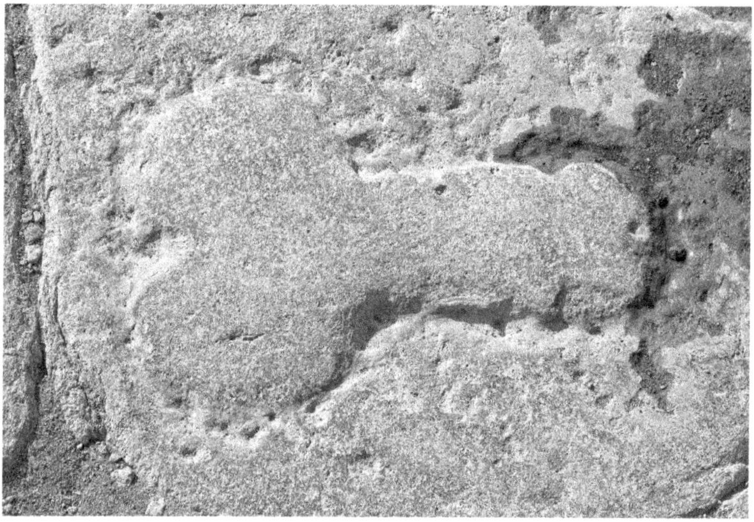

Figure 3.1 Sculpture of Phallus in Pompeii.

erotic depictions were soon stowed in private until the twenty-first century. Presently, erotic relics are housed in a secret museum and may be viewed by visitors by appointment.

Explicit and erotic themes are present in ancient Indian art. A few thousand years after Greek and Roman art depicted erotic themes, Indian art depicted orgies, child–adult sex, fellatio, lesbianism, masturbation, sodomy, and other potentially obscene themes (Bose, 2013). Interestingly, many of these depictions are carved on temples' outer walls. The public nature of these carvings demonstrates that they were not reserved for private view, and they were intended to be witnessed by the community in public. This notion is incompatible with present understandings of obscenity in the United States. Contemporary understandings hold that obscenity should be viewed exclusively only by adults in private. Presently, overlap between religious and explicit depictions is often treated like obscenity. However, ancient Indians also produced explicit educational materials (i.e., Kamasutra), and these depictions were grounded in their spiritual beliefs and religious texts. Ancient Indian depictions are still visible to the public and continue to defy perceived separations between private and public, sacred and profane, religion and eros, and art and obscenity.

Historical Influences on the Regulation of Obscenity

Social constructs of sexual boundaries have influenced depictions and definitions of art for thousands of years (Schrink, 1985). Scholars commonly analyze sexual themes in Renaissance art created during the fourteenth and fifteenth centuries to understand sexual boundaries. Throughout most of U.S. history, sodomy was classified as a crime against nature, and in the Renaissance, sodomy was also a crime. In the United States, enforcement of criminal law against those who committed sodomy was not rigorous even though acts were considered perverse and immoral. During the Renaissance, sodomy resulted in the greatest judgment and penalization. Sodomy posed the greatest threat to elite classes who governed the state and regulated family structure. Because sodomy caused God to destroy Sodom and Gomorrah by fire in the Judeo-Christian religious tradition, sodomites were put to death by fire during the Renaissance.

Sodomy increased during the Renaissance era, and erotic depictions did as well. Young, strapping men occupied city centers to replenish the labor force, which had been diminished by the plague. Cities, like Venice, were overrun with men (Schrink, 1985). Sex offenses increased, the abundance of males caused marriage rates to decrease among the population, and groups of rowdy men could not be disciplined by traditional institutions. Sex crimes included fornication, adultery, rape, sodomy, sex acts involving clergy or holy places, and sex between Christians and Jews. Once young males had run amok of morality and order, the state focused on stabilizing social order rather than on morality. For example, fornicators and rapists were required to marry, but they were not punished. These policies created additional avenues to marriage. Adultery was a crime, but it was punished using civil means. Sex crimes involving clergy were subject to church reprisal, not state action.

Sexual boundaries shifted during this era, and changes were expressed through art and memorialized by depictions. Depending on the location of art, mere nudity may have been considered obscene during the Renaissance. Sculptures, paintings, and literature depicting female nudity and sexuality proliferated. Themes that blurred lines between violence and homosexuality appeared in works. Sacred images hinted at incestuous affection. Labeling of inexplicit, nude art as obscene occurred recently during Attorney General Ashcroft's tenure. Similar to covering of public statues, including Lady Justice, during Ashcroft's era, during the Renaissance, Pope Paul III ordered fig leaves to be painted atop genitals appearing in frescos in the Sistine Chapel ("Censoring Art," 2010). During the Renaissance, art and sexuality experienced international blossoming. Pornographic depictions helped to normalize sexual deviance. Variations in culture and governmental responses to dramatic changes in moral landscapes illustrate how law bears on pornography production and perception of pornographic depictions.

Before the printing press was popularized, literacy, erotic literature, and visual depictions were consumed nearly exclusively by aristocrats (Wolfson, 1994). Upper classes and intelligentsia privately enjoyed explicit writings and paintings that were housed in secret chambers. Once literacy spread, people capitalized by selling explicit material to lower classes. This offended the upper classes, and they began to regulate dissemination of explicit materials. Perceived equalization of access to art elicited regulation of pornography.

In some capacity, pornography has always represented change and embodied conflict. From the Renaissance era through the French Revolution, pornography correlated with social revelations, religious revolutions, and underground cultures. Across Europe and North America, between 1660 and 1800, morality was challenged, and sexual privacy was claimed by the people (Dabhoiwala, 2012). Court cases, presses, personal writings, books, philosophy, art, sexual liberation, and intellectual revolutions were influenced by pornography. Just before the French Revolution, queens were drawn as harlots, and kings were depicted as depraved, comedic, and impotent (Wolfson, 1994). Women were viewed as being equally in control of sex as men, and sexuality was celebrated, yet women were belittled in depictions, and their personal power was mocked. After the French Revolution, political resistance waned, and pornography transitioned into its contemporary, mainly prurient, form.

Presses, writers, and publishers capitalized on the reformulation of pornography. Following the French Revolution, women were relegated to traditional roles in private, yet depictions of women engaged in pornography fueled males' beliefs that female sexuality was public. Pornography was viewed privately, often kept separate from a wife's sexual identity or marital activity. Thus, use and dissemination of pornography served to challenge traditional boundaries, even if messages were not intentionally political. Moral subversion eroded gender roles, as well as the ruling class's ability to control commerce and artistic aesthetics.

European ideas, morals, roles, and laws certainly undergird U.S. attitudes and policies. Reservation of deviance for upper classes is still evident in U.S. society. Wealthy classes can pay for better protection from the law (e.g., private spaces for viewing obscenity in groups), they have access to better-guarded distribution methods, they may afford better legal representation if they are prosecuted, and they may travel to jurisdictions where sexual commerce is legal or welcomed. Some critics argue that the ruling class in the United States (i.e., government) uses law and discretion to suppress cultural and sexual revolution by banning expressions of deviance, especially among nonelite classes.

U.S. History

When Europe first colonized America, Native tribes did not practice sexual shame (Northcraft, 2004). Sexuality was often affiliated with spirituality. Homosexuality, transvestism, and premarital sex were accepted among some tribes, and sexual violence and prostitution were unusual practices among Native American tribes. Natives' sex education practices were common and rooted in respect for community members and personal autonomy. European influences and Christian understandings of morality were eventually imposed on Native Americans, African Americans, and European Americans. However, for the first hundred years of U.S. history, pornography was commonly available.

In the mid-1800s, immoral or deviant objects and writings were considered to be obscene (Rabban, 1999). Obscenity was suppressed because it was blasphemous. Blasphemous obscenity posed a threat to public interests and social control. Anthony Comstock attempted to eradicate cultural and political speech that departed from religious norms. In 1873, Congress passed the Comstock Act to regulate speech. The Comstock Act was formally titled "An Act for the Suppression of the Trade in, and Circulation of, Obscene Literature and Articles of Immoral Use." It authorized prosecution of any person using the mail or interstate travel to transport obscenity. Almost half of the states passed laws like the Comstock Act. A special agent position was created for the U.S. Post Office (USPS) to monitor mail and enforce the Comstock Act. Comstock, who was first appointed to this position, held this position until 1915, when he died in office.

Comstock believed that pornography was a vice and a national death trap (Rabban, 1999). He believed that Satan, the ultimate Christian adversary, trapped people in vices. Satan allegedly used pornography because it did the greatest harm to children. Comstock compared pornographers to vultures preying on morality and youth. Comstock destroyed 160 tons of pornography in the name of Christian morals. Using evidence obtained by the USPS, hundreds of people were prosecuted, three-quarters of whom were convicted. Only a small portion of the material classified as obscene involved children, which was supposed to be one of Comstock's primary concerns.

The Federal Bureau of Investigation (FBI) heavily pursued obscenity crimes throughout the 1900s, but especially between the 1920s and the 1950s (Charles, 2012; Loftin, 2012). Ostensibly, the FBI intended to crack down on obscenity because agents believed that obscenity corrupted youth, led to delinquency, created sexual and racial tension, and contributed to social problems. The FBI's interest in pornography shaped cultural dynamics, politics, social relationships, and familial structure. During World War II and until 1953, J. Edgar Hoover's fascination with pornography influenced politicians, activists, and moral figures to participate in his inquisition against it. The FBI worked with local law enforcement and the public's watchful eye to prosecute. Agents amassed a collection of pornographic toys and materials as references; the FBI's collection also served as an arsenal to leverage against members of organized crime or politically unpopular people. The FBI's "Obscene File" was used to investigate and target organizations, activists, and artists, like the Kinsey Institute, gay rights organizations, and Andy

Warhol. In an interesting case, the nation's first openly homosexual magazine, *ONE: The Homosexual Magazine*, was seized by the USPS working with the FBI in Los Angeles in 1954. The U.S. Supreme Court held that the publication was not obscene, which led to some political shifts and interpretations of obscenity because it was the first time that the Court overtly protected homosexual consent (*One, Inc. v. Olesen*, 1958).

During the late 1800s and early 1900s, free speech challenges were routinely decided in favor of upholding the Comstock Act (Northcraft, 2004). Free speech organizations, for example, the Free Speech League and American Civil Liberties Union (ACLU), were developed during this time in response to the Comstock Act, which was considered to be a gag law. During the 1950s and 1960s, before the Comstock Act lost its power, several high-profile cases challenged obscenity laws. Many of these helped define contemporary obscenity law by teasing apart art from obscenity (White, 2011). Several cases involving banned books and literature, obscene performance, and immoral pornography were prosecuted. Notable cases include Allen Ginsberg's publisher, who was prosecuted for publishing Ginsberg's epic American poem *Howl*. In the 1950s, the publisher was acquitted because national standards held that *Howl*, which included explicit profanity and references to sodomy, possessed literary value. Lenny Bruce was arrested numerous times for using obscenity in his comedy act throughout the early 1960s. Following his final arrest, he was convicted for the first time, though he was eventually pardoned posthumously.

By today's standards, the Comstock Act may have violated free speech rights and other constitutional rights (Rabban, 1999). Some of the material classified as contraband included adult material created by free lovers and thinkers. Some literature disseminated medical information. The greatest controversy arose in Comstock's prosecution of dissemination of contraptions for birth control and literature about birth control and abortion. Feminism and family planning literature were treated as an affront to the state and morality; family planning literature was akin to pornography (*Four Star Publications, Inc. v. Erbe*, 1960). Margaret Sanger, founder of Planned Parenthood, was involved in a great deal of prosecution during this era (*Griswold v. Connecticut*, 1965; *U.S. v. One Package of Japanese Pessaries*, 1936). One of the most enduring provisions of the Comstock Act denying contraceptives was stricken under the right to privacy in 1965 (*Griswold v. Connecticut*, 1965). Shortly thereafter in 1969, contemporary interpretations of protected speech began to develop (*Stanley v. Georgia*, 1969). Contemporary standards are discussed later in this chapter. By the 1960s and 1970s, divergent sexuality had become more mainstream. This phenomenon was epitomized by the pornographic film *Deep Throat*, which won critical acclaim in 1972. *Deep Throat* is discussed further in Chapter 11.

Between the mid-1970s and 1990s, obscenity prosecutions substantially waned. However, controversial figures, like *Hustler*'s Larry Flynt and bondage and sadomasochistic photographer Robert Mapplethorpe, continued to bring obscenity prosecution into mainstream media. Then, former U.S. Attorney General John Ashcroft increased prosecution of obscenity and was accused of persecuting nude public art during the Bush era. Legislation was tightened, and efforts were ramped up to detect and prosecute all deviant sex and controversial public displays of sexuality. Attorney General Alberto Gonzales created a special task force for obscenity in the mid-2000s, and the government continues to increase obscenity prosecution and penalization at federal, state, and local levels (Loftin, 2012).

Black Letter Laws

Most speech is protected by the First Amendment. Very few classes of speech are unprotected. Obscenity is a class of speech that is unprotected. Obscenity is criminalized under federal case law and statutory law and is often criminalized under state case law and statutory law.

Miller v. California (1973) is a binding U.S. Supreme Court case, and it sets the standard for obscenity. It is discussed in full detail later in this chapter. The famous idiom supposedly used to delineate pornography, "I know it when I see it," is derived from *Jacobellis v. Ohio*, but *Jacobellis* is not Black Letter law (*Jacobellis v. Ohio*, 1964). The *Miller* test is Black Letter law. It is derived from *Miller v. California* (1973) and articulates a conjunctive three-prong test to be applied by the Court. Yet, in a sense, *Jacobellis*'s idiom is incorporated into the legal standard in two ways. First, probable cause for arrest arises from governmental agents' personal opinions about whether work is obscene. Agents are usually police, prosecutors, and judges. Second, "I" is like the jury composed of local community members. The *Miller* test states that if offensive prurient depictions meet local standards for obscenity but do not meet national values for art, literature, politics, or science, then the work can be ruled to be obscene and will be unprotected by the First Amendment (*Ginzburg v. U.S.*, 1966; *Hamling v. U.S.*, 1974).

Production, distribution, transmission, and receipt of obscenity are illegal throughout the United States. However, local standards used to define obscenity may vary according to geographic location. For example, depictions that are protected in California may be illegal in Kansas. If pornography is mailed from California to Kansas, and that material is considered to be obscene in those two states, then the state of Kansas, the state of California, and the federal government may prosecute for obscenity. A defendant may be prosecuted irrespective of where obscenity was produced or where a defendant lives. Local standards would be used to measure offense. In cases where depictions would be protected in California, recipients, producers, and distributors could still be prosecuted in Kansas.

Possessing, but not transmitting, a little obscenity in the privacy of one's home is legal. Under *Stanley v. Georgia* (1969), the right to privacy guarantees that people can view obscenity in their homes. This includes viewing magazines, DVDs, downloads, and other materials. The government cannot prosecute for possession of a single depiction of obscenity, though the government may prosecute for possession of several depictions. This is discussed in Chapter 20 in greater detail. The right to possess obscenity is not a First Amendment right. It is a substantive due process right to privacy that extends only to the home (*U.S. v. 12 200-Ft. Reels of Super 8mm. Film*, 1973). Outside the home, Congress has the power to regulate obscenity that may enter into the stream of commerce (*U.S. v. Orito*, 1973). The government cannot bootstrap prosecution for receipt, dealing, or production solely through evidence of possession of a single depiction found inside a home. However, consistent with *Stanley v. Georgia*, possession of a certain number of identical or similar obscene depictions (e.g., three duplicate files) can serve as prima facie evidence that one has dealt in obscenity.

Statutory definitions of *depiction* may be extensive and nearly all-inclusive. Where they are silent, defendants may challenge applicability of laws, but courts usually find in the government's favor. Florida's statutes offer an example of highly inclusive language explaining that *depict* can include the following:

> ...obscene book, magazine, periodical, pamphlet, newspaper, comic book, story paper, written or printed story or article, writing, paper, card, picture, drawing, photograph, motion picture film, figure, image, phonograph record, or wire or tape or other recording, or any written, printed, or recorded matter of any such character which may or may not require mechanical or other means to be transmuted into auditory, visual, or sensory representations of such character, or any article or instrument for obscene use, or purporting to be for obscene use or purpose; or who knowingly designs, copies, draws, photographs, poses for, writes, prints, publishes, or in any manner whatsoever manufactures or prepares any such material, matter, article, or thing of any such character; or who knowingly writes, prints, publishes, or utters, or causes to be written, printed, published, or uttered, any advertisement or notice of any kind, giving information, directly or indirectly, stating, or purporting to state, where, how, of whom, or by what means any, or what purports to be any, such material, matter, article, or thing of any such character can be purchased, obtained, or had; or who in any manner knowingly hires, employs, uses, or permits any person knowingly to do or assist in doing any act or thing mentioned above. (Fla. Stat. § 847.011, 2012)

Acts connected with obscenity are not black-and-white, but laws may be broad and generally inclusive. For example, Florida's obscenity statute punishes any person who does the following:

> …knowingly sells, lends, gives away, distributes, transmits, shows, or transmutes, or offers to sell, lend, give away, distribute, transmit, show, or transmute, or has in his or her possession, custody, or control with intent to sell, lend, give away, distribute, transmit, show, transmute, or advertise in any manner. (Fla. Stat. § 847.011, 2012)

Some states' laws may attempt to criminalize simple possession, but these laws likely lack constitutionality and are probably unenforceable. For example, Florida Statute § 847.011 (2) (2012) states the following:

> A person who knowingly has in his or her possession, custody, or control any obscene book, magazine, periodical, pamphlet, newspaper, comic book, story paper, written or printed story or article, writing, paper, card, picture, drawing, photograph, motion picture film, film, any sticker, decal, emblem or other device attached to a motor vehicle containing obscene descriptions, photographs, or depictions, any figure, image, phonograph record, or wire or tape or other recording, or any written, printed, or recorded matter of any such character which may or may not require mechanical or other means to be transmuted into auditory, visual, or sensory representations of such character, or any article or instrument for obscene use, or purporting to be for obscene use or purpose, without intent to sell, lend, give away, distribute, transmit, show, transmute, or advertise the same, commits a misdemeanor of the second degree. (Fla. Stat. § 847.011, 2012)

If obscene material is lawfully seized or confiscated, then it will be destroyed. However, material will be returned if it is held to be nonobscene or was improperly taken by the government.

Obscenity prosecution usually requires that defendants know that they transmitted obscenity. This is discussed further in Chapter 20. If defendants use lack of knowledge as a defense but then continue to transmit obscenity after they have been indicted, then knowledge will be inferred. If Internet service providers (ISPs) knowingly transmit obscenity, they are not prosecutable under obscenity statutes. Currently, only corporations or actual persons who knowingly transmit obscenity can be prosecuted, and ISPs are only required to report obscene pornography depicting children. This is discussed further in Chapter 9.

Miller Test

Obscenity is categorically unprotected speech. "Obscene" is a classification for certain depictions. Material is determined to be obscene using national and local standards. The court balances local sensitivities against national value using the *Miller* test to determine whether a work is obscene (*Miller v. California*, 1973). If a work is nonobscene, then the defendant will be acquitted. However, if the work meets standards set forth in *Miller*, then the defendant will be convicted.

In *Miller v. California* (1973), the defendant sent numerous pornographic flyers through the federal mail. The defendant was advertising material available at his adult bookstore. The flyers were mailed to local individuals and businesses that had not solicited them. The advertisements featured information and images for four books and one film. The books were titled *Intercourse*, *Man-Woman*, *Sex Orgies Illustrated*, and *An Illustrated History of Pornography*. The film was titled *Marital Intercourse*. In drawings and photos, the defendant's flyer explicitly and prominently depicted the genitals of people participating in group sex and partnered sex. Several recipients complained, and the defendant was arrested.

Following the defendant's criminal conviction, the U.S. Supreme Court granted *certiorari*. The Court held that when pornography enters the public sphere (e.g., mail or stores), then it is subject to prosecution for obscenity. The justices articulated a three-prong test: (1) whether the average person applying contemporary community standards would find that the work, taken as a whole, appeals to the prurient interest; (2) whether the work depicts or describes in a patently offensive way sexual conduct specifically defined by the applicable state law; and (3) whether the work, taken as a whole, lacks serious literary value, artistic value, political value, or scientific value. Several components of this conjunctive test have been challenged in different cases. The meaning or validity of the following components have been challenged:

1. a. Whether the average person,
   b. applying contemporary
   c. community standards
   d. would find that the work,
   e. taken as a whole
   f. appeals to
   g. the prurient interest;
2. a. Whether the work
   b. depicts
   c. or
   d. describes
   e. in a patently
   f. offensive way
   g. sexual
   h. conduct
   i. specifically
   j. defined
   k. by the applicable
   l. state law; and

3. a. Whether the work,
   b. taken as a whole,
   c. lacks
   d. serious
   e. literary value,
   f. artistic value,
   g. political value,
   h. or
   i. scientific value.

Members of the court decide the first two prongs of the *Miller* test. The following philosophical proposition breaks down how members of the court may analyze depictions:

> (A) X is appropriately classified as a member of a form or class of objects whose authorized purpose is to solicit and commend to us cognitive-affective responses which are (I) internalized as morally prohibited and (2) does so in ways found to be or which are held to warrant repulsion and (3) does so in order to (a) indulge first order desires held to be morally prohibited or (b) indulge the desire to be morally transgressive or the desire to feel repulsed or (c) afford cognitive rewards or (d) any combination thereof or (B) X successfully elicits cognitive-affective responses which conform to conditions (1)-(3). (Kieran, 2002, p. 31).

Local, state, and federal standards express internalized moral prohibitions and repulsion for obscenity. Jurors view transgressive depictions, experience repulsion, and recognize that their morals are violated.

Under *Miller*, the government may criminalize private or public transmission. However, the law has come to regulate privately transmitted obscenity as well. In *Miller*, the Court found the defendant's actions to be violative, especially because he forced explicit depictions into the hands and minds of unwilling community members. The Court found the defendant's aggressive campaign particularly offensive to the state's legitimate interest to keep obscenity out of the public eye. The Court seems to have used the lowest level of scrutiny in this sense, which seems to be atypical of the Court's use of strict scrutiny to analyze alleged constitutional violations. Strict scrutiny is judicially made and not required by the U.S. Constitution. The Court's use of rational review may possibly be because of the unsolicited nature of the defendant's mailings or because minors could have viewed the materials. However, neither recipients' unwillingness nor possession by minors is a factor in the *Miller* test. The *Miller* test applies even when all participants are willing and materials are solicited.

Some federal and state statutes codify *Miller*. For example, the Commonwealth of Virginia defines "obscene" in the following way:

> [Obscenity] considered as a whole, has as its dominant theme or purpose an appeal to the prurient interest in sex, that is, a shameful or morbid interest in nudity, sexual conduct, sexual excitement, excretory functions or products thereof or sadomasochistic abuse, and which goes substantially beyond customary limits of candor in description or representation of such matters and which, taken as a whole, does not have serious literary, artistic, political or scientific value. (Va. Code Ann., 2008)

This statute incorporates some concepts from the federal definition, case law, and other states' definitions of obscenity. It should be noted that this statute differs from *Miller* because it asks about the "dominant theme" of the work.

Authorities banning speech must not exceed the parameters of the *Miller* test. However, some states outright ban some speech that they believe meets the *Miller* test. Even when statutes do not outright ban sexually extreme, lewd, graphic, or explicit kinds of speech, courts may classify them as obscene. Virginia's statute per se criminalizes sadomasochism and excrement in pornography. Many states also criminalize bestiality statutorily. Notably, Virginia's statute allows mere adult nudity to be prosecuted as obscenity if the depiction appeals to "a shameful or morbid interest" (Va. Code Ann., 2008). However, nudity alone does not constitute obscenity under U.S. Supreme Court case *Jenkins v. Georgia* (1974). Depictions may become obscene when transmitted to minors. The state of Wyoming offers a definition that reflects *Miller* and case law. Obscenity is "material which the average person would find ... applying contemporary community standards, taken as a whole, appeals to the prurient interest ... depicts or describes sexual conduct in a patently offensive way" and "lacks serious literary, artistic, political or scientific value" (Wyo. Stat. Ann., 2005). "Patently offensive" means "representations or descriptions of ultimate sexual acts, normal or perverted, actual or simulated," including "sadomasochistic abuse" and "representations or descriptions of masturbation, excretory functions or lewd exhibitions of the genitals." The statutes specifically allow for bans of normal depictions. This law's breadth seems expansive.

Usually depictions of aberrant forms of sexuality are prosecuted under *Miller.* This is because material is judged by the sensitivities of the average community member, not the average deviant; yet, if material is so bizarre that it appeals only to a particular deviant group, then expert opinion may be presented about its prurience to the fact-finder (*Pinkus v. U.S.*, 1978). Local standards arising from the community, not cyberspace or fringe groups, will be used to define average sensitivities in determining prurience (*U.S. v. Thomas*, 1996). Local community is not limited by geographical descriptions or jurisdictions. Federal jurisdictions use local standards, not national standards, to determine prurience and shamefulness. Jurors residing in a federal jurisdiction in which the matter is heard must find that the material is patently offensive to an average member of their community (Glazer, 2008).

Art

Distinguishing between art and obscenity requires the criminal justice system to weigh local sensitivities against national value. If an average community member would feel that an offensive work appeals to prurient or shameful interests, then the work may be prosecutable. The *Miller* test requires the government to prove that the work in question lacks artistic value under national standards. The prosecution must carry this burden (*Ashcroft v. Free Speech Coalition*, 2002). The defendant does not need to prove that a work of art possesses artistic value under national standards. Boundaries of good taste may be part of local considerations, whereas value is decided using national standards (*Hamling v. U.S.*, 1974). Expert testimony may enter to help determine value using a national standard (*Pinkus v. U.S.*, 1978; *Pope v. Illinois*, 1987).

Several famous cases define differences between art and obscenity. In the late 1980s, artist Andres Serrano submerged a plastic crucifix in a jar of urine then photographed the jar. His work, called "Piss Christ," was controversial albeit legal under a U.S. Supreme Court case decided nearly four decades earlier that held that sacrilegious art was protected speech (*Joseph Burstyn, Inc. v. Wilson*, 1952). During the late 1980s, Robert Mapplethorpe explicitly photographed homosexual sexual deviance. Subject matter included anal penetration by a bullwhip and one man urinating into another's mouth. His photographs were criticized by conservative members of society and eventually banned from a gallery in Washington, D.C. Serrano's and Mapplethorpe's work prompted congressional revision of National Endowment for the Arts (NEA) rules. The NEA was required to consider "general standards of decency and respect for the diverse beliefs and values of the American public" (Munkittrick, 2009). Several artists sued the NEA because they could not receive grants, but the U.S. Supreme Court upheld Congress's revision because it did not impinge on free speech (*National Endowment for the Arts v. Finley*, 1998). The NEA's "decency clause" required considerations of factors; it did not require censorship of content (Heyman, 1999). To fairly enforce this requirement, the NEA formed advisory committees composed of members from diverse backgrounds, disciplines, ethnicities, and jurisdictions (Munkittrick, 2009). The Court held that artistic expression is vital to democratic society. Thus, governmental funding requires content neutrality (Leff, 1995).

The NEA may refuse grants to certain art submissions. Lack of funding may contribute to artists' failure to achieve national notoriety. In some circumstances, NEA standards may control which artwork becomes valued on a national scale. National recognition for certain kinds of art could potentially influence outcomes of obscenity trials applying the *Miller* test. Nevertheless, NEA suppression of some art could potentially influence local understandings of prurience and patently offensive content (*Brockett v. Spokane Arcades, Inc.*, 1985). On one hand, works that are known to possess national value may be less offensive on a local level. Local works that are comparable with nationally valued works may be less likely to be prosecuted. On the other hand, just as courts need not consider whether a work is obscene if comparable works have already been found to be nonobscene, courts may not fully apply the *Miller* test if comparable works have been devalued by the NEA's "decency clause" (*Hamling v. U.S.*, 1974). For example, a local artist depicting homosexual bondage may be more likely to be prosecuted because Mapplethorpe's work was rejected on a national level, which possibly reinforces the valuelessness of those kinds of depictions.

Around the same time that Serrano's and Mapplethorpe's questionably indecent artwork became the subject of congressional concern, 2 Live Crew, a musical rap group, produced a vulgar musical record titled *As Nasty as They Wanna Be*, which was the first allegedly obscene musical album put before the court (Germaine, 2001; Munkittrick, 2009). The record frequently and explicitly describes excretion, godlike genitalia, sodomy, orgies, masturbation, intercourse, prostitution, and abuse of women. Citizens complained about the lyrics, even though the rap group sold 1.7 million albums and played sanitized song versions in public. Broward Sheriff's Office (BSO) investigated, and Broward County Court found probable cause for obscenity charges. Local retailers were warned by BSO that album sales in Broward County would result in criminal prosecution. In the week following the ban, a recordstore owner was arrested for selling the album, and three 2 Live Crew members were arrested for performing a lewd version of the album at a nightclub. Their performance was described as "X-rated." They were arrested for defying a judge's order because the album was found to be obscene (Walker, 1990). Following their arrest, members of the rock band Too Much Joy protested by covering 2 Live Crew's music at the same nightclub (Walsh, 1991). They were subsequently arrested. 2 Live Crew was tried and acquitted. Jurors found the trial to be political, comical, and trivial (Clary, 1990). One juror said, "Everyday people use those words. … Maybe people ought to take a look at the obscenity law" (Clary, 1990). Another juror said, "It's certainly not something I want to see in the malls, or out in the open, but in a 21-year-old club, sure" (Clary, 1990). This juror's comment reflects the holding and facts in *Miller v. California* (1973). Too Much Joy members were also acquitted, but the ban remained in effect (Walsh, 1991). The recordstore owner was convicted and fined $1,000 (Hijek, 2010).

In response, 2 Live Crew filed civil suit. The civil court used the *Miller* test to determine whether the material was legally obscene. 2 Live Crew and its record label were defeated in the lower court (Smith, 1995). In this case, there were two issues. First, enjoinment or enforcement of BSO's restriction on album sales was decided as a civil matter (*Skyywalker Records, Inc. v. Navarro*, 1990). Second, 2 Live Crew claimed prior restraint on speech, that is, violation of First Amendment rights. The court stated that the burden of proof must be met by the preponderance of the evidence, not reasonable doubt, because it was a civil case. No jury was empanelled, and the case was decided by a single judge.

On the first issue, the judge required that BSO's sheriff prove the album was obscene. However, the judge specified that a civil determination was separate from a determination that 2 Live Crew's album was criminally obscene. Under the guise of considering cultural relevance and diversity, the court essentially considered whether the album should be evaluated by African American community members or residents of the tri-county area. The court applied the *Miller* test using the tri-county area. The court found that the album met all three prongs of the test by the preponderance of the evidence and by a higher standard of clear and convincing evidence.

On the second matter, the court considered whether BSO could continue criminalizing sales. The court noted that BSO consulted a judge, who found probable cause and then immediately issued an order. The court said, "There is no statutory or common law basis for such a procedure" (*Skyywalker Records, Inc. v. Navarro*, 1990, p. 598). Thus, the court found that this procedure was not rooted in law, and the work was presumptively constitutionally protected at the time that BSO threatened vendors. Seizure of 2 Live Crew's inventory in Broward County ran afoul of the Constitution, and BSO was enjoined from fulfilling threats to arrest.

At the appellate level, 2 Live Crew argued that music, that is, songs composed of notes and rhythms, is inherently artistic. Thus, any lyrics applied to music share the artistic value present in a song. The court tended to agree but decided that this was a nonissue of the appellate case. The appellate court focused on the fact that BSO did not overcome expert testimony. Two years after the lower court's judgment about the record's obscenity, the appellate court reversed (*Skyywalker Records, Inc. v. Navarro*, 1992). The district court judge misapplied *Miller* test's third prong. The Eleventh Circuit Court of Appeals held that the state failed to overcome expert testimony about the music's value presented by a psychologist, music critics, and scholars who testified that the album possessed literary, musical, social, and political value. Though the Constitution does not require expert testimony on this issue of value, to impinge speech the government must carry its burden to prove the prongs of the *Miller* test. 2 Live Crew presented expert testimony that overcame BSO's evidence. The single piece of evidence offered by BSO was *As Nasty as They Wanna Be*; though a work speaks for itself, the prosecution did not meet its evidentiary burden.

In the lower court, 2 Live Crew argued that they created explicit content warnings for their music that effectively provided notice to people who did not want to buy profane music. Unlike pornography, which may be viewed by the public in a store and cannot be unseen by vulnerable parties, music cannot be heard through the packaging. Thus, only those who purchase music have access to explicit lyrics. The court did not subscribe to the distinction raised between the case at bar and the facts of *Miller* because obscene music enters the community. However, warning labels continue to be affixed to the outside of packaging. Today, those stickers have become industry standard for music containing explicitly sexual and violent themes. Warning labels were discussed in Chapter 2.

Literature

Etymological roots of the English word *pornography* trace to the Greek word *pornographos*, meaning "writing about prostitutes" (Wolfson, 1994). In works like Henry Miller's *Tropic of Cancer* or *Under the Rooftops of Paris*, descriptions of prostitution may be pornographic, but depictions are not necessarily obscene. Explicit written descriptions of sex are protected under the First Amendment if they possess literary value. Literature that is sexually explicit, graphic, sadomasochistic, or depicts sexual abuse of minors to appeal to prurient interests may be prosecuted as obscenity if it meets the *Miller* test. Acquittal results if courts find that literature possesses more than *de minimis* literary value.

Many works of literature that are considered to be American classics or culturally significant have been persecuted or banned as obscenity. Examples include Theodore Dreiser's *An American Tragedy*, D. H. Lawrence's *Lady Chatterly's Lover*, and Allen Ginsberg's *Howl*, which have gained national popularity. In the late 1800s, Walt Whitman published "Song of Myself" and other exceptional poems in a collection called *Leaves of Grass*. Today, these poems are taught to high school students along with other once-persecuted works. However, at the time, the collection's discussion of sex, masturbation, prostitution, and other sordid and prurient themes led a Boston prosecutor to intervene into the poems' publication. Whitman's publisher was persuaded by the prosecutor to request that Whitman censor his collection. When Whitman refused, he was forced to find an alternate publisher. Yet, he capitalized on the resulting controversy, and obscenity charges were never filed.

Count Leo Tolstoy published *The Kreutzer Sonata* in the late 1800s (*In re Arentsen*, 1890; *U.S. Ex Rel. Milwaukee Social Democratic Publishing Company v. Burleson*, 1921). That work described extramarital sex. It was declared to be indecent and, thus, excluded from the U.S. mail. Supportive periodicals published the work in installments and popularized the work.

The court stated that it need not consider whether each published section was obscene because the entire work was already considered to be obscene. The court discussed how the book was immoral, in some regards, because it questioned Christian marriages. However, it was determined that the text was nonobscene and that anti-Christian contemplations of marriage are protected by the First Amendment. The court said that the book denounced obscenity because it advocated that celibacy was better than extramarital sex. The court stated that the work possessed no literary value, but because it was not lewd or obscene, it could not be banned.

Nearly 50 years after Whitman was threatened with prosecution and Tolstoy was persecuted by the government, James Joyce's *Ulysses* was famously persecuted by the government. The work had been published in sections through a periodical (*U.S. v. One Book Entitled Ulysses by James Joyce*, 1934). The government argued that obscene portions were disconnected from other content. Each section was considered to be a whole publication, and, thus, some publications were considered to be obscene. Two of *Ulysses*'s publishers were convicted of obscenity. The work was officially banned, though it continued to be popular. Approximately one decade later, a book compiled the publications, but again, the government prosecuted the content. The court and appellate court found that the book contained explicitly sexual passages, some of which were obscene; however, the work was found to possess artistic value, and obscene passages were necessary to develop the book's characters. This case stood for the proposition that the government cannot homogenize literature and sanitize human existence.

> [The court is] not of a mind, nor [does it] have the authority, to require an author to write about one kind of people and not about another, nor [does it] object to [an author's] effort to paint a complete picture of those whom [the author] has chosen. Certainly [the court] will not say that it is not a good thing to look deeply into life and people, regardless of the shadows that are to be found there. (*Commonwealth v. Gordon et al.*, 1949, p. 8)

In 1973, the year in which the *Miller* test was created, a court held that the Constitution does not require the government to rely on expert testimony to allege that material is obscene. This determination is made by local police and prosecutors. The material speaks for itself and is the best evidence of its violation of community standards (*Kaplan v. California*, 1973). The state must convince the court that national standards for literary value are not met and that any literary value possessed by the work is *de minimis*. Named after Supreme Court Justice William J. Brennan, Jr., nationalization of obscenity standards are sometimes known as "the Brennan doctrine" (McDonald, 2008). In 1987, *Pope v. Illinois* considered an objective national standard. In that case, an adult bookstore owner sold to local police three magazines titled *Anal Animal*, *Full Throttle*, and *Fuck Around*. The Court found that the Constitution requires the jury to apply an objective, national standard to determine whether literary work possesses sufficient value. Literary value may be established by expert testimony. Literary critics, publishers, scholars, authors, and others may offer expert testimony. As a matter of law, a defendant is not required to prove anything. However, defendants typically provide experts to overcome the government's experts. Previously, under the Comstock Act, judges were not required to recognize expert testimony about literary value (Glass, 2006). Though there are some potential drawbacks to using national standards to determine artistic value, rights guaranteed under the federal Constitution are best protected by the inclusion of this requirement (Elkin, 1987; *Pope v. Illinois*, 1987).

Politics

If a works fails the first two prongs of the *Miller* test, but as a whole, the work possesses political value, then it will be protected under the First Amendment. One important case discussing political value was *Federal Communications Commission v. Pacifica Foundation et al.* (1978). In that case, comedian George Carlin's routine "Filthy Words" was played by a radio station. In his routine, Carlin listed words that he believed were forbidden from public broadcast: "shit, piss, fuck, cunt, cocksucker, motherfucker, and tits." A listener complained to the Federal Communications Commission (FCC) after his son heard the broadcast played during daytime hours. The FCC found the broadcast to be indecent, and *Pacifica Foundation* brought suit. The appellate court held that the words likely contained political value because they are used in public interest programming, for example, live news broadcasts and plays. Because the words had political value and did not appeal to prurient interests, then they were nonobscene and were entitled to full First Amendment protection on the airwaves. The holding was reversed by U.S. Supreme Court on the grounds that the words were indecent. Though they were nonobscene, they were still subject to regulation under the FCC. The issue before the Court was whether the FCC could regulate the content of a broadcast in which patently offensive language was used to inexplicitly depict sex and excretion. Public offense to political content is insufficient grounds for suppressing free speech. However, vulgar language, whether explicit or inexplicit, is offensive, like obscenity. While obscenity possesses *de minimis* political value, and receives no First Amendment protection, vulgar language may possess political value in context. "Time, place, manner" regulation of vulgar content is within the FCC's power. The government has an interest in regulating indecent broadcasts on public airwaves because public airwaves enter people's homes and private spaces.

Political speech cannot merely intend to shock the public's conscience. Civil disobedience is not protected political speech. Works that attempt to push legal limits to protest those limits will not likely be found to possess political value. Civil disobedience cannot be protected speech for safety and policy reasons.

On occasion, antipornography feminists have displayed sadomasochistic depictions in public to illustrate misogynistic or patriarchal themes in pornography (Reddington & Kreisel, 2009). Displaying these images in a political context may not likely convert hard-core depictions to political speech. Though feminists' purpose is not to titillate viewers, the sadomasochistic depictions displayed were likely produced to appeal to prurient interests. Sadomasochistic depictions may be banned in jurisdictions and are frequently held to be obscene. Antipornography feminists argue that they are patently offensive. Thus, the first and second prongs of *Miller*, admittedly, may be met. Taken as a whole, the works do not possess political value apart from their use within feminists' political lectures. Indecent language may receive context-specific protection, but typically, obscenity does not. Thus, the third prong may likely be met.

Science

Theoretically, every intangible and tangible depiction, including objects, art, literature, performances, occurrences, and phenomenon, possesses scientific value. The quantity or quality of the scientific value present in a depiction may be *de minimis* to society or the court. Value must be more than *de minimis* under the *Miller* test to merit First Amendment protection.

These images do not possess scientific value as much as educational value. Educational value is not protected by *Miller*, but courts have protected it. Nevertheless, depictions of artificial insemination may not be produced or used as a pretext. Images depicting penetration of animals' sex organs may be obscene or protected (Cusack, 2013b). For example, images graphically or explicitly depicting artificial insemination of animals may possess scientific value if the depictions are produced by the farming industry and are possessed for a scientific purpose.

> The circumstances of presentation and dissemination of material are equally relevant to determining whether social importance claimed for material in the courtroom was, in the circumstances, pretense or reality—whether it was the basis upon which it was traded in the marketplace or a spurious claim for litigation purposes. Where the purveyor's sole emphasis is on the sexually provocative aspects of his publications, that fact may be decisive in the determination of obscenity. (*Ginzburg v. U.S.*, 1966)

Child pornography is not normally analyzed under *Miller.* However, depictions of child sex abuse may be prosecuted as obscenity in some cases. Under *New York v. Ferber*, the U.S. Supreme Court upheld a statute forbidding depictions of children in sexually explicit scenarios irrespective of scientific value (*New York v. Ferber*, 1982). The Court held that these depictions hold *de minimis* scientific value. Bona fide scientific value may be *de minimis.* State laws may prohibit possession of child pornography depictions, regardless of bona fide scientific value, because children suffer psychological harm when depictions that memorialize abuse are distributed. The Court held that adults can simulate these depictions when necessary.

Educational depictions of sex may be prosecuted (Northcraft, 2004). In *Rees v. Texas*, two defendants were convicted for promoting obscenity (Closen, 1998; *Rees v. Texas*, 1995). They played on cable television a call-in TV show, called *Infosex*, which explicitly depicted same-sex sodomy. Though the show aired after midnight and was allegedly educational about HIV transmission and safe-sex practices, the content included homosexual depictions that traditionally have been considered to be obscene. The court found that scientific value was not substantive insofar as it was a pretense for promoting hard-core pornography, including mutual masturbation, anilingus, and oral sex. The court added, "The overall educational value, if any, of exposure to pornography does not create scientific value" (*Rees v. Texas*, 1995, p. 272). Explicit educational materials risk prosecution especially when they expose the public to nonnormative sex acts (*Bowen v. Kendrick*, 1988; Cusack, 2013a).

Expert witnesses have testified that pornographic depictions serve therapeutic purposes (*Video Village v. Kentucky*, 1992). However, expert witness testimony is not always admissible or may not establish value (*Stancil et al. v. State*, 1980). Experts must possess specialized training or knowledge to be admitted as experts. If expertise cannot be established, then scientific value cannot be established. Admissible expert testimony must convince the court that depictions possess scientific value. Experts have failed to convince the court, even after presenting expert testimony, that depictions possess scientific value, lack of frivolity, possess therapeutic value, and provide definite, measurable, and demonstrable aid to patients who experience sexual dysfunction and to professionals in the field of sexology and sex therapy (*Showcase Cinemas, Inc. et al. v. State*, 1980).

Sexism, Racism, Culturalism, and Speciesism

Some critics of the *Miller* test argue that the government and society sanction normative pornographic themes and strictly regulate deviant sexual narratives allegedly to reinforce heterosexual, white male's moral control over sex, family, women, men of color, homosexuals, children, animals, and society (*Lawrence v. Texas*, 2003; *Miller v. California*, 1973). Depictions may offend the establishment because they challenge traditional notions of who has power over pleasure and who is entitled to pleasure. The collateral effect of *Miller* and obscenity case law has been institutionalization of normality, which may authorize discrimination against minorities and politically powerless groups (Glazer, 2008). Depictions are criminalized by a process that considers the dominant groups' offense toward prurience that violates norms and criminal statutes. These statutes were created by, interpreted by, and enforced by dominant groups and local political agents. The dominant group in the United States has traditionally been wealthy, adult, Anglo, heterosexual, Protestant men. Their values are "normal." "Normal" sex upholds their values and maintains their power.

Under *Lawrence v. Texas* (2003), all nonharmful, consensual sex acts between adults became legal under a right to privacy, but public obscenity analyses are not governed by privacy law. It may be a crime to depict non-normative sex acts performed in private. However, in some cases, acts and depictions may be illegal (e.g., pedophilia and sadomasochism). Depictions of legal activities may be prosecuted as obscenity. Some examples are excretion, interracial sex, group sex, sex with legally consenting minors, facial ejaculation performed by men or women, and lactation (Cusack, 2013c). These examples may demonstrate that some depictions of women, racial and political minorities, children, and animals receiving pleasure or possibly in positions of sexual dominance offend the establishment. These depictions contravene normal pornography, which predominantly depicts white European or European American men in dominant positions receiving pleasure.

White people's right to marry nonwhite people was established in 1967 in *Loving v. Virginia* (1967). Depictions of interracial couples are never per se obscene, like bestiality and excretory functions; however, they may be persecuted. In at least one case, interracial pornography was so offensive that it led to attempted murder. Larry Flynt, founder of *Hustler* magazine, has been arrested and convicted of obscenity on several occasions since founding *Hustler* in 1974. In 1978, officials in the state of Georgia bought a copy of *Hustler* magazine and prosecuted Flynt for obscenity in county court. During the trial, Flynt was shot by a sniper while standing in front of the courthouse. The attack paralyzed Flynt. Following the shooting, an investigation failed to reveal the identity of the shooter, but authorities were certain that the shooting related to *Hustler* magazine. Years after the shooting, Joseph Paul Franklin confessed to attacking Flynt. Franklin committed several racially motivated attacks and murders. He attacked Flynt because of an interracial depiction featured in *Hustler*. This shooting was an extreme act of violence, but during that era in the South, racism was normal. Such depictions were offenses and violated the law. Interracial marriages between whites and nonwhites were legalized only 11 years before Flynt was shot. Yet, approximately five decades later, depictions of interracial sex may continue to inflame the establishment.

Conclusion

Members of the government and community decide whether depictions are obscene. Case-by-case determinations are made to protect speech as much as possible. National standards may redeem depictions found at the local level to be shameful, prurient, and offensive. Artistic, political, scientific, and literary value may be demonstrated by experts who testify about national standards. However, certain kinds of depictions, like bestiality or explicit cartoons of child rape, are rarely found to possess more than *de minimis* value. Critics have argued that the law allows dominant groups to infringe on nonharmful speech that threatens the status quo.

References

Ashcroft v. Free Speech Coalition, 535 U.S. 234 (2002).

Bose, P. (2013, October 24). Love, cast in stone: Temples in India depicting erotic art. DNA. Retrieved from http://www.dnaindia.com/lifestyle/report-love-cast-in-stone-temples-in-india-depicting-erotic-art-1907716

Bowen v. Kendrick, 487 U.S. 589 (1988).

Brockett v. Spokane Arcades, Inc., 472 U.S. 491 (1985).

Censoring art: During the renaissance and today. (2010, August 29). Escuela Honors History Block D. Retrieved from http://escuelahonorshistory-block-d.blogspot.com/2010/08/censoring-art-during-renaissance-and.html

Charles, D. M. (2012). *The FBI's obscene file: J. Edgar Hoover and the Bureau's crusade against smut*. Lawrence: University Press of Kansas.

Clary, M. (1990, October 21). Jurors acquit 2 Live Crew in obscenity case. *Los Angeles Times*. Retrieved from http://articles.latimes.com/1990-10-21/news/mn-4279_1_live-crew

Closen, M. L. (1998). The decade of Supreme Court avoidance of aids: Denial of certiorari in HIV-AIDS cases and its adverse effects on human rights. *Albany Law Review*, *61*(3), 897–987.

Commonwealth v. Gordon et al., Pa. D. & C. Dec. LEXIS 242 (1949); 66 Pa. D. & C. 101 (1949).

Cusack, C. M. (2012). Boob laws: An analysis of social deviance with in gender, family, or the home (etudes 2). *Women's Rights Law Reporter*, *33*, 197–217.

Cusack, C. M. (2013a). Comparative sexology: Nonconsensual insemination in the United States and the European Union. *Sexologies*, *23*(1), e19–e23.

Cusack, C. M. (2013b). Feminism and husbandry: Drawing the fine line between mine and bovine. *Journal for Critical Animal Studies*, *11*(1), 24–45.

Cusack, C. M. (2013c). Obscene squirting: If the government thinks it's urine, then they've got another think coming. *Texas Journal of Women and the Law*, *22*, 45–69.

Dabhoiwala, F. (2012). *The origins of sex: A history of the first sexual revolution*. New York: Oxford University Press.

Elkin, S. (1987). Taking serious value seriously: Obscenity, *Pope v. Illinois*, and an objective standard. *University of Miami*, *41*, 855–877.

Federal Communications Commission v. Pacifica Foundation et al., 438 U.S. 726 (1978).

Fla. Stat. § 847.011 (2012).

Four Star Publications, Inc. v. Erbe, 181 F. Supp. 483, 485 (S.D. Iowa 1960).Germaine, D. (2001). Regulating rap music: It doesn't melt in your mouth. *Journal of Art and Entertainment Law*, *11*, 83–132.

Ginzburg v. U.S., 383 U.S. 463 (1966).

Glass, L. (2006). Redeeming value: Obscenity and Anglo-American modernism. *Critical Inquiry*, *32*, 341–361.

Glazer, E. M. (2008). When obscenity discriminates. *Northwestern University Law Review*, *102*, 1379–1439.

Greek Islands. (n.d.) Sex in ancient Greece. Greek-Islands.us. Retrieved February 2, 2014, from http://www.greek-islands.us/ancient-greece/sex-in-ancient-greece/

Greek "obscene art" trial delayed. (2005, June 3). *BBC News*. Retrieved from http://news.bbc.co.uk/2/hi/europe/4606533.stm

Griswold v. Connecticut, 381 U.S. 479 (1965).

Gye, H. (2013, September 30). Nude paintings, obscene sculptures and gods having sex with animals: Pompeii's treasure trove of erotic artefacts which prudish scholars kept locked up. *Daily Mail*. Retrieved from http://www.dailymail.co.uk/news/article-2439371/Nude-paintings-obscene-sculptures-gods-having-sex-animals-Pompeiis-explicit-artefacts-kept-secret-prudish-scholars-19th-century-Europe.html

Hamling v. U.S., 418 U.S. 87 (1974).

Heyman, B. J. (1999). *The National Endowment for the Arts v. Finley*: The Supreme Court's artful yet indecent proposal. *New York Law School Journal of Human Rights*, *16*, 439–473.

Higgins, C. (2009, November 24). Catullus still shocks 2,000 years on. *The Guardian*. Retrieved from http://www.theguardian.com/culture/charlottehigginsblog/2009/nov/24/catullus-mark-lowe

Hijek, B. (2010, October 20). 20 years ago today three members of the rap group 2 Live Crew acquitted of obscenity charges. *Sun Sentinel*. Retrieved from http://articles.sun-sentinel.com/2010-10-20/entertainment/sfl-2-live-crew-20-years-ago-102010_1_obscenity-charges-e-c-records-mark-brother-marquis-ross

In re Arentsen, 26 W. N. C. 359 (1890).

Jacobellis v. Ohio, 378 U.S. 184 (1964).

Jenkins v. Georgia, 418 U.S. 153 (1974).

Joseph Burstyn, Inc. v. Wilson, 343 U.S. 495 (1952).

Kaplan v. California, 413 U.S. 115 (1973).

Kieran, M. (2002). On obscenity: The thrill and repulsion of the morally prohibited. *Philosophy and Phenomenological Research*, *64*(1), 31–55.

Lasker, S. (2002). Sex and the city: Zoning "pornography peddlers and live nude shows." *UCLA Law Review*, *49*, 1139–1185.

Lawrence v. Texas, 539 U.S. 558 (2003).

Leff, T. P. (1995). Implications of government funding to the arts in the aftermath of *Rust v. Sullivan*. *American University Law Review*, *45*, 353.

Loftin, C. (2012). J. Edgar Hoover's smutty obsession. H-Histsex. Retrieved from http://www.h-net.org/reviews/showrev.php?id=36738

Loving v. Virginia, 388 U.S. 1 (1967).

McDonald, B. P. (2008). If obscenity were to discriminate. *Northwestern University Law Review Colloquy*, *103*, 72–87.

Miller v. California, 413 U.S. 15 (1973).

Munkittrick, D. (2009). Music as speech: A First Amendment category unto itself. *Federal Communications Law Journal*, *62*(3), 665–690.

National Endowment for the Arts v. Finley, 524 U.S. 569 (1998).

New York v. Ferber, 458 U.S. 747 (1982).
Northcraft, D. M. (2004). A nation scared: Children, sex, and the denial of humanity: A review essay on Judith Levine's *Harmful to minors: The perils of protecting children from sex* [Book review]. *American University Journal of Gender, Social Policy and the Law, 12*, 483.
One, Inc. v. Olesen, 355 U.S. 371 (1958).
Pinkus v. U.S., 436 U.S. 293 (1978).
Pompeii: Erotic art and roman sexuality. (2012, May 21). Ancient digger. Retrieved from http://www.ancientdigger.com/2012/05/pompeii-erotic-art-and-roman-sexuality.html
Pope v. Illinois, 481 U.S. 497 (1987).
Rabban, D. M. (1999). Cultural speech and political speech in historical perspective. *Boston University Law Review, 79*, 717.
Reddington, F. P., & Kreisel, B. W. (Eds.). (2009). *Sexual assault.* Durham, NC: Carolina Academic Press.
Rees v. Texas, 909 S.W.2d 264, 265-66 (Tex. Ct. App. 1995).
Robson, J. (2009, November 25). The Ancient Greeks were the true masters of obscenity. *London Evening Standard.* Retrieved from http://www.standard.co.uk/news/the-ancient-greeks-were-the-true-masters-of-obscenity-6732498.html
Schrink, J. (1985). The boundaries of Eros: Sex crime and sexuality in renaissance Venice. By Guido Ruggiero. *Journal of Criminal Law and Criminology, 76*(4), 1156–1158.
Showcase Cinemas, Inc. et al. v. State, 156 Ga. App. 225 (1980).
Skyywalker Records, Inc. v. Navarro, 739 F. Supp. 578, 582 (S.D. Fla. 1990).
Skyywalker Records, Inc. v. Navarro, 960 F.2d 134 (1992).
Smith, E. (1995, June 2). As obscene as they wanna be? *Entertainment Weekly.* Retrieved from http://www.ew.com/ew/article/0,,297450,00.html
Stancil et al. v. State, 155 Ga. App. 731 (1980).
Stanley v. Georgia, 394 U.S. 557 (1969).
U.S. Ex Rel. Milwaukee Social Democratic Publishing Company v. Burleson, 255 U.S. 407 (1921).
U.S. v. 12 200-Ft. Reels of Super 8mm. Film, 413 U.S. 123 (1973).
U.S. v. One Book Entitled Ulysses by James Joyce, 5 F. Supp. 182 (S. D. N. Y., 1933).
U.S. v. One Book Entitled Ulysses by James Joyce, 72 F.2d 705 (2d Cir. 1934).
U.S. v. One Package of Japanese Pessaries, 86 F.2d 737 (2d Cir. 1936).
U.S. v. Orito, 413 U.S. 139 (1973).
U.S. v. Thomas, 74 F.3d 701, 704-05 (6th Cir. 1996).
Va. Code Ann. § 18.2-372 (2008).
Video Village v. Kentucky, 825 S.W.2d 288 (1992).
Walker, M. (1990, June 11). 2 Live Crew singers arrested after show deputies cite lyrics, obscenity. *Sun Sentinel.* Retrieved from http://articles.sun-sentinel.com/1990-06-11/news/9001130225_1_lyrics-band-deputies
Walsh, B. (1991, January 18). Rock group not guilty of obscenity. *Sun Sentinel.* Retrieved from http://articles.sun-sentinel.com/1991-01-18/news/9101030982_1_club-futura-obscenity-jurors
White, J. N. (2011). Kiddie porn in the gallery: Defending the artist's corpus or invading the corporal integrity of the subject. *Villanova Sports and Entertainment Law Journal, 18*(2), 683–710.
Wolfson, N. (1994). Eroticism, obscenity, pornography and free speech. *Brooklyn Law Review, 60*, 1037.
Wyo. Stat. Ann. § 6-4-301(a)(iii-v) (2005).

Pornography Production and the U.S. Criminal Justice System

4

Overview

Throughout the United States, commercial production of pornography is typically illegal. It may be criminalized under prostitution statutes or obscenity statutes. Production of obscenity is illegal in every jurisdiction. However, interpretations of what constitutes obscenity may vary widely between jurisdictions. Child pornography production is almost invariably illegal. Hard-core depictions of children may also constitute obscenity. In a few jurisdictions, for example, Nevada and Los Angeles, California, production of pornography is legal, but may be regulated. When production is illegal, any participant may be liable.

Obscenity

Production and distribution of obscenity in the United States is forbidden. Within pornographic films, some scenes may depict protected speech acts, but other scenes may depict explicit acts that are obscene. Because the *Miller* test, discussed in Chapter 3, evaluates work as a whole, some offensive scenes can effectively tarnish an entire work, leading to prosecution under obscenity statutes (*Miller v. California*, 1973).

Though some production may be illegal per se in certain jurisdictions (e.g., sadomasochism or excretory functions), other depictions are prosecuted on case-by-case bases (Va. Stat. § 18.2-372, 2014). Pornographers have tried to up the ante or push the envelope by producing explicit or fetishistic films that are intended to be legally distributable. Others have intentionally broken boundaries with full expectations of being prosecuted. Their goals may be to create new art, expand First Amendment protection, generate publicity, or sell hard-core pornography for profit. Their work may embody various intentions simultaneously.

Some companies producing explicit films have survived obscenity prosecution. In the case of *U.S. v. Stagliano*, director John "Buttman" Stagliano and his corporation, Evil Angel Productions, Inc., were charged with distribution of obscenity (*U.S. v. Stagliano*, 2010). The government prosecuted Stagliano over films titled *Milk Nymphos* and *Storm Squirters 2 "Target Practice."* FBI

Agent Daniel Bradley testified that he believed that these films obscenely depicted excretory functions, that is, in a patently offensive manner appealing to prurient interests (Brint, 2010). In the films, performers pump milk using syringes and tubes into women's anus and vaginas (Hess, 2010a, 2010b). Female actors expel fluid into other actors' mouths. Scenes depict actors squirting fluid over great distances for target practice. Some controversy exists because Agent Bradley and the state moved forward with prosecution under the belief that these scenes seemed to depict excretion. However, some scenes depicted milk squirting and others depicted female ejaculation, which is distinguishable from excretion (Cusack, 2013d). The state argued that Stagliano's depictions were obscene irrespective of supposed use of milk or depictions of ejaculation because they depicted or seemed to depict excretory functions. Stagliano argued that the liquid used was not urine. Judge Richard Leon held that the government failed to carry its burden. The court did not rule on free speech claims because the case was dismissed because of insufficient evidence (Brint, 2010; Hess, 2010a; Hsu, 2010; *Jenkins v. Georgia*, 1974; *Pope v. Illinois*, 1987). Judge Leon also dismissed other charges against Stagliano relating to the films' accessibility to minors (Hsu, 2010). Police were able to click links to pornographic trailers for films on Stagliano's website (Hess, 2010a, 2010b; *U.S. v. Stagliano*, 2010). These links were not protected by membership passwords or privacy portals. They were accessible to the public from a hotel lobby in Washington, D.C. The government argued that a movie trailer titled *Belladonna: Fetish Fanatic Chapter 5* was obscene and potentially accessible to minors. The government failed to sufficiently prove its case, and those charges were also dismissed for lack of evidence.

Some production companies unsuccessfully defend against encounters with the U.S. criminal justice system. Fetishist and pornography film director Marco Fiorito produced a trailer advertisement for his movie *Hungry Bitches* (MFX Video, 2007). The trailer was known as "2 Girls 1 Cup." In the trailer, two women engage in coprophagia and, ostensibly, fecalphelia. The film *Hungry Bitches* depicts performers consuming vomit in addition to feces. Like Stagliano's trailer, Fiorito's trailer was freely and openly available to the public. The trailer became an Internet sensation that inspired viral reaction-videos (Cusack, 2012). Countless shocked viewers watched the trailer and recorded their reactions to it. Then, viewers posted their reaction-videos on mainstream websites, like Youtube.com. Reaction-videos to "2 Girls 1 Cup" created an enormous nexus between mainstream social media and hard-core pornography, which seemed to demonstrate that the film trailer possessed some social value. Nevertheless, the work was deemed to be obscene by the government (i.e., possessing *de minimis* value).

Danilo Simones Croce, who served as the agent for Fiorito's Brazilian production company in the United States, was charged by the U.S. federal government (*U.S. v. Croce*, 2006; *U.S. v. Croce*, EFC No. 98, 2007; *U.S. v. Croce*,

EFC No. 107, 2007). Croce was charged with selling, broadcasting, and transporting obscenity. Though federal statutes do not per se criminalize the excretory sex acts depicted in Fiorito's film or trailer, pornography involving excretory functions has commonly been criminalized at the state level, which plays a part in the *Miller* test and federal prosecution (Va. Code Ann. § 18.2-372, 2008; Wyo. Stat. Ann. § 6-4-301(a)(iii), 2005). Furthermore, availability of excretory pornography to minors is criminalized under federal statutes (18 U.S.C. §§ 1460–1470, 2006). In response to prosecution, Fiorito first unsuccessfully asserted that he used chocolate ice cream to simulate excrement. Then, he claimed that he did not intend to produce prurient pornography, but intended to produce fetishistic shock art. Finally, he stated that, in Brazil, his speech acts are protected. Each of these contentions failed. Croce pleaded guilty and was sentenced to three years of unsupervised probation. The production company, established in Florida, forfeited $98,000 of assets.

Condoms

San Fernando Valley in Los Angeles, California, is a major U.S. hub for pornography production. Production regulations have increased in the Valley because of numerous incidents of sexually transmitted disease (STD) transmission between actors (Lin, 2012; Shahbazi, 2013). Additional regulations were opposed by the Free Speech Coalition and other advocates for pornography, but their opposition was overcome by support from the American Medical Association, California Conference of Local AIDS Directors, American Public Health Association, National Coalition of STD Directors, California STD Controllers Association, National Association of City and County Health Officials, California Medical Association, and AIDS Healthcare Foundation. These groups rallied city voters to further regulate STD transmission by requiring pornography actors to use condoms (Section 12.22.1(e), 2012). The City of Los Angeles Ordinance 181989, also called Measure B, Safer Sex in the Adult Film Industry Act, and Adult Film Industry Act, was passed with 56% of the vote, demonstrating that a significant portion of voters opposed the measure (Adult Film Industry Act, 2012; "Measure B Passes," 2012).

California Code of Regulations Title 8, Section 5193, mandates barrier protection from contact with blood or other potentially infectious material. Condoms must be used during production of adult films. Yet, producers routinely violate worker safety provisions. HIV and STDs transmitted during production have undermined policy rationales. The City of Los Angeles Ordinance requires production companies to apply for permits to film pornography. All film permitting is overseen by the Los Angeles Police Department and City of Los Angeles. Permits will be granted only if actors use condoms and condom-safe, water-based or silicone-based lubricants during production. Permitting fees help pay for inspectors to randomly visit production sets, as set forth in Section 12.22.1 (The City of Los Angeles Ordinance 181989, 2012). Enforcement includes civil fines, and misdemeanor charges may be brought against recidivists or egregious violators (Measure B Passes, 2012). Requests for permits to film decreased by 95% in 2013 because of the new law (Associated Press, 2014).

This law may impact U.S. pornography production and audiences. When the law was first proposed, production companies threated to relocate outside Los Angeles or California (Lin, 2012; Measure B Passes, 2012). Some production companies may have little alternative to production within the state of California because pornography production in other states is not feasible or protected under the First Amendment (Minn. Stat. § 609.321, 2013). Some companies have successfully relocated to Nevada where prostitution is legal and regulated, and production may be more cost-effective than in California (Associated Press, 2014). Some companies have moved to tolerant jurisdictions in Florida, but worker safety complaints in Florida have followed the industry. Relocating does not address the prevalence of HIV transmission among pornographers.

Requirements for condom use add some educational value to films. Though educational messages cannot be required by the government because of free speech protections, the incidental benefit provided to viewers can encourage safer sex, especially among uneducated or young viewers (Cusack, 2013b). Increased education about condom use could potentially reduce other crimes, such as reproductive coercion, intentional disease transmission, or nonconsensual insemination (Cusack, 2013c). Condom use in pornography may encourage viewers to perceive actors as being in control and consenting to sex (Cusack & Waranius, 2012). However, it is well established that some rapists wear condoms. Thus, condom use in pornography may not actually correlate with consent. Furthermore, false perceptions that pornography production is always consensual may obfuscate the role of sex trafficking in production. Yet, viewers who are becoming educated about sex and self-efficacy by watching pornography may not be informed about more complex issues, and they may likely benefit from educational messages about safe sex (Cusack, 2013a).

Producers, Distributors, and Performers

There are numerous reasons why people involved in pornography could be prosecuted. Depending on the content of the scenes, ages of actors, and other factors, producers, distributors, and actors could be prosecuted for multiple offenses. Jurisdictional variations between statutory definitions, severity of offenses, and local opinions about erotic depictions can greatly influence prosecution and outcomes of cases.

Many jurisdictions may prosecute production of pornography using commercial sex laws; the government may prosecute performers or anyone deriving income from commercial sex (Fla. Stat. § 796.05(1), 2013). Some cases have articulated a difference between prostitution and pornography production. Pornography production differs from prostitution because, during production, money is paid to actors who permit others to record them having sex; prostitution occurs when others are paid to perform sex acts (*People v. Freeman*, 1988). Some jurisdictions directly ban pornography production and distribution (Minn. Stat. § 609.321, 2013; NY CLS Penal § 230.15, 2013; *People v. Kovner*, 1978). For example, New York statutes explicitly define prostitution to include hiring actors to film sexual conduct. Minnesota prostitution statutes prosecute businesses or individuals who hire people to commit sexual contact. These statutes also allow for prosecution of people who maintain establishments that allow pornography production. Laws could reach lessors, lessees, security guards, and property managers. Some statutes may be so inclusive that they could possibly include chauffeurs who transport performers. In some cases, participants may be liable even if they are not certain that pornography production occurs on the premises.

Some states are more inclusive than others. Many states, like Minnesota, prosecute any parties involved in child pornography production. One may not assist in concealing a crime, yet in most jurisdictions, there is no general duty to aid victims of crimes or to report crimes. Special relationships may create a duty; for example, parents have a duty to protect their children. Thus, parents can be prosecuted in most jurisdictions for negligently allowing their children to become victims of commercial sexual abuse. In Washington, anyone who permits commercial sexual abuse of a minor can be prosecuted; anyone who permits commercial sexual abuse of a minor on his or her property can be charged with a misdemeanor even if the minor voluntarily engages in sex (Wash. Rev. Code § 9.68A.103, 2013). Possessing or controlling premises known to be used for commercial sexual abuse of a minor requires intervention to stop the abuse and reporting to the authorities.

Distributing child pornography is a crime in every jurisdiction. However, some parties may incidentally distribute child pornography. In California, this would be a misdemeanor (Cal Lab Code § 1309.5, 2014). If distribution is incidental, then a distributor's identity will be discovered and confidentially becomes available to law enforcement for three years. If a retailer buys images of minors, then the dealer's name and vendor's name confidentially will become available to law enforcement for the same period. Any person who induces a minor to model for any product that is associated with child pornography may be prosecuted under felony statutes even if the sexual content in the depiction is computer generated or is of another child. Simulated pornography is discussed in detail in Chapter 16. Knowledge or belief of a minor's age by a producer may be necessary for felony prosecution. Lack of knowledge may be no excuse (HRS § 712-1218, 2013). In some jurisdictions (e.g., Hawaii), failure to maintain a record of a performer's age may be a felony.

Child pornography prosecution is not limitless. For example, in California, producers, parents, or other parties cannot be prosecuted under commercial child sexual abuse statues more than 10 years after production of pornographic material (Cal Pen Code § 801.2, 2014). This limitation does not apply to possessing, selling, buying, or distributing images. Statutes of limitations are discussed further in Chapter 18. Commercial child sexual abuse statutes may not legally emancipate minors or lawfully married minors who depict sex with their spouses (Cal Pen Code § 311.4(e), 2014). Several jurisdictions exempt married minors and their spouses from child pornography production statutes. Exemptions may permit minors and spouses to distribute explicit images of the married minor. However, production and distribution of these images may amount to obscenity, even if they are not child pornography. Child pornography laws are designed to protect children, but obscenity laws are designed to protect viewers in the community (White, 2011).

Prosecution for obscenity between adult spouses may occur under circumstances that seem to merit constitutional protection (Furry Girl, 2011). For example, an adult married couple, Warren and Theresa Taylor, were prosecuted in Polk County, Florida. They were charged with numerous misdemeanors for selling obscenity and a single felony charge for commercial distribution of obscenity. The couple produced pornographic films in their home, which they sold online. Films included scenes between the couple and between Theresa and male actors, lesbian scenes featuring Theresa, and solo fantasy scenes in which Theresa would simulate sex while talking to paying viewers throughout what is described as point-of-view (POV) cinematography. POV scenes did not physically involve customers, and the couple was never charged with prostitution. A neighbor placed an anonymous tip with police that pornography was being produced in the couple's home. Police posed as clients and ordered pornography online. The couple was arrested, and their production equipment was seized. Theresa Taylor says that she does not believe that their work was obscene and did not understand why she was arrested for obscenity. "We have NEVER done fisting, rape-style content, underage people, BDSM or bondage with sex. We do not understand [our prosecution] when we can get all this stuff on DishNetwork on TV now!" (Furry Girl, 2011). Perspectives like Theresa's are discussed in detail in Chapter 3. The couple pleaded to a misdemeanor charge of selling obscenity, they agreed to pay a small fine, and the remaining charges were dropped (Schottelkotte, 2012). The Taylors forfeited some videotapes, though their equipment was returned. After they pleaded, the Taylors moved to California, where production of pornography is legal, and they continued to sell the same depictions online.

First Amendment protection of free speech can be invoked only if defendants plead not guilty. Pornography may be found to be legal if defendants win at trial. However, most defendants plead to crimes in exchange for a plea deal with the government. Defendants often plead to avoid trial and costs of litigation. Plea deals may involve reduced charges, fines, and probation instead of jail time. Defendants who plead are unable to invoke any applicable First Amendment protection and occasionally accept fines or sentences to end the stress and cost of prosecution. In some cases, it has been argued that material that is believed to be obscene by police officers, judges, and prosecutors would be found to be nonobscene by jurors under the *Miller* test. Nevertheless, if cases do not go to trial, then the argument is moot.

International Production and Distribution

Controlling or stopping production of child pornography is much more difficult than interrupting pornography distribution chains (White, 2011). The U.S. government uses federal laws and resources to combat international child pornography. This is discussed further in Chapter 22. Dozens of U.S. federal agencies investigate and prosecute international production and distribution of child pornography. Agencies fighting against child pornography include, but are not limited to, the following: U.S. Attorney's Offices, Office of Justice Programs, Federal Bureau of Investigation (FBI), U.S. Marshals Service, International Criminal Police Organization (INTERPOL), Federal Trade Commission, Internet Crimes Against Children Task Force (ICAC), Department of Homeland Security, U.S. Postal Inspection Service (USPIS), Department of Health and Human Services, Military Criminal Investigative Organizations (MCIO), National Center for Missing and Exploited Children (NCMEC), U.S. Immigration and Customs Enforcement (ICE), and Child Exploitation and Obscenity Section of Department of Justice (CEOS/DOJ) (CEOS, 2014; DOJ, 2010).

ICAC is composed of 61 separate task forces that are affiliated with 2,500 law enforcement agencies at every level (U.S. Sentencing Commission [USSC], 2012). Training, investigations, prosecutions, and forensic examinations are conducted by ICAC. In 2010, federal grants given to ICAC allowed law enforcement to investigate 32,000 cases and arrest 5,300 suspects for child pornography. The FBI investigates, conducts counterinitiatives, and analyzes evidence. In 2010, the FBI investigated 6,070 cases and arrested 1,094 people suspected of child pornography crimes. Attorneys from CEOS advise, investigate, assist with prosecution, and train prosecutors in federal U.S. Attorney's Offices. NCMEC is a federally funded nonprofit organization that is governed by the Missing Children's Assistance Act of 1983. NCMEC focuses on child abduction, exploitation, and rescue. It manages the CyberTipline and Child Victim Identification Program (CVIP). Since 1998, 1,300,000 tips have been reported to CyberTipline. Between 2005 and 2009, tips about production and dealing increased by 69%. When new images are produced and distributed online, they are tagged by CVIP, which has reviewed approximately 30 million depictions. Worldwide, 190 countries contribute information, training, and international strategies to INTERPOL.

Most online advertisement and distribution of child pornography occur outside the United States (DOJ, 2010). Chapter 22 discusses this in greater detail. Child pornography is produced for recreation and commercial gain. The Internet Watch Foundation (IWF) reports that 26% of child pornography sites are recreational purveyors. Among National Drug Intelligence Center (NDIC) professionals interviewed, 46% reported no serious financial component exists for U.S.-based websites. However, it reported that a financial component exists for websites based in Eastern European countries, which may tolerate or legalize portions of child pornography dealing. International sellers and clientele usually anonymize their activities, making investigation by U.S. authorities difficult. Information shared by foreign governments becomes crucial to U.S. investigations of proxy servers and payment sites that delete transactional records to protect users. This is discussed in further detail in Chapter 9. Though international groups may engage in unregulated or lawful child pornography activities abroad, availability of their content to U.S. citizens allows U.S. agencies to intervene and collaborate with foreign agencies (DOJ, 2010; USSC, 2012).

Every year, 1,536 domains offer child pornography, but most operate for only a few weeks or months on a limited basis. Short-lived websites present unique challenges to investigators. ICE reports that 250 sites actively maintain child pornography displays at any moment online. Networked groups distribute massive amounts of content. Single images can be downloaded or displayed thousands of times. Eradicating voluminous copies can drain law enforcement resources. When law enforcement arrest individuals in various countries, operations may continue because groups are transnational. This difficulty supports users' access to and confidence in online pornography distribution. Ending an international commercial enterprise online does not necessarily eliminate distribution. Commercial child pornography enterprises utilizing mail order catalogs are frequently detected by USPIS. E-mail advertisements and catalogs also are used by distributors, who then use federal mail to ship child pornography. These offenders typically have collected child pornography for years and have higher prevalence of hands-on offenses.

Though Secretary General John Ashcroft prosecuted more than 300 people for obscenity using the Obscenity Prosecution Task Force during his tenure, prosecution for obscenity has not been nearly as common as prosecution for child pornography or obscenity charges relating to child pornography (Clark-Flory, 2012). Because greater need exists to prosecute child pornography production and distribution, all resources once allocated to the Obscenity Prosecution Task Force have been redirected to CEOS (CEOS, 2014). Many obscene works are produced outside the United States but distributed within the United States. One well-known case arose with Ira Isaacs, who distributed explicit films, some involving excrement. Isaacs claimed films were avant-garde and protected by the First Amendment as art (Cusack, 2012). However, Isaacs also allegedly distributed a bestiality film, *Japanese Doggie 3 Way*, which seems to fall squarely within average understandings of obscenity throughout the United States (Clark-Flory, 2012). He was convicted and sentenced to four years in federal prison and three years of supervised probation (Gallegos, 2013). He was ordered to pay approximately $11,000 in fines. Chapter 16 further discusses prosecution of receipt of obscene images produced abroad.

Conclusion

Pornography production has increased significantly in recent years to accommodate growing demand online. In response, regulation of pornography production has increased in recent years. Though some jurisdictions have accommodated the growing market by regulating pornography production, many jurisdictions continue to criminalize it. Essentially, morality is a primary concern underlying criminalization policies, but participants' health and safety are grounds for criminalization and regulation. The government continues to expend greater resources to investigate and prosecute illegal depictions, especially when obscenity production involves children. Since the early 1900s, numerous obscenity prosecutions have reached the U.S. Supreme Court or been the subject of mainstream media attention. Landmark cases have carved new distinctions between legal and illegal depictions. Some of the Court's decisions have favored free speech protection, while others have favored regulation. Many highly publicized cases have resulted in successful prosecution despite public support, media attention, tenacious advocacy, or crafty constitutional claims.

References

18 U.S.C. §§ 1460–1470 (2006).

Adult Film Industry Act. (2012). Los Angeles, CA, Ordinance 181989.

Associated Press. (2014, January 17). Porn production moves to Las Vegas after California condom law. *Fox News*. Retrieved from http://www.foxnews.com/entertainment/2014/01/17/porn-production-moves-to-las-vegas-after-california-condom-law/?intcmp=features

Brint, J. (2010, July 14). Buttman trial: Courthouse porn shows milk enemas, racial epithets to D.C. jurors. *Washington City Paper*. Retrieved from http://www.washingtoncitypaper.com/blogs/sexist/2010/07/14/buttman-trial-courthouse-porn-shows-milk-enemas-racial-epithets- for-dc-jurors/

Cal Lab Code § 1309.5 (2014).

Cal Pen Code § 311.4(e) (2014).

Cal Pen Code § 801.2 (2014).

Child Exploitation and Obscenity Section (CEOS), Department of Justice. (2014). Retrieved January 16, 2014, from http://www.justice.gov/criminal/ceos/

Clark-Flory, T. (2012, February 28). My obscenity trial subpoena. Salon.com. Retrieved from http://www.salon.com/2012/02/28/my_obscenity_trial_subpoena/

Cusack, C. M. (2012). Two films, one law. *Entertainment, Art, and Sports Law Journal, 23.*

Cusack, C. M. (2013a). Comparative sexology: Nonconsensual insemination in the United States and the European Union. *Sexologies, 23*(1), e19–e23.

Cusack, C. M. (2013b). How the content of online pornography depicts expressed consent for insemination. *Online Journal of Communication and Media Technologies, 3*(3), 91–110.

Cusack, C. M. (2013c). Nonconsensual seminal transmission. *Criminal Law Bulletin, 49*(1).

Cusack, C. M. (2013d). Obscene squirting: If the government thinks it's urine, then they've got another think coming. *Texas Journal of Women and the Law, 22*, 45.

Cusack, C. M., & Waranius, M. (2012). Nonconsensual insemination and pornography: The relationship between sex roles, sex crimes, and "STRT," "Gay," and "Shemale" films on Youporn.com. *Journal of Research in Gender Studies, 2*(2), 15–33.

Department of Justice (DOJ). (2010, August). The national strategy for child exploitation prevention and interdiction. Retrieved from http://www.justice.gov/psc/docs/natstrategyreport.pdf

Fla. Stat. § 796.05(1) (2013).

Furry Girl. (2011, July 27). *The People vs. Kimberly Kupps*. Tits and Sass. Retrieved from http://titsandsass.com/the-people-vs-kimberly-kupps/

Gallegos, E. G. (2013, January 16). "Japanese Doggie 3 Way" producer sentenced to 4 years in prison in obscenity case. LAist. Retrieved from http://laist.com/2013/01/16/shock_artist_poop_producer_gets_pri.php

Hess, A. (2010a, July 14). Buttman trial: Courthouse porn viewing turns to squirting. *Washington City Paper*. Retrieved from http://www.washingtoncitypaper.com/blogs/sexist/2010/07/14/buttman-trial-courthouse-porn-viewing-turns-to-squirting/.

Hess, A. (2010b, July 13). Opening arguments in the *U.S. v. John "Buttman" Stagliano*. *Washington City Paper*. Retrieved from http://www.washingtoncitypaper.com/blogs/sexist/2010/07/13/opening-arguments-in-the-u-s-vs-john-buttman-stagliano/

HRS § 712-1218 (2013).

Hsu, S. S. (2010, July 17). U.S. district judge drops porn charges against video producer John A. Stagliano. *Washington Post*. Retrieved from http://www.washingtonpost.com/wp-dyn/content/article/2010/07/16/AR2010071605750.html

Jenkins v. Georgia, 418 U.S. 153 (1974).

Lin, R., II. (2012, July 4). L.A. County voters to decide on requiring condoms in porn. *LA Times*. Retrieved from http://latimesblogs.latimes.com/lanow/2012/07/la-county-voters-could-decide-on-requiring-condoms-in-porn.html

Measure B passes, forcing porn actors to wear condoms. (2012, November 7). *CBS Los Angeles*. Retrieved from http://losangeles.cbslocal.com/2012/11/07/measure-b-passes-forcing-porn-actors-to-wear-condoms/

MFX Video. (2007). *Hungry Bitches*.

Miller v. California, 413 U.S. 15 (1973).

Minn. Stat. § 609.321 (2013).

NY CLS Penal § 230.15 (2013).

People v. Freeman, 46 Cal.3d 419, 250 Cal.Rptr. 598, 758 P.2d 1128 (1988).

People v. Kovner, 96 Misc 2d 414, 409 NYS2d 349 (1978).

Pope v. Illinois, 481 U.S. 497 (1987).

Schottelkotte, S. (2012, February 28). Former Lake Wales couple plead no contest in pornography case. *The Ledger*. Retrieved from http://www.theledger.com/article/20120228/news/120229245?tc=ar#gsc.tab=0

Shahbazi, R. (2013, September 18). Former pornography performers urge condom use in industry. *Los Angeles ABC News*. Retrieved from http://abclocal.go.com/kabc/story?id=9253665

The City of Los Angeles Ordinance 181989 (2012).

U.S. Sentencing Commission. (2012). Report to the Congress: Federal child pornography offenses: Technology and investigation by law enforcement in child pornography cases. Retrieved from http://www.ussc.gov/Legislative_and_Public_Affairs/Congressional_Testimony_and_Reports/Sex_Offense_Topics/201212_Federal_Child_Pornography_Offenses/Chapter_03.pdf

U.S. v. Croce, No. 06-00182 (M.D. Fla. Sep. 5, 2006), ECF No. 1 (Affidavit).

U.S. v. Croce, No. 06-00182 (M.D. Fla. Aug. 27, 2007), EFC No. 98 (Criminal Complaint).

U.S. v. Croce, No. 06-00182 (M.D. Fla. Aug. 29, 2007), ECF No. 107 (Judgment in a Criminal Case).

U.S. v. Stagliano, 693 F. Supp. 2d 25; 729 F.Supp.2d 222 (2010).

Va. Code Ann. § 18.2-372 (2008).

Va. Stat. § 18.2-372 (2014).

Wash. Rev. Code § 9.68A.103 (2013).

White, J. N. (2011). Kiddie porn in the gallery: Defending the artist's corpus or invading the corporal integrity of the subject. *Villanova Sports and Entertainment Law Journal, 18*(2), 683–710.

Wyo. Stat. Ann. § 6-4-301(a)(iii) (2005).

Children, Pornography, and the Law

5

Overview

Societal constructions of childhood sexuality influence legal understandings of children. Most minors cannot legally consent to sex. They may engage in sex voluntarily, but sometimes the law classifies voluntary sex as rape rather than consensual sex. One legal premise for prosecuting child pornography is the government's perception that children are vulnerable, forced, or violated victims of sexual abuse rather than willing participants in pornography. Children's alleged sexual purity and naïveté provide rationales for the government's prohibition against children possessing pornography.

Societal Constructions of Childhood Sexuality

Traditional morals may be threatened by childhood sexuality. Though prepubertal sexual experimentation and postpubertal relationships are somewhat common, tradition opposes sexualization of children by adults or other children. However, authorities claim that policies limiting childhood sexuality are designed to protect children from several harms, such as exploitation and sexual abuse, emotional trauma, physical damage, intimate partner violence, unintended pregnancy, and sexually transmitted disease (STD) (Cusack, 2013a; Fischer, 2005; Wurtele, 2009). Yet, critics argue that excessive control and institutionalized denial of childhood sexuality may harm children.

Historical focus on the importance of marriage and procreative marital relations may be at the root of strong prohibitions against child sexuality and pornography (Northcraft, 2004). General understandings of adult sexuality guide law (*Pinkus v. U.S.*, 1978). Law is more deeply influenced by tradition than science in many regards. Objective knowledge about childhood sexuality is lacking. Research studies investigating childhood sexuality are rare because children are considered to be a vulnerable population (Fischer, 2005). Institutional review boards rarely authorize researchers to directly study childhood sexuality because children are allegedly placed at risk by studies about sex, for a few reasons. First, when children self-report sexual experiences, possible breaches of anonymity or confidentiality could lead to unwanted consequences for respondents. Second, exposing children to information about sex may raise moral and ethical considerations. Third, survey questions could cause more than minimal discomfort or trauma. However, little research demonstrates that surveying children about sexual experiences results in trauma unless children are reliving past trauma during an interview.

Childhood sexuality is most frequently studied through adults' memories, which may be tainted by time, experience, emotions, knowledge, analysis and reflection, substance use, and faultiness. When children are studied directly, inclusion criteria typically require children to have a history of risky sexual behavior. These studies tend to target children who suffer from sexual trauma, highlight deviant behaviors, and increase existing literature and attitudes linking social ills to childhood sexuality. Thus, throughout U.S. history, studies about healthy or pleasant childhood desires, sexual practices, and experiences have been infrequent.

Traditionally, churches produced reports about sex and promoted marriage, which was sponsored and regulated by the church (Northcraft, 2004). Procreative sexuality was emphasized as a primary purpose for martial relations. U.S. colonists taught children about normal sexuality through religious education and family discussions or role modeling. Some children may have witnessed parents or married adults copulating in their homes, which provided little privacy. Women were thought to be more susceptible to sexual weakness than men, and colonists subscribed to these beliefs. Court records and journals from that era, however, reveal that unmarried couples experimented sexually, and planter-class white men fornicated with servants or slaves.

By the 1700s, anachronistic relationships between marriage and pregnancy developed, such that one-third of brides were pregnant (Northcraft, 2004). Pregnancy expedited courtship. Bundling pregnancy and marriage benefited society during this era because it ensured marriages. This is evidenced by the fact that during this era, couples needed only to publicly confess their sin of premarital sex to receive forgiveness and condonation. Public intervention into sexual relationships was common. Far worse than pregnancy out of wedlock was extramarital sex or bastardized births, which were included in a class of impropriety that could be met by severe consequences (e.g., corporal punishment, fines, and humiliation).

During the Victorian era, circa the nineteenth century, value was allotted to pleasurable aspects of sex (Northcraft, 2004). In relation to the fact that reproduction was not the sole purpose of sex, women reproduced fewer offspring. At the same time, society focused on purity, which resulted in increased age requirements for consensual sex. Statutory rape laws raised the age of legal consent from 10 years old to between 14 years old and 18 years old. Female genital mutilation was practiced in the United States at that time to control female sexuality. Focus on purity dovetailed with society's concern that men would force female children into prostitution and subservience. One-third of Victorian boys reportedly had premarital sex. Some of this sexual activity occurred with prostitutes. Among Victorian girls, only 7% experienced premarital sex. Society held diverse and conflicting perceptions of women, sex, reproduction, and children's sexuality during this era. These research findings may legitimize Victorian society's concerns about prostitution and sexual predation at that time. Three-fifths of Victorian boys reported that they experienced masturbation. Almost half of women, 40%, reported childhood and adolescent masturbation. Researchers discovered strong correlations between lack of sex education among women, distaste toward sex, and marital unhappiness. Throughout the century, same-sex relationships were believed to be platonic. Late in the 1900s, homosexuality was publicly identified and distinguished from heterosexual norms.

In 1905, Sigmund Freud argued that sexual desires begin long before adulthood, marriage, or puberty; they begin in infancy (Kern, 1973). Freud's research indicated that small children regularly experience erections, masturbate, and engage in activities that are like coitus. Many of Freud's studies were of adults' memories of childhood, and much of Freud's psychoanalytical work has been refuted or abandoned by the scholarly community. However, Freud's research helped develop processes for analyzing biological sexuality among young children.

Childhood sexuality may be biological, as Freud suggested, but to some extent, it may also be a social construct managed by adults. Freud theorized that urges to suckle, anal stimulation, genital stimulation, and other forms of sexuality manifested during the three stages of development are biological. Contextualized social responses to biological urges train children to behave as members of society. For example, without society's acceptance of breast-feeding and women's willingness to nurse, infants could not explore oral-stage urges with nipples. If infants were prohibited from contacting breasts, bottles, pacifiers, or any other nipple-like objects, then their sexual development may deviate. Children may innately suck their thumbs, toes, fingers, and other objects, but caretakers could prevent this by covering or binding children's feet and hands until the oral stage passed. Elimination of any opportunity to suckle could cause infants to experience anxiety or other problems, like antisocial behavior and greed. Society's permissive attitude toward suckling allows children to entertain or satisfy biological impulses. Furthermore, adults' perceptions of childhood sexuality may influence social responses to children.

In the 1920s, approximately half of dating-age youth were allegedly engaging in premarital sex (Northcraft, 2004). Mixed-gender school environments provided youth with access to intimacy and potential targets for their desires. Automobiles granted youth with access to privacy and independence. Booming urban environments limited parents' abilities to shelter children. Gendered morality classified sexually active girls as bad girls even when they participated in monogamous, heterosexual relationships. Homosexuals sought out single-sex environments, like the military, where they could disguise intimate relationships.

In the mid-1900s, Alfred Kinsey revolutionized science by studying sexual behavior. Kinsey discovered that the great majority of male respondents engaged in masturbation and heterosexual fondling. Almost all had intercourse. Three-fifths of women had masturbated, the great majority had experienced fondling, and half engaged in premarital coital intimacy. This suggested that purity among youth was a myth. Males either were more truthful in their responses or experienced sexual activity with partners unidentified by this study (e.g., women in other cultures, prostitutes, etc.). It also strongly suggests that males were involved in significantly more homosexual activity than society condoned or discussed. Later that century, the sexual revolution inspired women to become more sexually active or as honest about their sexual experiences as men. Women experienced greater rates of homosexuality and adultery. Young children's sexuality was discussed more openly, and some communities encouraged nonsexual nudity to be shared by nonfamilial adults and children. Traditional stereotypes about relationships between pedophilia and homosexuality were denied by the sexual revolution, but some sexually liberated youths engaged in intergenerational sexual activities, which justified the establishment's fears.

By the 1980s, traditional ideas connecting nude youth and perversion had outlasted the sexual revolution (Mirkin, 2009; Wilgoren, 2002). In *New York v. Ferber* (1982), the U.S. Supreme Court held that nude photos of youth do not merit First Amendment protection under *Miller* (*Miller v. California*, 1973).

Ashcroft v. Free Speech Coalition (2002) questioned society's promotion of illusory understandings of teens' purity, safety, and morality. The Court recognized that there is some social and commercial interest in depicting childhood sexuality for adult consumption. However, use of children to depict childhood sexuality continued to be banned, while adults' depictions of childhood sexuality (e.g., role play or acting) were upheld. The Court protected depictions of childhood sexuality as long as members of the public do not believe that they actually transmit or possess authentic child pornography. Though *Free Speech Coalition* (2002) protects children from sexual exploitation, it also protects adults' control of childhood sexuality, it invades children's private sexual matters, and it continues to reserve depictions of sexuality for those who are postpubertal, procreative, and legally capable of marrying.

Child Pornography: Black Letter

Child pornography seems to be easily definable and prosecutable, but Black Letter law and persuasive case law demonstrate some variability. In *Osborne v. Ohio* (1990), the U.S. Supreme Court differentiated between obscenity and child pornography. Unlike obscenity, there is no pronged test, community-based standard, or determination of national value. Child pornography is unprotected per se. Unlike obscenity, simple possession of child pornography is illegal. Children are victimized by mere possession because possession increases demand for production. Simple possession demeans victims because it memorializes victimization, and children suffer knowing that their images are used for masturbation. Possessors of child pornography may be held strictly liable even when a depicted child was honestly believed to be an adult. This is because child pornography is viewed as a serious affront to morality, a crime of moral turpitude, a breach of social duties owed to children, and a violation society's mores (*Grant v. California*, 2014; *Outmezguine v. Maryland*, 1994).

"Child porn usually isn't subtle" (Korosec, 2003). Generally, "child pornography" depicts the exhibition of a child's genitals or partially covered genitals (Pa. Code §§ 311.3-311.4, 2011). Depictions may include simulated or actual sexual contact with children, masturbation, or lewd exhibition of the genitals (*New York v. Ferber*, 1982). "Genitals" may possibly include buttocks, female areolas, or area of a female breast below the areola. Exhibition of a child's genitals may be distinguishable from nudity. Depiction of child nudity is not necessarily pornography. For example, a photo of children in a bathtub or naturist periodicals may not exhibit children sexually. Generally, depictions must be sexually explicit or exploitative to meet state and federal definitions of child pornography. However, cases have arisen in which defendants have been prosecuted for photographing bathing children or photographing otherwise lawful activity, like breast-feeding. In *Osborne v. Ohio* (1990), an Ohio statute defined nudity in child pornography as lewd exhibition of a child's genitals. This definition is common. The statute also criminalized depictions that placed upon genitals graphic focus. This definition of child pornography is also standard in First Amendment jurisprudence, though statutory language and definitions vary.

Production, possession, transmission, and promotion of a depiction are distinct units of prosecution (*Vineyard v. State*, 1998). Generally, possession must be knowing. Knowing possession is distinguishable from possession. Possession may occur when a person accidentally downloads depictions, receives an unsolicited e-mail, or otherwise has the option to view child pornography on his or her computer (*Ohio v. Hurst*, 2009). Knowing possession likely occurs when a downloaded file has been viewed or knowingly could be viewed. This is discussed further in Chapter 23. In most jurisdictions, the state must prove that an offender knowingly possessed depictions. Pornographers may be held strictly liable for viewing, producing, or promoting child pornography in some jurisdictions. The law tends not to permit pornographers to defend with ignorance of a child's age. Some jurisdictions prosecute offenders if the child's age should have been reasonably known, but acquit defendants who had a reasonable belief that an image depicted an adult (Fla. Stat. § 847.0137, 2013; 720 ILCS 5/11-20.1, 2014; Tex. § 43.26, 2014). Knowledge of the child's age may not be required (*Johnson v. State*, 1998). In some jurisdictions, possession or promotion offenses are affirmatively defended against when the victim is no more than a certain number of years younger than the defendant.

The state must prove every element of the crime. Statutory affirmative defenses will result in acquittal if defendants claim the defense and the state fails to overcome it with proof beyond a reasonable doubt. One common defense is that the subject of the depiction is an adult. Defendants are not required to prove victims' ages (*State v. Cannady*, 2007). Affirmative defenses may shift the burden of production, which means that defendants may be required to produce evidence. However, affirmative defenses may not shift the burden of persuasion. Some courts have held that some victims are so young that they cannot possibly be adults. Thus, the state may carry its burden without identifying victims' ages. When subjects depicted cannot be identified and ages are unknown, the government may not carry its burden beyond a reasonable doubt if subjects appear to be adults. The U.S. Supreme Court held in *Ashcroft v. Free Speech Coalition* (2002) that if the government cannot prove that a child is depicted, then prosecution will not succeed. If the government has difficulty proving the subject's age, then it would be even more difficult for a defendant to prove it, especially in cases where a defendant did not produce the depiction. Sufficiency of evidence may be decided by the jury.

The federal government bars solicitation of child pornography. The First Amendment does not protect those who solicit or offer child pornography, even when no actual child pornography is available (*U.S. v. Williams*, 2008). Offering to transmit child pornography when one only possesses adult images is prosecutable under child pornography statutes when the offeror or the recipient believes that images are of children. There is an objective and subjective component to belief. This is discussed in greater detail in Chapter 22.

Simulated child pornography involving computer-generated images that do not depict actual children may be obscene, but simulated images do not violate child pornography statutes (Prosecutorial Remedies and Other Tools to End the Exploitation of Children Today Act [PROTECT Act], 2003). Simulations are discussed in Chapter 16. In some jurisdictions, the fact-finder may infer that depictions are of real children unless evidence is presented to the contrary. However, other jurisdictions require the state prove that depictions are of actual children (*Ohio v. Tooley*, 2006). Expert testimony is not required, but experts may persuade the jury to believe that depictions are authentic (*Illinois v. Normand*, 2004). Ultimately, the fact-finder must decide if subjects are actual children. However, the fact-finder need not determine whether sexual contact depicted was simulated or actual if the child is determined to be an actual child (18 U.S.C. § 2256, 2012). Depictions are unprotected if they involve actual children simulating sex acts.

In some jurisdictions, an affirmative defense to sexual contact with a child and production offenses is that the defendant was married to the minor at the time of the offense. This means that defendants who are the same sex as their victims may not prevail with this defense in states where same-sex marriage is void (*Vann v. State*, 2011). This gender-based preclusion to the affirmative defense may violate constitutional due process or equal protection. When defendants invoke this affirmative defense, the state must prove that the defendant was not married to the victim. However, some juries may infer that children are not married by court order or with parental permission to prepubescent minors and minors younger than the legal age to marry. Marriage may also be an affirmative defense to possession and promotion of child pornography (Tex. § 43.26(c), 2014). This kind of affirmative defense, which is not available at the federal level, may indicate that married children are emancipated from all child pornography laws that provide such a defense. Thus, child exploitation could result from pretextual marriages, particularly those involving prostitution.

Some jurisdictions provide an affirmative defense to child pornography production and promotion offenses if "the conduct was for a bona fide educational, medical, psychological, psychiatric, judicial, law enforcement, or legislative purpose" (Tex. § 43.26(2), 2014). When the defendant raises this defense at trial, a court record is created. A defendant who is guilty of possessing child pornography in one jurisdiction that does not offer this affirmative defense may submit the court record to a court in another jurisdiction where this affirmative defense exists. The defendant may not be guilty of a sex offense in a jurisdiction that accepts the affirmative defense if the offender moves to that jurisdiction.

Art and Other Material Approaching the Bright Line

The PROTECT Act is restrictive legislation prohibiting obscene depictions of children and child pornography. Child erotica may be legal. Nude and sexual depictions of children may be artful, but artistic value may not be present in obscene depictions of children, however. Some erotic fiction literature available on North American Man Boy Love Association's (NAMBLA's) website offers examples of material that sexually depicts children, but may be legal. This material is not child pornography because it does not depict actual children and is inexplicit. Children are not harmed during the production of fictional literature (Bristol, 2007). Explicit nonfiction may be child pornography if it meets statutory definitions by graphically depicting sexual abuse, exploitation, or child nudity. Photos of nude children may be artistic. For example, artistic images of a 10-year-old Brooke Shields wearing full makeup and bathing while nude are not considered to be child pornography or obscenity in the United States. However, the Tate Museum in Great Britain once withdrew the photos after authorities questioned whether the depictions were obscene (Singh, 2009).

Drawings, sculptures, cartoons, and paintings that depict a minor explicitly engaged in sexual conduct, including but not limited to sodomy, genital contact, bestiality, and sadomasochism, are illegal. Under the PROTECT Act, possessing three or fewer hard-core depictions of children and surrendering them promptly to law enforcement or destroying the material is an affirmative defense. If an artistic depiction is part of a collection that includes graphic or explicit content, then it may be evaluated as obscenity (Cusack, 2011; United States Sentencing Commission [USSC], 2012; *U.S. v. Whorley*, 2008). Naturist films and periodicals have been held to be outside the scope of child pornography or obscenity statutes because they are not sexually explicit and do not exhibit genitals in a graphic or lewd manner. Thus, genitals partially covered by a bathing suit may be pornographic, while videos of a nude child in a steam bath may be lawful. Modeling photos of children, for example, catalog models wearing bathing suits, are not normally proscribed unless they are modified in a manner that creates obscenity or child pornography. This is discussed further in Chapter 16.

Simple nudity may not be explicit, and nude dancing is not necessarily sexual conduct. For example, nude dancing broadcast on television may not necessarily be sexual conduct, demonstrate lascivious intent, or create harm (April, 2012; Bristol, 2007; Cusack, 2012). However, explicit depictions of children engaged in sexual activity may be obscenity irrespective of whether actual children perform. For example, films may not use body doubles to explicitly portray sex with a minor if audiences are made to believe that the activity occurred. The motion picture industry tends to vet film scenes at the production stage, although many final products are questionable, especially among foreign films imported into the United States or viewed online (Bristol, 2007; Cusack, 2011). Inexplicit, commercial motional pictures also were discussed in Chapter 2.

Courts may use the *Dost* factors as a guide to decide whether genitals or pubic areas are exhibited lasciviously in depictions (*U.S. v. Dost*, 1986; *U.S. v. Knox*, 1994). Juries may use these factors to make a determination, though every factor is not always considered. It is often called the *Dost* test, but the *Dost* factors are not a test, the factors are not conjunctive or balanced, and individual factors are not dispositive. *Dost* factors are a guide that should take into consideration minors' ages. Jurors may examine the following:

1. Whether the focal point of the visual depiction is on the child's genitals or pubic area
2. Whether the setting of the visual depiction is sexually suggestive, that is, in a place or pose generally associated with sexual activity
3. Whether the child is depicted in an unnatural pose or in inappropriate attire, considering the age of the child
4. Whether the child is fully or partially clothed or nude
5. Whether the visual depiction suggests sexual coyness or willingness to engage in sexual activity
6. Whether the visual depiction is intended or designed to elicit a sexual response in the viewer

Retribution, SORNA

Convicted sex offenders may be required to register with a sex offender registry under the Sex Offender Registry and Notification Act (SORNA). Registration may occur with local authorities, state authorities, federal authorities, or a combination of these depending on convictions, offender location, and jurisdictional requirements. Producing, possessing, or transmitting child pornography or distributing pornography to minors may be registerable offenses. Offense levels at which an offender must register may vary. Even misdemeanor offenses may carry mandatory registration requirements. Some critics have complained that ostracism resulting from publication of crimes is excessive, especially for first-time or low-level offenders. Levels of registration may be discretionary. For example, juvenile offenders may not be required to register (R.C. 2152.83(B)(2), 2012). Production of child pornography is not necessarily the most serious-level offense. Voyeurism and video voyeurism may be grouped with the most serious sex offenses even if voyeurism occurs pursuant to a prank perpetrated by a minor.

Obscenity convictions unrelated to minors are not generally registerable sex offenses (Iowa Code § 692A.102, 2013; USSC, 2012). When obscenity or pornography is shown to minors, it results in a registerable sex offense (*Shoemaker v. Harris*, 2013). In terms of registration requirements, some statutes do not differentiate between promoting obscenity to minors and wholesaling obscenity (Mo. Rev. Stat. 573.020, 2013; Mo. Rev. Stat. 589.400(2), 2013). Introducing minors to obscenity is usually considered to be a lower-level offense than pandering or soliciting photos from youth (Adam Walsh

Child Protection and Safety Act, 2008). Pandering may be the same level offense as trafficking (Louisiana State Police, 2010).

Certain sex offender registries may be more restrictive than others. Some lower-level offenses may not require notification to the community, but registration information may be available with authorities. Higher-level offenses, like solicitation and contact offenses, may require direct notification to day cares, schools, nursing homes, and so on (Whatcom County, 2007). At a minimum, notification may require offenders' residence, name, convictions, and other information to be available to the public. Many jurisdictions provide information on the Internet to the public. Offenders may be required to register every so often for a specified amount of time (USSG §§2A3.5, 2012). For example, hands-on offenders may be required to register every 90 days for life (Adam Walsh Child Protection and Safety Act, 2008). Failure to register is a separate criminal offense. In 2010, 364 federal offenders criminally violated SORNA (USSC, 2012).

All registries typically share one central feature. Offenders register locally with police or other authorities. Then, information is compiled at the state level. Under Megan's Law, the public must be notified that offenders are present in the community. Notification may be a passive process or an active process. For example, some registries may collect publicly accessible information, while others may inform past victims of the offender's presence in the community. The amount of information available to the public varies between states. A physical description, a driver's license number, a birthdate, a place of employment, and other identifying information may be published along with the name and location; however, certain information, for example, the Social Security number and victims' names, remain confidential (*Connecticut Department of Public Safety v. Doe*, 2003; *Smith v. Doe*, 2003). Controversially, some jurisdictions have imposed severe restrictions on sex offenders. For example, several states, including North Carolina, Tennessee, Ohio, Missouri, and Texas, have prohibited offenders from participating in Halloween festivities ("Halloween Sex Offender Laws," 2014).

Flaws in the SORNA system may be problematic to governmental goals and society. The first flaw results because some sex offender registries list offenders' names and addresses. This provides pornographers with their own "little black book" (Furniss, 1991). Recidivists may use publicly available contact information to connect with each other to physically share photos, files, or information about local children.

A second flaw results from varying definitions and affirmative defenses (*Fraser v. Sleeper*, 2007; *New York v. Fraser*, 2001). In New York, a social worker who specialized in child sex abuse was reported by a computer technician for possessing images of sex abuse on his computer (*New York v. Fraser*, 2001). The images were not necessarily related to cases worked on by the social worker. Child pornography is categorically unprotected speech in New York, and New York offers no affirmative defense for researchers or experts. The court held that the state only needed to provide a rational interest for strict liability laws. Nevertheless, the state proved a compelling interest in protecting children. The defendant was required to register as a sex offender in the state of New York. This flaw highlights the severity of registries. A person who had an extensive record of treating victims and offenders may be grouped socially and legally with abusers.

A third flaw results when convicted sex offenders may continue to lawfully possess child pornography in some states because of jurisdictional variations among sex offender registries. The same defendant who was convicted in New York for possessing images relating to social work moved to Vermont (*Fraser v. Sleeper*, 2007). Though the defendant had not been convicted in Vermont, he was required to register in Vermont because of his conviction in New York. In Vermont, it is an affirmative defense that the defendant had a bona fide purpose for possession of child pornography (e.g., scientific research). He produced court records demonstrating that he had raised the defense at trial in New York. Because he produced court records, and because Vermont accepted that affirmative defense, he was not required to register as a sex offender in Vermont. Thus, under some circumstances, offenders may legally possess child pornography in some states because of the availability of affirmative defenses. In this scenario, the defendant's crime in New York was undermined by the state of Vermont. Some may argue that this creates legal and social justice when the defendant made a mistake of law. Yet, offenders who are sexually aroused by child pornography may legally possess it if they also prove a bona fide purpose, and they may be exonerated from social ostracism if they move to a permissive jurisdiction.

Critics raise other flaws, including excessive punishment, absence of reintroduction opportunities for offenders, constructive homelessness resulting from compliance with local SORNA requirements, moral panic in communities, harassment toward offenders by the public, destruction of families and community life, and unfairness toward pranksters, intoxicated perpetrators, and young offenders. Though these arguments claim that sex offender registries may violate the Constitution in some respects, the Court has repeatedly held that they do not.

Registries announce to the public that law and society will not tolerate deviance, moral decay, sex abuse, and violation. Registries and notification may serve to validate and reinforce society's power, legal compliance, social cohesion, morality, and safety. Retributive punitive principles underlie the registries to some extent. Though they warn and potentially protect the public, the retributive penological purpose is to publicize offenders' information. Some supporters argue that offenders' humiliation, ostracism, and discomfort are part of the punishment.

Victims' Rights, Remedies, and Compensation

Remedies are available for victims of child pornography. Most children who are victimized by production offenses also are victimized by distribution offenses (USSC, 2012). Among child sex abuse experts interviewed by the Department of Justice (DOJ), 95% reported that victims of pornography suffer lifelong psychological trauma and damage (DOJ, 2010). Three-quarters of experts reported that victims suffer for three reasons: (1) images circulate in perpetuity, (2) offenders are presently viewing their photos, and (3) offenders may encounter victims in public. Congress and the U.S. Supreme Court have recognized harm suffered by victims as depictions are reposted on the Internet hundreds, thousands, or millions of times (*New York v. Ferber*, 1982). Victims experience deep uncertainty about who has seen their photos and which perverts will attempt to contact them. Some victims have reported that they have been stalked by pornographers (USSC, 2012). Victims are haunted throughout their lives by past abuse and the threat of being confronted by those who have viewed a record of their victimization. They suffer from anxiety, depression, low self-esteem, post-traumatic stress disorder, guilt, inferiority, relationship problems, addiction, substance abuse, suicidal ideation, and delinquency. Victims' trauma may be exacerbated knowing that their right to privacy is continually violated and that new victims may be groomed using their images (*New York v. Ferber*, 1982).

Under the Victims' Rights and Restitution Act (VRRA), child victims of pornography offenses may be eligible for services (VRRA 63 42 U.S.C. § 10607, 2012). Under the Crime Victims' Rights Act (CVRA), victims may have certain rights that may be enforced during prosecution (CVRA 64 18 U.S.C. § 3771, 2012). Victims must be informed about federal processes, including investigation, victims' services, and enforceable rights. Rights include reasonable notification about proceedings, a reasonable right to be heard at proceedings, restitution, conference with prosecutors, freedom from unreasonable delays in proceedings, and fair, respectful, and dignified treatment. The most important right may be the "gateway right" of reasonable notification of proceedings, which initiates victims' awareness about governmental processes. The most complicated right may be the right to be heard, because a single victim could potentially be involved in hundreds or thousands of proceedings each year because pornographers circulate many of the same victims' images. To help victims retain privacy, the DOJ presents victims' signed victim impact statements (VISs) prior to sentencing in every prosecution involving a depiction of the victim. A VIS may be withdrawn or updated at any time (DOJ, 2010).

Restitution provided for victims may be mandatory and complete (18 U.S.C. § 2259, 2012). Restitution may be the same for victims harmed by production, possession, or transmission offenses (USSC, 2012). For example, in Florida and Kansas, victims who suffer psychological or physical harm for production or nonproduction offenses will be awarded no less than $150,000 (Fla. Stat. § 847.01357, 2012; K.S.A. § 60-5001, 2012). Victims must file claims within three years of the disposition of their criminal cases. Some statutes do not delimit the number of defendants or proportion of compensation to be paid by each defendant. However, in Minnesota, *restitution is mandatory only for production offenses* (Minn. Stat. § 609.321, 2013). *Victims of production offenses may be awarded* gross income generated from production offenses, the value to the defendant, or minimum wage and overtime as required. Social services also are provided to victims.

Amy, whose image is one of the most circulated images online, has collected $1.75 million over the course of 4.5 years from 182 defendants. She suffered $3.4 million worth of damage, and she collected $1.2 million from a single defendant. However, estimates show that approximately 70,000 pornographers have viewed pornographic depictions of Amy. Amy argued that any offender who possesses one or two images depicting her as a victim ought to be liable for the entire amount of damages because psychological injuries are indivisible. Even if each offender could be held liable for and was capable of paying $3.4 million, Amy's damages are capped at $3.4 million by the court because she was awarded restitution damages. Restitution damages are designed to place a victim in the same position that he or she was in before damages occurred. The U.S. Supreme Court heard Amy's case, and in a plural opinion, it held that offenders should compensate victims for their criminal conduct, but not for damage caused by others' crimes (*Paroline v. U.S.*, 2014). District courts ought to exercise discretion when determining the amount of restitution damages owed to victims by particular offenders. Judgments are sound when courts evaluate the amount of losses caused to a victim by production offenses and online circulation of child pornography depicting the victim. Other relevant factors should be weighed, and awards should be relatively based on causality, that is, how much damage was caused by a particular offender's conduct. Thus, an offender cannot be held liable for total damages caused to a victim if an offender did not cause all of the damage. Some offenders may be ordered to pay greater damages than others. For example, production offenders and distributors may be ordered to pay greater damages than those who only view or possess images. Compensation may be tabulated according to the number of images of a victim possessed by an offender.

Damages, including counseling and medical treatment, can total millions of dollars (Barnes, 2014). Yet, some district courts have failed to order restitution for nonproduction offenses because they do not believe that they are the proximate cause (i.e., legal cause) of a victim's injury. Other courts have refused to order restitution because they are unable to appropriately apportion a percentage of a victim's damage to a particular defendant. Appellate courts have been split about restitution for nonproduction offenses. Among the appellate court circuits, the Second, Seventh, Ninth, Eleventh, and D.C. Circuits have ordered restitution to be paid by defendants who were the proximate cause of particular losses created by nonproduction offenses. The Fifth Circuit held that victims of nonproduction offenses need not show proximate cause for damages relating to medical and mental problems, income loss, and expenses incurred by participating in legal processes.

Children Producing, Viewing, and Possessing Pornography: Black Letter

Differences between nudity, graphic nudity, sexual excitement, explicit sexual conduct, sadomasochism, and other types of speech lie along a spectrum. The differences between mere nudity and sadomasochism are clear, but fine distinctions between simple nudity and graphic nudity may be a matter for the courts. Some parents and community members may feel that verbally depicting nudity to children is inappropriate, even to warn children about online solicitation offenses or texting (Todt & Scolforo, 2013). These community members may believe that average sensibilities are conservative. Other parents may believe that exposure to pornography and obscenity is a normal part of sexual development and may provide children with such materials (Chetty & Basson, 2006). These parents may believe that average sensibilities are liberal and that they have a fundamental right as parents to educate their children about pornography (*Meyer v. Nebraska*, 1923). Minors may be permitted by their parents to view sexual nudity in some circumstances (Fla. Stat. § 847.013, 2013).

When potentially erotic, nonobscene material present in the community is brought to the attention of the state, a prosecutor may ask a court to determine whether the material is erotic, and a hearing for the vendor will be set (Fla. Stat. § 847.013, 2013; Wash. Rev. Code § 9.68.060, 2013). If the material is found to be erotic, then an order may be issued conspicuously labeling the material as "adults only." Front covers of publications and recordings may be labeled, or signs will be posted at the place where material is being exhibited. "Adults only" material may not be displayed in a manner that makes erotic content accessible or visible to minors. Vendors are enjoined from selling erotic material to children. Selling or distributing erotic material to children usually violates the law, except in some circumstances where erotic material is merely stored on a server or is under the state's control, for example, at public libraries, historical societies, and so on. Adult material is discussed in

Chapter 3 and Chapter 13. The presence of pornography in a cache may be under sufficient control to amount to distribution to a minor in some jurisdictions; however, other jurisdictions hold that cached pornography does not equate with distribution. Minors commit a crime by misrepresenting their ages to gain access to pornography or exhibitions labeled "adult only." Vendors may not be held liable if minors misrepresent their ages, minors gain access through parents, a nonparental adult falsely represents to be a minor's parent, or the vendor has a bona fide belief about the minor's age (Fla. Stat. § 847.013, 2013; Wash. Rev. Code § 9.68.070, 2013).

Generally, children seem to have no right to possess pornography and likely do not have a privacy right to view obscenity. The right to view and possess obscenity is a privacy right that likely belongs only to adults, who have a right to view pornography in private. It would be a crime for a child to transmit obscenity or child pornography. The law does not routinely punish children who merely view pornography. It may be illegal for children in some jurisdictions to consensually exchange nude images on cell phones or other devices, though authorities typically only prosecute minors who distribute nude depictions of other minors in an exploitative manner (Illinois' Child Pornography Act 720 ILCS 5/11-20.1, 2013; Stone, 2014). Sexting is discussed further in Chapter 23. For policy reasons, authorities usually do not prosecute victims of solicitation even though transmission is illegal. Child prostitution may be an exception because the government may have an interest in incapacitating suppliers. Prosecution of child prostitutes is discussed in Chapter 7. Sometimes minors victimize other minors by committing voyeuristic production offenses. Minors who surreptitiously record their intimate experiences are not exempted from voyeurism laws. Even if their sex partners are adults, minors may also be subject to child pornography production laws for recording themselves performing sexual conduct. The government seriously opposes voyeurism and may provide criminally and civil remedies (*Boyles v. Kerr*, 1993). Criminal punishment may be as severe as punishments for rape in some cases. Voyeurism is discussed further in Chapter 8 and Chapter 14.

Erotic materials online may be required to be password protected or have age-verification mechanisms. Popular sites like Youporn.com or Pornhub.com do not require age verification even though they potentially make content available to minors. Thus, laws that prohibit commercial establishments from giving pornography to teens act as *parens patriae* under circumstances that protect the moral dignity of public life, but they do little to prevent modern teens from accessing harmful material and erotica online. This may be because major pornography websites managed in foreign countries fall outside the control of U.S. law.

Numerous studies have found that a significant percentage of youth view pornography online. One study examined minors' use of and exposure to

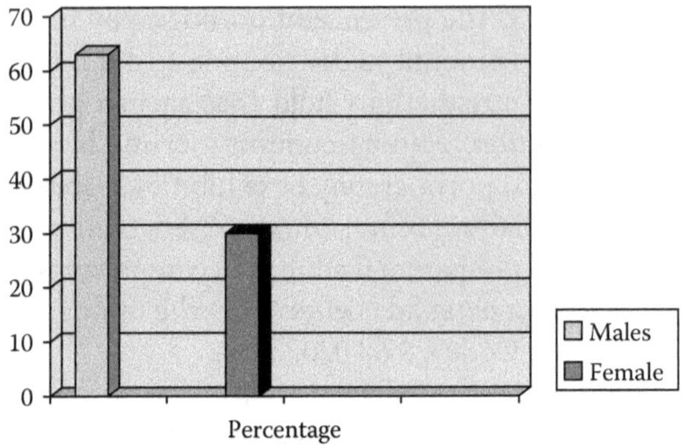

Figure 5.1 Percentage who viewed pornography as minors.

pornography online in Spain (González-Ortega & Orgaz-Baz, 2013). An online survey sampled college students. Researchers found that 63% of males and 30% of females had seen pornography online as minors (Figure 5.1).

Girls were more likely to have been exposed involuntarily to pornography on the Internet. Boys tended more than girls to have been exposed for longer time periods (i.e., up to 30 minutes). Males were more likely to report deliberate use of and sexual excitement to pornography, whereas females were more likely to report disgust, avoidance, or concern. Males and females reported that, as minors, they viewed bondage, rape, and child pornography. The explicitness of these depictions may have varied between viewers. One-sixth of respondents remembered experiencing strong reactions to the material. Of minors between the ages of 9 years and 19 years who use the Internet at least once a week in the United Kingdom, 57% were exposed to pornography (Chetty & Basson, 2006). Thirty-eight percent had been exposed to “pop-ups” of pornography, and 36% accidentally navigated into pornographic websites. One-quarter received pornography through e-mail or instant messaging. In the United States, approximately three-quarters of 10-year-old to 17-year-old minors could access pornography through unsolicited e-mails and instant messaging, or they were accidentally exposed to it online. More than one-quarter were redirected from one website to a pornographic website. Half of French minors older than 11 years had accidentally witnessed pornography online. One-third of boys in Sweden, but only 3% of girls, watched pornographic material at least one time each week. Canadian parents reported that one-fifth of their children between the ages of 6 years and 16 years had been exposed to sexual content on home computers. Approximately one-third of 9 year olds to 16 year olds across Europe had accidentally viewed violent or offensive pornography online.

Conclusion

The government's current interest in child pornography indicates that, in comparison to years past, minors' exposure to production offenses and access to online pornography has reached epidemic proportions. Significant resources have been allocated to investigating and prosecuting offenders, as well as providing appropriate remedies to child victims. Many members of society have questioned the government's denial of child sexuality, though many victims of child pornography attest to the severity of trauma inflicted on child participants. Some children have resisted government intervention into their sexuality by voluntarily, independently, and illegally producing, possessing, and distributing obscenity and child pornography.

References

18 U.S.C. § 2256 (2012).

18 U.S.C. § 2259 (2012).

720 ILCS 5/11-20.1 (2014).

Adam Walsh Child Protection and Safety Act. (2008).

April, K. (2012). Cartoons aren't real people, too: Does the regulation of virtual child pornography violate the First Amendment and criminalize subversive thought? *Cardozo Journal of Law and Gender, 19*, 241–271.

Ashcroft v. Free Speech Coalition, 535 U.S. 234, 258 (2002).

Barnes, R. (2014, January 22). Supreme Court weighs how much one person should pay pornography victim. *Washington Post.* Retrieved from http://www.washingtonpost.com/politics/supreme-court-weighs-how-much-one-person-should-pay-pornography-victim/2014/01/22/551db36c-838c-11e3-bbe5-6a2a3141e3a9_story.html

Boyles v. Kerr, 855 S.W.2d 593 (1993).

Bristol, J. E. (2007). Free expression in motion pictures: Childhood sexuality and a satisfied society. *Cardozo Arts and Entertainment Law Journal, 25*(1), 333–365.

Chetty, I., & Basson, A. (2006). Report on Internet usage and the exposure of pornography to learners in South African schools. Film and Publication Board. Retrieved from http://www.cie.org.za/images/uploads/Report_on_Internet_Usage_2006.pdf

Connecticut Department of Public Safety v. Doe, 538 U.S. 1 (2003).

Crime Victims' Rights Act 64 18 U.S.C. § 3771 (2012).

Cusack, C. M. (2011). Busting patriarchal booby traps: Why feminists fear minor distinctions in child porn cases, an analysis of social deviance with in gender, family, or the home (etudes 4). *Southern University Law Review, 39*, 43–70.

Cusack, C. M. (2012). Boob laws: An analysis of social deviance with in gender, family, or the home (etudes 2). *Women's Rights Law Reporter, 33*, 197–217.

Cusack, C. M. (2013a). Comparative sexology: Nonconsensual insemination in the United States and the European Union. *Sexologies, 23*(1), e19–e23.

Cusack, C. M. (2013b). How the content of online pornography depicts expressed consent for insemination. *Online Journal of Communication and Media Technologies, 3*(3), 91–110.

Department of Justice. (2010, August). The national strategy for child exploitation prevention and interdiction. Retrieved from http://www.justice.gov/psc/docs/natstrategyreport.pdf

Fischer, N. L. (2005). The more things change … the Kinsey Institute on Child Sexuality. *Journal of Sex Research, 42*(3), 271–273.

Fla. Stat. § 847.013 (2013).
Fla. Stat. § 847.0137 (2013).
Fla. Stat. § 847.01357 (2012).
Fraser v. Sleeper, 2007 VT 78 (2007).
Furniss, T. (1991). *The multi-professional handbook of child sexual abuse: Integrated management, therapy, and legal intervention*. Florence, KY: Taylor & Frances/Routledge.
González-Ortega, E., & Orgaz-Baz, B. (2013). Minors' exposure to online pornography: Prevalence, motivations, contents and effects. *Anales De Psicología*, *29*(2), 319–327.
Grant v. California, 58 Cal. 4th 469 (2014).
Halloween sex offender laws. (2014). FindLaw.com Retrieved from http://criminal.findlaw.com/criminal-charges/halloween-sex-offender-laws.html
Illinois' Child Pornography Act 720 ILCS 5/11-20.1 (2013).
Illinois v. Normand, 345 Ill. App. 3d 736 (2004).
Iowa Code § 692A.102 (2013).
Johnson v. State, 967 S.W.2d 848 (1998).
Kern, S. (1973). Freud and the discovery of child sexuality. *History of Childhood Quarterly: The Journal of Psychohistory*, *1*(1), 117–141.
K.S.A. § 60-5001 (2012).
Korosec, T. (2003, April 17). 1-hour arrest. *Dallas Observer*. Retrieved from http://www.dallasobserver.com/2003-04-17/news/1-hour-arrest/3/
Louisiana State Police. (2010). Department of Public Safety and Corrections, Public Safety Services: Offenses. Retrieved from http://www.lsp.org/socpr/offenses.html
Miller v. California, 413 U.S. 15 (1973).
Minn. Stat. § 609.321 (2013).
Mirkin, H. (2009). The social, political, and legal construction of the concept of child pornography. *Journal of Homosexuality*, *56*, 233–267.
Mo. Rev. Stat. 573.020 (2013).
Mo. Rev. Stat. 589.400(2) (2013).
Meyer v. Nebraska, 262 U.S. 390 (1923).
New York v. Ferber, 458 U.S. 747 (1982).
New York v. Fraser, 96 N.Y.2d 318 (2001).
Northcraft, D. M. (2004). A nation scared: Children, sex, and the denial of humanity: A review essay on Judith Levine's *Harmful to minors: The perils of protecting children from sex* [Book review]. *American University Journal of Gender, Social Policy and the Law*, *12*, 483.
Ohio v. Hurst, 181 Ohio App. 3d 454 (2009).
Ohio v. Tooley, 114 Ohio St. 3d 366 (2006).
Osborne v. Ohio, 495 U.S. 103 (1990).
Outmezguine v. Maryland, 335 Md. 20 (1994).
Pa. Code §§ 311.3-311.4 (2011).
Paroline v. U.S., 2014 U.S. LEXIS 2936 (2014).
Pinkus v. U.S., 436 U.S. 293 (1978).
Prosecutorial Remedies and Other Tools to End the Exploitation of Children Today Act of 2003 (PROTECT Act) §§2252B (2003).
R.C. 2152.83(B)(2) (2012).
Shoemaker v. Harris, (2d Dist 2013) 2013 Cal App LEXIS 234.
Singh, A. (2009, September 30). Brooke Shields picture withdrawn from Tate exhibition after police visit. *Telegraph*. Retrieved from http://www.telegraph.co.uk/news/celebritynews/6248384/Brooke-Shields-picture-withdrawn-from-Tate-exhibition-after-police-visit.html
Smith v. Doe, 538 U.S. 84 (2003).
State v. Cannady, 727 N.W.2d 403 (2007).

Stone, E. (2014, May 1). Sexting charges brought against 2 Barrington middle schoolers. *Barrington Patch*. Retrieved from http://barrington-il.patch.com/groups/schools/p/sexting-charges-brought-against-2-barrington-middle-schoolers

Tex. § 43.26 (2014).

Todt, R., & Scolforo, M. (2013, September 26). Porn, al-Qaida mentions put end to Pa. web lessons. *CNS News*. Retrieved from http://www.cnsnews.com/news/article/porn-al-qaida-mentions-put-end-pa-web-lessons

United States Sentencing Commission. (2012). Report to the Congress: Federal child pornography offenses. Retrieved from http://www.ussc.gov/news/congressional-testimony-and-reports/sex-offense-topics/report-congress-federal-child-pornography-offenses

USSG §§2A3.5 (2012).

U.S. v. Dost, 636 F.Supp. 828 (S.D.Cal.1986).

U.S. v. Knox, 32 F.3d 733 (3d Cir. 1994).

U.S. v. Whorley, 550 F.3d 326, 330 (C.A. 4 12/18/08).

U.S. v. Williams, 553 U.S. 285 (2008).

Vann v. State, 2011 Tex. App. LEXIS 3417 (2011).

Victims' Rights and Restitution Act 63 42 U.S.C. § 10607 (2013).

Vineyard v. State, 958 S.W.2d 834 (1998).

Wash. Rev. Code § 9.68.060 (2013).

Wash. Rev. Code § 9.68.070 (2013).

Whatcom County. (2007). Sheriff's office: Risk level classification and notification. Retrieved from http://www.co.whatcom.wa.us/sheriff/sexoffenders/classifications.jsp#level1notify

Wilgoren, J. (2002, April 30). Scholar's pedophilia essay stirs outrage and revenge. *New York Times*. Retrieved from http://www.nytimes.com/2002/04/30/education/30MISS.html

Wurtele, S. K. (2009). Preventing sexual abuse of children in the twenty-first century: Preparing for challenges and opportunities in preventing sexual abuse. *Journal of Child Sexual Abuse*, *18*, 1–18.

Pornography and Viewers' Crime

6

Overview

Correlations between viewing pornography, various criminal offenses, and paraphilia are well established. However, causal relationships have not been proved. Numerous scientific studies about offenders and nonoffenders demonstrate that pornography plays a significant role in sexual deviance and crime, but it is not solely responsible for them.

Fetishistic Masturbation, Pornography, and Crime

Sexually deviant behaviors (i.e., paraphilia) have repeatedly correlated in research studies with compulsive masturbation, aberrant masturbation, viewing pornography, or pornography addiction (Laws & O'Donohue, 2008). Serious crimes, including murder, rape, child molestation, and intimate partner violence (IPV), have correlated with viewing artistic pornography (Bourke & Hernandez, 2009; Hald, Malamuth, & Yuen, 2010; Salmon & Diamond, 2012). Pornography use also correlates with victimless sex crimes, for example, clandestine public masturbation (Flood, 2009; Laws & O'Donohue, 2008).

Etiological pathways for sexually abusive behaviors may be developed while viewers watch conventional or deviant pornography if viewers' fantasies are aberrant. The majority of viewers who consume illegal pornography also consume legal pornography (Department of Justice [DOJ], 2010). Among viewers who solely consume obscenity and child pornography, addiction to pornography is high. Yet, viewers may experience aberrant or aggressive fantasies or memories while viewing normal pornography; they may also rehearse victimizing others (Laws & O'Donohue, 2008; Salmon & Diamond, 2012). Numerous scientific studies demonstrate relationships between addiction to violent fetishistic pornography, rehearsing crime while fantasizing, and perpetration of deviant fantasies, that is, sex crimes (Bourke & Hernandez, 2009; Salmon & Diamond, 2012). People, especially youth, who are already prone to risk taking, lack impulse control, suffer from trauma, or demonstrate rape-supportive cultural attitudes or beliefs are more prone to commit sex crimes in conjunction with pornography use, especially if depictions are hard core (Flood, 2009). Violent pornography may encourage viewers to harbor rape myths and rape-supportive attitudes and encourage viewers to act out deviant fantasies (Cusack & Waranius, 2012; Ryan, 2011; Salmon & Diamond, 2012).

Researchers hypothesize that fantasizing to pornography could relate to completion of contact offenses. In the United Kingdom, indecent images of children (IIOC) are criminalized at five levels (Long, Alison, & McManus, 2013). Level one criminalizes depictions that feature children posing but do not depict sexual activity. The second level includes nonpenetrative solo sexual activity, activity between children, or depictions of children masturbating. The third level involves nonpenetrative sexual contact between adults and children. The fourth level involves penetrative sexual contact between children or adults with children. Level five includes sadomasochistic abuse, bondage, or penetrative bestiality. Reportedly, 66% of child pornography websites feature some level four and level five content. However, these images are least prevalent. Dual offenders, that is, those who had committed pornography and contact offenses, possessed far fewer photos of level one and level two content.

Eighty percent of sexual murderers reported that their crimes related to their most common fantasy (Arkin, 2014; Long et al., 2013). These findings are supported by James Dobson's interview with famous serial killer Ted Bundy. In the documentary *Natural Porn Killer*, Bundy blames his violence, rape, murder, and necrophilia primarily on hard-core, sadistic pornography. Bundy claims that all pornography corrodes the psyche and that hard-core pornography addiction directly relates to sexual violence and murder. Numerous other serial killers' addictions, rituals, collections, or deviant behavior involved pornography. John Wayne Gacy, Jeffrey Dahmer, Anthony Sowell, Heriberto Seda, and Zodiac killer suspect Arthur Leigh Allen are a few examples. Notably, the vast majority of serial killers have no serious mental disorders, even though they may engage in mutilation, flagellation, vampirism, necrophilia, torture, anthropophagy, and other paraphilia (Fox & Levin, 1998). Often, serial killers may be driven by strong fantasies, but they are not delusional. Serial killers, who are frequently rapists, typically understand the wrongfulness of their actions, but they fail to control their impulses using will power or conscience. Lack of impulse control may contribute to viewing pornography excessively or may be worsened by overindulgence. Rather than control their impulses, these individuals may control their fantasies by compartmentalizing victims (e.g., good people vs. bad people, known people vs. strangers, children vs. adults). They may choose to kill victims within a specific group (e.g., children or bad people).

Cognitive distortions about inappropriate sex partners and courtship disorders may develop or worsen in conjunction with viewing conventional or fetish pornography (Laws & O'Donohue, 2008). Control fantasies cultivated while viewers watch pornography may validate courtship disorders, for example, wherein offenders truly believe that a victim's "no" response to sexual advances genuinely grants consent. Within seconds of meeting victims for the first time, offenders who suffer from courtship disorders may believe that victims are sexually enticed or are making sexual advances. Pornographic scenes depicting strangers who meet then spontaneously have sex could contribute to courtship disorders (Cusack & Waranius, 2012).

Stalking can correlate with courtship disorders, trauma, and control issues (Fla. Stat. § 847.0141(4), 2012; Mullen & Pathé, 2002). Pornography use may correlate with multiple aspects of stalking and paraphilias, like exhibitionism, peeping, fantasies of closeness, voyeurism, sadistic satisfaction achieved by inducing fear, and thrill experienced by humiliating a victim (Mullen & Pathé, 2002). In one study, a quarter of stalking victims experienced trauma, feelings of powerlessness, and aggressive fantasies. The presence of trauma, as well as aberrant masturbation, is a significant factor in sex crimes. Thus, cycles of violence may correlate with viewing pornography and sex crimes.

Relationships Between Kinds of Pornography

Viewing any kinds of hard-core depictions correlates with viewing other kinds of hard-core depictions including sadomasochism, bondage, snuff, bestiality, or child pornography (DOJ, 2010; *U.S. v. Davidson*, 2002). Relationships between violent pornography, child pornography, and bestiality pornography have remained constant. For example, research of 9,800 pornographic images found in Usenet news groups during the mid-1990s demonstrates this relationship (Mehta, 2001). Usenet allows exchanges of free pornography, and a few of the most popular groups offer illegal pornography (King, 1999). Usenet is not managed by a central body (United States Sentencing Commission [USSC], 2012). Bulletin boards, like Usenet, permit image sharing and allow child abusers to network about specific children and perpetration of hands-on offenses. Over a five-year period on Usenet, commercial pornography posts increased along with depictions of child pornography (Mehta, 2001). Though bondage and discipline images decreased, other hard-core and deviant depictions were available, including depictions of multiple participants, sodomy, ejaculation, and homosexual sex. The number of paraphilic fetish photos exchanged did not change. This study found that depictions of bondage and discipline decreased in the early 2000s, but more recent studies have found that sadomasochistic pornography and other hard-core depictions have increased. For example, a survey of National Drug Intelligence Center (NDIC) personnel found that 15% of respondents observed increased bestiality pornography and child pornography in recent years (DOJ, 2010). Among respondents, 63% reported increased depictions of violence against children; 42% reported an increase in bondage pornography, and 38% reported more sadomasochistic depictions. No respondents reported decreased depictions of sexual violence.

Offenders who view one kind of hard-core pornography are likely to view other kinds of hard-core depictions. Courts have accepted this relationship as evidence of defendants' intent or *modus operandi*. In *U.S. v. Caldwell* (2009), the defendant was charged with downloading numerous bestiality videos and possessing 17 child pornography videos. The defendant claimed that he was unaware that either kind of pornography was downloaded to his computer. The state presented evidence that the defendant's computer was in the process of downloading "animal sex Brazilian girl fucking dog" when agents entered his home. The download was visible on the computer screen. The defendant was the only person home at the time. Because the defendant knowingly downloaded bestiality using LimeWire, the evidence was probative of his interest in explicit pornography (i.e., child pornography) and intent and ability to download child pornography using the same program.

In 2006, 68% of child pornography offenders possessed adult pornography. In one study of 261 law enforcement officers and citizens involved in crime-watch meetings, researchers discovered that approval of adult pornography and misunderstandings about the law may contribute to some child pornography offenses (McCabe, 2000). Researchers theorized that because males were less likely to oppose adult pornography, they were less likely to oppose sexual images of minors. Males were more likely to perceive child pornography distribution as legal. Among the 261 respondents, women were more likely to feel that legal pornography was exploitative of women and opposed distribution of legal images (McCabe, 2000). The same number of respondents who indicated an understanding that child pornography possession is illegal also stated that viewing synthetic pornography may be legal. Synthetic images, discussed further in Chapter 16, may be classified as obscenity in most jurisdictions (Cusack, 2011). Synthetic pornography could potentially contribute to demand for actual child pornography, but it cannot be criminalized as child pornography when specific children are not victimized by it.

Depiction of Crime in Pornography

Some pornography depicts crime. Crimes commonly depicted include victimless public exhibitionism and lewd public sex (Cusack, 2013). Depictions of victimless crimes are rarely described as obscenity and do not seem to be as offensive to society as hard-core depictions. Yet, exhibition may actually occur in public places where filming permits were not granted. Even if these films are evidence of actual crimes, the acts are victimless because actors exhibit themselves to parties involved in production.

Serious crimes, including rape and murder (i.e., snuff films), are less commonly depicted. Simulated crimes are discussed in Chapter 16. Depiction of actual crimes could encounter persecution and prosecution. Videos available on social media and through the press depict actual sex crimes and murder (Drunk Woman Molested by Man in Street, n.d.; Killer Caught on Camera, 2011). Nevertheless, pornographic films of actual violent crimes have been the focus of intense legal and public scrutiny.

There is no free speech right to create actual snuff, even when victims consent to be murdered and filmed (*People v. Freeman*, 1988; *State v. Theriault*, 2008). Planning to produce snuff of a third party probably creates criminal liability (e.g., abetting, aiding, conspiracy, complicity, etc.). First Amendment considerations will not shield anyone connected to the origination of the film if the conduct depicted is illegal (*People v. Kovner*, 1978). Furthermore, this argument may hold water only if the films are found to be nonobscene, but these films are probably susceptible to proscription under the *Miller* test in most jurisdictions. Obscenity production is illegal. Theoretically, if material is considered to be nonobscene in some jurisdictions, then the speech content could still be protected even if the attendant circumstances resulted in separate prosecutions (*People v. Freeman*, 1988). In any case, watching adult obscenity is legal, thus watching pornographic rape and murder films is legal regardless of whether content is simulated or actual.

Witnesses and victims may record rape or violent sex acts (Trial for Canadian Webcam Murder Suspect Begins, 2014). Their speech rights, as incidental witnesses or victims, may be protected, and they may not be enjoined from distributing depictions. Distribution and purchase of these films could be protected or prosecuted as obscenity depending on how or where the film is marketed. Prosecution is likely if the depiction is marketed or distributed as pornography. Sexually violent depictions are usually considered to be obscene.

Forty states restrict sale of "murderabilia," which are items that are valuable because of their connections to famous crime (Mauro, 2012). In these states, actual rape and murder films could be restricted as murderabilia. A full ban of murderabilia may violate constitutional rights when nonobscene objects are considered to be an offender's speech. Explicit details of crimes produced by criminals may be protected. If a criminal produced offensive pornographic narratives or drawings of crimes, then the speech could possess redeeming value under *Miller* (*Simon & Schuster, Inc. v. Members of New York State Crime Victims Board*, 1991). In *U.S. v. Williams* (2008), Justice Stevens said that media photos of a soldier raping a child may violate child pornography statutes. Thus, no exceptions to criminal statutes are guaranteed, except in states that provide affirmative defenses for bona fide purposes.

In some cases, courts forbid criminals from profiting from their crimes, for example, selling movie rights (Mauro, 2012). These laws would apply to pornographic biographies or other works. Criminals can produce the speech acts or work with others who produce films or literature, but in some states they cannot profit from them. In some jurisdictions, antiprofiting speech restrictions have been invalidated because they target individuals based on their identities.

Bondage and Sadomasochism

Generally, the law does not permit parties to consent to violent sexual activity. While the law protects private consensual sexual activity, it only protects nonharmful sexual activity (*Lawrence v. Texas*, 2003). Voluntary sadomasochistic sex is not equivalent to consensual sex. Pornography produced in the United States that depicts actual voluntary sadomasochism and bondage may be evidence of breach of peace, battery, aggravated battery, domestic violence, attempted murder, and other relevant crimes (Krueger, 2010).

A significant body of literature demonstrates that sexual sadism is a paraphilic disorder in which people inflict harm and injury on others. The American Psychiatric Association (APA, 2013) groups sexual masochism with sadism. Like sadism, sexual masochism is a disorder. Studies often analyze sadistic behavior. However, studies rarely analyze masochistic behavior. Sex offenders (i.e., forensic populations) have been studied at length, but as of 2010, only three studies had examined sexual masochism among forensic populations (Krueger, 2010). In one study of 45 pedophiles, none suffered from sadism; of 120 civilly committed sex offenders, only 2% suffered from sexual sadism; and of a group of 166 offenders guilty of sexual homicide, only 5.4% suffered from paraphilic sexual sadism. Among this population, 14.8% of male offenders who suffered from paraphilic sexual sadism also had sexual masochism. In nonforensic populations (e.g., outpatient treatment), sadism is consistently low, for example, about 10%. In this population, the number of people who suffer from sadism is similar to that of those who suffer from masochism. Nearly one-quarter of community members not receiving any treatment for sexual disorders reported that they may enjoy being bitten. In another study of 2,026 respondents, researchers found that only 4.8% of males and 2.1% of females ever derived pleasure from sadism, and only 2.5% of males and 4.6% of females ever derived pleasure from masochism. Thus, sadomasochistic pornography misrepresents the normalcy or prevalence of this behavior in society. Low prevalence of sadomasochism in society may partly explain why depictions of violent sex are offensive to average members of the community.

Deviant sexual interests do not necessarily indicate that a person suffers from a mental disorder (APA, 2013). Diagnosis of sexual sadism or sexual masochism requires (1) that apart from social disapproval, a person feels personal distress because of his or her sexual desires or behavior; (2) that a person experiences sexual desire or behavior involving psychological distress, injury, or death inflicted on another person; or (3) that a person desires to become sexually involved with an unwilling person or a person who cannot legally consent. Thus, problematic sexual sadism involving psychological or physical harm is a paraphilic disorder. However, problematic sexual sadism is also a paraphilic disorder because partners cannot legally consent to violent sexual activity. Sexual masochism also requires dominant partners to engage in sexual activity to which they cannot consent (i.e., inflicting harm). In this sense, sexual sadism disorder is defined by laws prohibiting voluntary violent sex. In forensic contexts, this definition could be used to bootstrap.

Broader historical analyses demonstrate some prejudices against sadomasochistic sexuality and pornography that could explain why they are considered to be harmful by the APA and the law. Sadomasochistic sex and bondage have been associated with homosexuality and gay pornography. Prejudices against nonprocreative sex and moral resistance to homosexuality likely influence policies (Chiesa, 2011; Ridinger, 2006). Moral prejudices derived from traditional Anglo Christian perspectives were discussed in Chapter 1. Since 1959, under the Obscene Publications Act, England had successfully prosecuted every case of gay sadomasochistic and bondage pornography until 2012. One well-known case, the *Spanner* case, involved a raid on a gay club offering bondage and sadomasochism activity (*The Spanner Trust*, n.d.). In 1987 during Operation Spanner, police seized video evidence of numerous men enslaving and beating each other and inflicting genital abrasions and lacerations. Because of the seriousness of the bondage, Operation Spanner included murder investigations, which were ultimately cleared without charges. Though defendants claimed that activities were lawful because they were voluntary, 16 defendants were convicted of assault causing actual bodily harm and grievous bodily harm. Supreme Court of Canada held that intent and causation comprise the crime of bodily harm (Deckha, 2007). A victim's voluntary participation does not amount to legal consent.

Further analyses are necessary about relationships between depictions of voluntary sexual slavery and depictions of sex trafficking victims. Some victims may be forced to participate in pornography. If conventional and nonharmful sex is depicted, and slavery is not advertised, then it is unlikely that any crime would result from selling, transmitting, or buying pornography featuring actual sex slaves. However, explicit images depicting willing sex slaves could be subject to criminal prosecution (e.g., obscenity or aggravated assault), depending on the content and jurisdiction (*People v. Samuels*, 1967). This dichotomy is discussed further in Chapter 1 and Chapter 16.

Some jurisdictions (e.g., Oregon) specifically criminalize sadomasochistic sexual conduct or abuse in live shows. Statutes directly outlaw production of films depicting and exhibiting sexual slavery (Or. Rev. Stat. § 167.062, 2009). Even when statutes are silent about sadomasochism or bondage pornography production, courts throughout the United States tend to uphold convictions for aggravated assault pursuant to voluntary sexual slavery depicted in films (*Commonwealth v. Appleby*, 1980). This tendency should provide a strong rationale to prosecute transmitting or dealing films that involve actual sexual slavery even if sex scenes depict nonviolent sex. Under the Harm Principle, it could be argued that the government should tolerate voluntary sadomasochistic sex and pornography and focus investigative and prosecutorial resources on locating victims of human trafficking. The government should ensure that every adult performer consensually participates in pornography (Cusack, 2011). Yet, depictions of voluntary sexual slavery potentially contribute to demand for depictions of actual slavery, as well as contribute to sexual and moral denigration in society. Thus, the government's prosecution of violent sex acts and depictions may be compelling.

Though the federal government relies on the *Miller* test to define obscenity featuring adults, the government stipulates that child pornography depicting minors in bondage are considered to be both child pornography and obscenity (U.S. 18 § 1466A(i), 2014). Children need not be violently assaulted for depictions of sadism and bondage to be prosecuted as obscenity. Statutory definitions are met when simulations involve actual children. Both child pornography and obscenity charges could result from a single depiction, and this would not result in double jeopardy. From a policy standpoint, this provision is important to fully punish people who psychologically or physically torture children, especially considering that victims are likely to develop severe trauma.

Fisting

Consensual digital penetration is lawful. Depictions of nonharmful digital penetration between heterosexual consenting adults are likely lawful. However, at some point between penetration using one finger, multiple fingers, all fingers, and a fist, society may draw a line. Fisting is an extreme sexual act that may be grouped with sadomasochism and other harmful acts by the government. Depictions of fisting may be classified as obscene because often they are produced to appeal to the homosexual community. For example, in England, Michael Peacock was prosecuted under the Obscene Publications Act 1959 for selling depictions of fisting and other fetishes (Hodgson, 2012). Peacock challenged traditional classifications of hard-core homosexual pornography as obscenity. In 2012, he was the first defendant to plead not guilty to charges relating to selling hard-core gay pornography. The jury found him not guilty.

Fisting is not necessarily violent, although depictions deviate from normal sexual behavior and normal pornography. Hard-core gay male pornography depicts fisting, and it is usually considered to be an extreme sexual act or fetish within gay communities (Lumpkin, 2011). Mainstream lesbianism does not generally qualify fisting as a deviant sexual act or fetish, but mainstream lesbian pornography does not depict it. These trends are consistent with findings that any mainstream pornography is less likely to include hard-core acts, but homosexual pornography is more likely to contain hard-core elements than heterosexual pornography (Cusack & Waranius, 2012). Salmon and Diamond (2012) selected 60 best-selling pornographic heterosexual and homosexual films. They found that almost no hard-core sex acts were depicted in best-selling films. In a study of amateur pornography on Youporn.com, a website that allows viewers to select hard-core film scenes, including fisting, 10% of heterosexual films and 80% of homosexual films depicted sex crimes and hard-core content, like rape (Figure 6.1) (Cusack & Waranius, 2012).

"Rough sex" is a defense that could be invoked if criminal charges were brought against pornography actors who fist (Ridinger, 2006). This defense has been attempted against breach of peace and battery charges or as a mitigating factor to more serious charges, like aggravated battery or kidnapping. Under battery laws in some jurisdictions, prosecutions could turn on whether a court found that a victim was harmed by fisting. If no harm can be demonstrated, then the defense may prevail, but if harm can be imputed or inferred, then charges may be sustained irrespective of the victim's voluntary participation. "Rough sex" may be no excuse in obscenity prosecutions

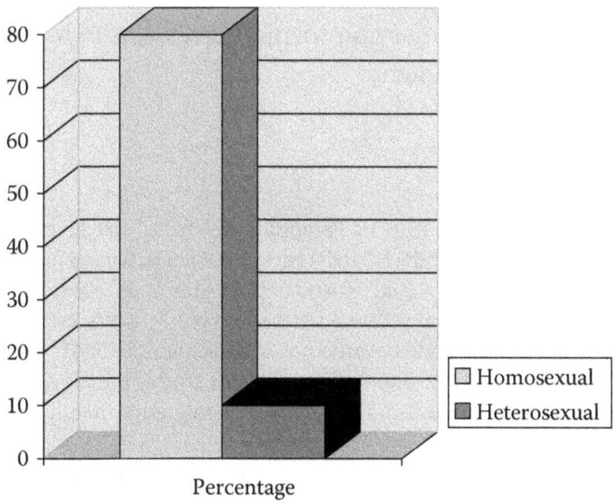

Figure 6.1 Percentage of amateur pornography scenes depicting hard-core themes or illegal behavior.

unless it defends against statutes that triggered obscenity prosecution under *Miller*'s first prong, that is, bans of violent sexual speech.

Under some state statutes, definitions of obscene sadomasochistic pornography seem broad enough to include nonviolent fisting because it may be considered physically "abusive or substantially beyond customary limits of candor," and depictions of it would "not have serious … political … value." Depictions of gentle or nonviolent fisting are not customary, and perhaps any political value derived from the fact that images could reflect the sexual behavior of a minority political group may not sufficiently demonstrate nationally recognized political value (Va. Code Ann. § 18.2-372, 2008). Even if fisting were mainstream, "normal or perverted" depictions can be classified as sadomasochistic or patently offensive (Wyo. Stat. Ann. § 6-4-301(a)(iii), 2005).

Conclusion

Generally, sexually violent depictions are unprotected speech. A number of researchers have demonstrated relationships between crime and pornography. Neither causality nor a definitive degree of probability between correlations has been proved. Frequent fantasizing to violent and hard-core pornography may permit viewers to rehearse violent crimes. Depictions of victimless crime in pornography (e.g., public exhibitionism) do not seem to directly inspire viewers to commit crimes. Aberrant masturbation to hard-core depictions may have deleterious effects on viewers, and viewers may fantasize about and rehearse engaging in sadomasochistic sex. Voluntarily violent sex is nonconsensual sex because the law does not protect harmful sex acts. The court may consider nonnormative sex acts to be harmful even if acts are voluntary and nonviolent.

References

American Psychiatric Association. (2013). Paraphilic disorders. Retrieved from http://www.dsm5.org/Documents/Paraphilic%20Disorders%20Fact%20Sheet.pdf

Arkin, D. (2014, February 21). Child pornography found at accused Missouri killer's home. *NBC News*. Retrieved from http://www.nbcnews.com/news/us-news/child-pornography-found-accused-missouri-killers-home-n35841

Bourke, M. L., & Hernandez, A. E. (2009). The "Butner study" redux: A report of the incidence of hands-on child victimization by child pornography offenders. *Journal of Family Violence*, *24*(3), 183–191.

Chiesa, L. E. (2011). Consent is not a defense to battery: A reply to Professor Bergelson. *Ohio State Journal of Criminal Law*, *9*(1), 195–208.

Commonwealth v. Appleby, 380 Mass.296 (1980).

Cusack, C. M. (2011). Busting patriarchal booby traps: Why feminists fear minor distinctions in child porn cases, an analysis of social deviance with in gender, family, or the home (etudes 4). *Southern University Law Review, 39*, 43–70.

Cusack, C. M. (2013). How the content of online pornography depicts expressed consent for insemination. *Online Journal of Communication and Media Technologies, 3*(3), 91–110.

Cusack, C. M., & Waranius, M. (2012). Nonconsensual insemination and pornography: The relationship between sex roles, sex crimes, and "STRT," "Gay," and "Shemale" films on Youporn.com. *Journal of Research in Gender Studies, 2*(2), 15–33.

Deckha, M. (2007). Pain, pleasure, and consenting women: Exploring feminist responses to S/M and its legal regulation in Canada through Jelinek's the piano teacher. *Harvard Journal of Law and Gender, 30*, 425–459.

Department of Justice. (2010, August). The national strategy for child exploitation prevention and interdiction. Retrieved from http://www.justice.gov/psc/docs/natstrategyreport.pdf

Drunk woman molested by man in street. (n.d.). Youtube.com. Retrieved January 22, 2014, from http://www.youtube.com/watch?v=-cuwMzYyIZ0

Fla. Stat. § 847.0141 (2014).

Flood, M. (2009). The harms of pornography exposure among children and young people. *Child Abuse Review, 18*(6), 384–400.

Fox, J. A., & Levin, J. (1998). Multiple homicide: Patterns of serial and mass murder. *Crime and Justice, 23*, 407–455.

Hald, G. M., Malamuth, N. M., & Yuen, C. (2010). Pornography and attitudes supporting violence against women: Revisiting the relationship in nonexperimental studies. *Aggressive Behavior, 36*(1), 14–20.

Hodgson, N. (2012, January 6). Michael Peacock's acquittal is a victory for sexual freedom. *The Guardian*. Retrieved from http://www.theguardian.com/commentisfree/libertycentral/2012/jan/06/michael-peacock-obscenity-trial

Killer caught on camera. (2011, April 27). *New York Post*. Retrieved from http://www.youtube.com/watch?v=-WPcLI40r2k

King, S. A. (1999). Internet gambling and pornography: Illustrative examples of the psychological consequences of communication anarchy. *CyberPsychology and Behavior, 2*(3), 175–193.

Krueger, R. B. (2010). The DSM diagnostic criteria for sexual masochism. *Archives of Sexual Behavior, 39*(2), 346–356. doi:10.1007/s10508-010-9613-4

Lawrence v. Texas, 539 U.S. 558 (2003).

Laws, D. R., & O'Donohue, W. T. (2008). *Sexual deviance*. New York: Guilford Press.

Long, M. L., Alison, L. A., & McManus, M. A. (2013). Child pornography and likelihood of contact abuse: A comparison between contact child sexual offenders and noncontact offenders. *Sex Abuse, 25*(4), 370–395.

Lumpkin, J. (2011, October 20). The forbidden lesbian sex act. *Huffington Post*. Retrieved from http://www.huffingtonpost.com/jincey-lumpkin/the-forbidden-lesbian-sex-act_b_1018585.html

Mauro, J. C. (2012). Rethinking "murderabilia": How states can restrict some depictions of crime as they restrict child pornography. *Fordham Intellectual Property, Media and Entertainment Law Journal, 22*, 323–358.

McCabe, K. A. (2000). Child pornography and the Internet. *Social Science Computer Review, 18*(1), 73–76.

Mehta, M. D. (2001). Pornography in Usenet: A study of 9,800 randomly selected images. *CyberPsychology and Behavior, 4*(6), 695–703.

Mullen, P. E., & Pathé, M. (2002). Stalking. *Crime and Justice, 29*, 273–318.

Or. Rev. Stat. § 167.062 (2009).

People v. Freeman, 46 Cal. 3d 419 (1988).

People v. Kovner, 96 Misc 2d 414 (1978).
People v. Samuels, 250 Cal. App. 2d 501 (1967).
Ridinger, R. B. (2006). Negotiating limits: The legal status of SM in the United States. *Journal of Homosexuality*, *50*(2), 189–216.
Ryan, K. M. (2011). The relationship between rape myths and sexual scripts: The social construction of rape. *Sex Roles*, *65*(11–12), 774–782.
Salmon, C., & Diamond, A. (2012). Evolutionary perspectives on the content analysis of heterosexual and homosexual pornography. *Journal of Social, Evolutionary, and Cultural Psychology*, *6*(2), 193–202.
Simon & Schuster, Inc. v. Members of New York State Crime Victims Board, 502 U.S. 105 (1991).
State v. Theriault, 158 N.H. 123; 960 A.2d 687 (2008).
The Spanner Trust. (n.d.). The history of the Spanner case. Retrieved January 24, 2014, from http://www.spannertrust.org/documents/spannerhistory.asp
Trial for Canadian webcam murder suspect begins. (2014, March 24). MSN. Retrieved from http://news.msn.com/crime-justice/trial-for-canadian-webcam-murder-suspect-begins
United States Sentencing Commission. (2012). Report to the Congress: Federal child pornography offenses: Technology and investigation by law enforcement in child pornography cases. Retrieved from http://www.ussc.gov/news/congressional-testimony-and-reports/sex-offense-topics/report-congress-federal-child-pornography-offenses
U.S. 18 § 1466A(i) (2014).
U.S. v. Caldwell, 586 F.3d 338 (2009).
U.S. v. Davidson, 283 F.3d 681 (2002).
Va. Code Ann. § 18.2-372 (2008).
U.S. v. Williams, 553 U.S. 285 (2008).
Wyo. Stat. Ann. § 6-4-301(a)(iii) (2005).

7 Relationship Between Pornography and Trafficking

Overview

Numerous criminal justice agencies, researchers, and nonprofit organizations present concrete and undeniable connections between pornography and forced sex work involving human trafficking. Familial relatives, corrupt public officials, members of organized crime, and gangs are involved in commercial human trafficking. Human trafficking is the second-largest illegal market in the world (Tanagho, 2007). The market for human traffic generates $19 billion each year; most of the revenue is produced from commercial sex sales of women and children (Initiative against Sexual Trafficking, n.d.). Approximately 500,000 to 1 million children and adults are internationally trafficked annually (Tanagho, 2007). Intranationally, thousands more are trafficked each year. Annually, thousands of victims from Asia, Eastern Europe, and Latin America are trafficked into the United States. Some victims are kidnapped; others are held as indentured servants to repay the costs of trafficking. Thus, some trafficked individuals voluntarily travel across borders. A portion of these people knowingly and successfully hire or barter with traffickers to be transported covertly across borders.

Adult Pornography and Human Trafficking

Contract girls are the face of pornography. They are highly paid pornography superstars who project an image of being healthy, lucrative, and empowered businesswomen. However, the majority of participants in pornography are not contract girls. Many of these noncontract girls are independent contractors who do not usually enjoy the same glamour as contract girls. It has been theorized that many of these noncontract girls are prostitutes who are essentially forced or coerced to perform by human traffickers or pimps.

The Federal Bureau of Investigation (FBI), local and state law enforcement, and victim-centered advocacy organizations have formed hundreds of task forces to combat human trafficking (Department of Justice [DOJ], 2010). Federal and state laws classify trafficking as a felony (11 Del. Code § 787, 2013). Trafficking in commercial sexual activity includes trade, sale, recruitment, or promises (11 Del. Code § 787, 2013; Minn. Stat. § 609.321,

2013). Sexually explicit performances are a form of commercial sexual activity. During live public shows, actors intend to arouse prurient interests or sexually satisfy desire. Public places may include hotel rooms (D.C. Code § 22-2708, 2013). Pornography production may be evidence of statutory violations. When victims are forced to perform, then they may be considered to be victims of human trafficking because they are subjected to involuntary labor or servitude (11 Del. Code § 787, 2013; Minn. Stat. § 609.321, 2013). Enslavers may use threats, physical restraint, and physical force to coerce performances. Traffickers may blackmail victims by threatening to report victims' undocumented status or participation in sex work. To add credibility to threats, traffickers may destroy or confiscate victims' identifications or passports. Victims may believe that authorities have conspired with their captors or would fail to help them if they escaped. Victims may be controlled through drug addictions, whereby pimps ply victims with drugs or withhold drugs to achieve compliance. Over time, victims may voluntarily participate in trafficking operations or become pimp-like in their behavior (e.g., "bottom bitches"). Sex workers who transform from victims to abusers independently evade authorities to protect their stakes in trafficking operations.

Victims are forced by intimate partners to participate in commercial sex work, exotic dancing, and pornography (D.C. Code § 22-2708, 2013; Utah Code Ann. § 76-5-308, 2013). However, some statutes restrict definitions of trafficking to victims who are undocumented or unlawfully residing in the United States. Thus, intranational victims of trafficking may be protected only by lesser statutes, such as domestic violence statutes, rape laws, or promotion of prostitution statutes, if those apply. Pornography producers who pimp their spouse also could be charged with patronizing prostitutes if they hire individuals to perform in pornographic depictions with their spouse (Minn. Stat. § 609.321, 2013). Some jurisdictions specifically protect spouses from forced prostitution (A.R.S. § 13-3205, 2013; D.C. Code § 22-2708, 2013). Yet, jurisdictions may not consider commercial pornography production to be prostitution, especially when force is not evident. Prior human trafficking-related convictions may serve as evidence of trafficking. Withholding earnings from spouses or defrauding spouses of their share of pornography production earnings may also be evidence of trafficking (D.C. Code § 22-2708, 2013). In jurisdictions that specifically recognize spouses as victims of prostitution, the government may attempt to provide services similar to those provided for rape victims (Okla. Stat. Ann. § 75:15-13-25, 2012). Governmental and private organizations may offer specific services to sex trafficking victims (Wash. Rev. Code § 43.280.091, 2013; Wash. Ann. Code § 246-324-010, 2013). Medical and mental health treatment, food, shelter, English-language training, employment training, detox treatment, and legal support may be necessary. Undocumented residents may be permitted to reside in the United States to testify against abusers if they can provide evidence of a requisite level of intimacy with traffickers. In some cases, victims will be sexually trafficked by family members other than spouses or intimate partners, and the state may prosecute this using a variety of relevant laws (e.g., human trafficking, kidnapping, false imprisonment, prostitution, sexual assault, etc.).

Child Pornography, Sex Trafficking, and Adult Human Trafficking

Approximately 90% of child victims of sexual assault are personally acquainted with their offenders (Office of the Attorney General, 2013; Veronica's Voice, 2013). Abducted children are often transformed into prostitutes. They may grow up in the commercial sex industry and participate in pornography, willingly or unwillingly. Some voluntarily assist traffickers to recruit other children. Two-thirds of cases brought to authorities' attention may be unprosecuted (Report: 20 Cases of Child Trafficking, 2013). Many of these cases come to the authorities' attention after children are arrested for sex work. Child sex workers are prosecuted more frequently than traffickers. Once sex workers have criminal records, they are more likely to continue prostituting themselves. On average, U.S. prostitutes begin at 12 years of age, but commonly remain in the industry and bear children of their own. Thus, adults and parents involved in pornography and human trafficking may also have children who are involved. Second-generation prostitutes effectively become native, local prostitutes operating within the community.

Forty-three percent of National Drug Intelligence Center (NDIC) experts responded that foreign tourists commit hands-on offenses with American children in the United States (DOJ, 2010). More than one-fifth of experts reported that these tourists spread sexually transmitted diseases, and 14% reported that U.S. tourists who abuse children abroad may be more likely to abuse children domestically after becoming desensitized to child abuse. Fourteen percent of exploitation experts reported that commercial sex tourism encourages domestic and foreign parents to involve their children in commercial sex trade. Sixteen percent of child exploitation experts reported that sex traffickers are frequently men older than 20 years, but younger than 50 years, who often have children of their own.

Child pornography is a $3 billion industry that is frequently linked with commercial sex trafficking; the commercial sex trade is a multibillion-dollar business (Commercially Sexually Exploited Children [CSEC], 2013; Washington State Office of the Attorney General, 2013). One estimate showed that 55% of the total child pornography on the Internet, including commercial and free websites, depicts U.S. children and pornography produced in the United States (CSEC, 2013).

> Some may consider child pornography less concerning than sex trafficking, perhaps because it is a graphic representation of a child, and not necessarily actual physical abuse. However, evidence increasingly shows that graphic images can be an exploiter's inducement into other forms of commercial sexual exploitation. (CSEC, 2013, p. 4)

Campaigns to crack down on commercial trafficking of children and child pornography mostly target male offenders (DOJ, 2010). Yet, these men are not the only offenders forcing victims to participate (Freedom Youth Project Foundation, 2011). Millions of married and single women contribute to the demand for young children by viewing child pornography and participating in prostitution. One study found that 68% of production cases were perpetrated by people in trusted positions, relatives, or family friends (United States Sentencing Commission [USSC], 2012). Pornography producers may train children to perform sadomasochistic sex acts, endure bondage and humiliation, and participate in violent pornography (Stevens, n.d.). Children may be routinely tortured, coerced, and sold. Subjection to violent pornography production may result in severe mental and physical trauma. A single victim may suffer from dissociative identity disorder, depression, posttraumatic stress disorder, suicidality, and Stockholm syndrome.

Among NDIC interviewees, 15% reported that female children are paid $1,000 to $3,000 per night of prostitution, and they will earn additional money for pornography production (USSC, 2012). However, 75% of NDIC experts reported that traffickers keep all of the profits, and children do not retain any profits. One-fifth of experts specified that children barely survive while traffickers may live lavishly. Despite these incongruities, many children remain in captivity though they have opportunities to leave. The Dallas, Texas, police department reports that 80% of chronic female runaways become involved in commercial sex work, that is, prostitution (DOJ, 2012). Poor family structure, poverty, exposure to crime, and other factors may lead children to become involved with local gangs or street life. Traffickers may be street-level drug dealers who prey on vulnerable children after they become disconnected from their families. Fifteen percent of DOJ experts reported local street gang involvement in federal child trafficking (DOJ, 2012). Child prostitutes who consider returning to their families may remain in captivity if they believe that traffickers will find them no matter where they flee.

Well-intended members of law enforcement prosecute child prostitutes to incapacitate and deter operations. However, many child prostitutes are younger than the legal age required to grant sexual consent, which effectively transforms every sexual encounter into rape. Criminal prosecution of children may further disenfranchise children by failing to provide them with services, while stigmatizing them with criminal records (Smith, Vardaman, & Snow, 2009). Still, criminal justice intervention provides children with opportunities to contact the justice system, escape captivity, and possibly seek rehabilitation. However, many child sex workers are financially, psychologically, and physically unprepared to take these steps.

Localized Child Sex Trafficking

Some victims of child pornography are shuffled locally between abusers. Abuse may involve parents and community members. Between 2003 and 2004, Operation Cybersafe investigated records of federal sex offenders in Illinois (DOJ, 2010). Seventeen offenders had victimized over 200 children. More than 70 computers were analyzed for offenders' involvement in online networking, child exploitation, pornography production, sexting, texting, e-mailing, distribution, enticement, private chatting, in-person meetings, and hands-on abuse. The main connection between offenders was their involvement in pedophilia, interest in child pornography, and motivations for law breaking. It was discovered that these offenders, who had been prosecuted for federal charges, often competed with each other locally. At times, they worked with each other to increase the number of exploited children. They shared information about particular victims and recruitment strategies. One defendant was identified as having had sex with more than 125 children in the area, and he maintained that he had sex with over 500 local children.

Half of experts participating in a study published by the DOJ reported that traffickers operate semiformal networks; only a quarter of respondents reported child trafficking operations to be large and well organized (DOJ, 2010). However, among child exploitation experts surveyed throughout the country, approximately one-quarter stated that they possessed no data about where to physically locate local child prostitutes (DOJ, 2010), though 14% stated that truck stops may feature local child prostitutes who circulate among sex offenders and pornography producers. The same percentage reported the availability of local children at brothels. Local child prostitutes are often shuffled to areas hosting major events, for example, sports tournaments (Weinreich, 2014).

The following cities are known for widespread availability of local child sex workers: Atlanta, Georgia; Bridgeport, Hartford, and New Haven, Connecticut; Washington, D.C.; Miami and Orlando, Florida; New York City; Arlington, Dallas, Fort Worth, Garland, Houston, and Mesquite, Texas (DOJ, 2010). A few of these cities contain international airports where predators may arrive in search of local child victims (Figure 7.1).

Orlando, Florida, may be one of the most attractive cities for pedophiles and local sex trafficking. The city is home to Disney World, which has been the place of employment of several online solicitors at the time of their arrest (Black, 2014). In response to severe sex trafficking and local commercial sex

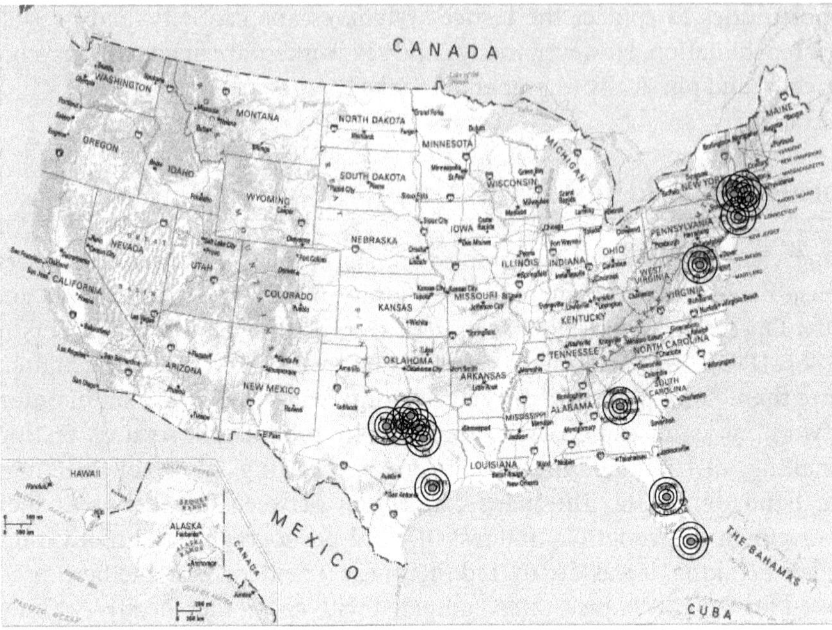

Figure 7.1 U.S. cities with highest prevalence of child sex workers.

work, Florida has developed comprehensive statutes that criminalize trafficking and traveling to meet a minor for sex. Eleven percent of DOJ interviewees reported that online solicitors travel any distance to meet with children (DOJ, 2010). Thus, Florida, and other jurisdictions, prohibit traveling any distance within the state, to the state, or from the state to meet a child to commit sexual acts, including sharing pornography or production offenses (Fla. Stat. § 847.0135 (4), 2013). It is a crime to entice or lure children's parents or custodians to sexually sell, transfer custody, or traffic children (Fla. Stat. § 847.0145, 2013). A few states directly prohibit enterprises from generating tourism for child sexual work (720 ILL. 5/10A-10(a), 2006). Charges and sentences depend on the jurisdiction, statutory language, and degrees of crimes committed (720 ILL. 5/10A-10(a), 2006; Wash. Rev. Code § 19.138.340, 2013).

Much local trafficking results from families offering their children for trade. Parents and foster parents may trade children with community members or other parents for access to new child victims, drugs, pornography, money, power, or favors. For example, two parents in Tennessee rented their four female children to support addictions to the designer-drug bath salts (Charged, 2013). Their children ranged from 6 years old to 16 years old. Federal authorities charged the parents, who forced their daughters to perform in pornographic sexual activity at several locations throughout Johnson City, Tennessee. Federal agents became involved when one daughter was shuffled to South Carolina. These children were ill, and they suffered from dental decay, which is typical of child victims of trafficking. When authorities found them, the children also suffered from lice, fleabites, and ringworm. Sometimes, child care or child welfare groups are infiltrated by traffickers. Money may not be directly exchanged for services, but money or favors may be laundered to organizations directed by traffickers (Sewell & Farrar, 2013; Swanson, 2014). This is discussed in Chapter 19.

Conclusion

Pornography has two faces. The public face is of actors who consent to perform, are paid, and enjoy their work. The hidden face is of victims who are abused, exploited, prostituted, and trafficked. Many participants in commercial pornography have been abused and victimized. After months or years of victimization, victims may voluntarily participate in commercial sex industries and prey on new victims. Traffickers, pimps, and conspirators may victimize spouses, foster children, grandchildren, and biological children in exchange for benefits, power, money, and drugs.

References

11 Del. Code § 787 (2013).

720 ILL. COMP. STAT. ANN. 5/10A-10(a) (West Supp. 2006).

A.R.S. § 13-3205 (2013).

Black, J. (2014, February 12). Disney world workers among 22 nabbed in child-sex sting. *NBC News*. Retrieved from http://www.nbcnews.com/news/us-news/disney-world-workers-among-22-nabbed-child-sex-sting-n28916

Charged: Tennessee couple sells their 6-year-old daughter and three others to pornographers. (2013, October 20). FreakOut Nation. Retrieved from http://freakoutnation.com/2013/10/20/charged-tennessee-couple-sells-their-6-year-old-daughter-and-three-others-to-pornographers/

Commercially Sexually Exploited Children (CSEC). (2013). Report problem statement. California Health and Human Services Agency. Retrieved from www.chhs.ca.gov/Documents/CSEC_Report-Problem_Statement.docx

D.C. Code § 22-2708 (2013).

Department of Justice. (2010, August). The national strategy for child exploitation prevention and interdiction. Retrieved from http://www.justice.gov/psc/docs/natstrategyreport.pdf

Farley, M. (2006). Prostitution, trafficking, and cultural amnesia: What we must not know in order to keep the business of sexual exploitation running smoothly. *Yale Journal of Law and Feminism*, *18*, 109–144.

Fla. Stat. § 847.0135 (4) (2013).

Fla. Stat. § 847.0145 (2013).

Freedom Youth Project Foundation. (2011, July 21). Pornography: A gateway to human trafficking. Retrieved from http://www.freedomyouthproject.org/2011/07/pornography-and-child-sex-trafficking.html

Initiative against Sexual Trafficking. (n.d.). Sexual trafficking facts. Retrieved May 5, 2013, from http://www.iast.net/thefacts.htm

Minn. Stat. § 609.321 (2013).Office of the Attorney General. (2013, May 5). Megan's Law: Facts about sex offenders. Retrieved from http://www.meganslaw.ca.gov/facts.htm

Okla. Stat. Ann. § 75:15-13-25 (2012).

Report: 20 cases of child trafficking investigated in Kentucky in four-month period. (2013, December 23). *Fox News*. Retrieved from http://www.foxnews.com/us/2013/12/22/report-20-cases-child-human-trafficking-investigated-in-kentucky-in-four-month/?intcmp=latestnews

Sewell, D., & Farrar, J. (2013, February 24). Rape of adopted Ohio kids unusual, haunting case. Yahoo.com. Retrieved from http://news.yahoo.com/rape-adopted-ohio-kids-unusual-haunting-case-165818115.html

Smith, L. A., Vardaman, S. H., & Snow, M. A. (2009). The national report on domestic minor sex trafficking: America's prostituted children. Shared Hope International. Retrieved from http://sharedhope.org/wp-content/uploads/2012/09/SHI_National_Report_on_DMST_2009.pdf

Stevens, M. (n.d.). Scared selfless: An autoethnographic account of enslavement in a pedophilic sex ring. *Dissertation Abstracts International: Section B: The Sciences and Engineering*. (Order No. AAI3509463)

Swanson, L. (2014, January 23). New lawsuit details "tag team of abuse" at St. Louis de Montfort. *Oak Lawn Patch*. Retrieved from http://oaklawn.patch.com/groups/police-and-fire/p/new-lawsuit-against-archdiocese-details-tag-team-of-abuse-at-st-louis-de-montfort

Tanagho, J. (2007). New Illinois legislation combats modern-day slavery: A comparative analysis of Illinois anti-trafficking law with its federal and state counterparts. *Loyola University Chicago Law Journal, 38*(4), 895–962.

United States Sentencing Commission. (2012). Report to the Congress: Federal child pornography offenses: Technology and investigation by law enforcement in child pornography cases. Retrieved from http://www.ussc.gov/news/congressional-testimony-and-reports/sex-offense-topics/report-congress-federal-child-pornography-offenses

Utah Code Ann. § 76-5-308 (2013).

Veronica's Voice. (2013, May 5). Informational resources, statistics. Retrieved from http://www.veronicasvoice.org/statistics.html

Wash. Ann. Code § 246-324-010 (2013).

Wash. Rev. Code § 19.138.340 (2013).

Wash. Rev. Code § 43.280.091 (2013).Washington State Office of the Attorney General. (2013). Human trafficking. Retrieved from http://www.atg.wa.gov/HumanTrafficking/SexTrafficking.aspx#.UV_I_hzvun8\

Weinreich, M. (2014, April 9). FBI makes arrests in Augusta sex trafficking sting. *Sports Illustrated Wire*. Retrieved from http://tracking.si.com/2014/04/09/augusta-fbi-masters-sex-trafficking-arrests-golf/?xid=si_topstories

Commonalities and Comorbidities Within Child Pornography

8

Overview

Viewers and producers of child pornography participate in some similar behaviors (United States Sentencing Commission [USSC], 2012). They tend to experience similar or predictable comorbidities, recidivism risks, sexual deviancy, and interests in violence and penetration. In general, child pornography offenders may be analyzed using five variables. First, their degree of interest in sexualizing children encompasses a range. Second, their motives may vary for collecting child pornography. Third, they may or may not engage in sex offending, that is, production offenses, hands-on offenses, and contact offenses. Fourth, child pornography viewers are not necessarily pedophiles. Fifth, technology may influence the level of interest in child pornography, acceptance for their behavior, community participation, and degree of contact with children. Kinds of technology and frequency of technology used may be separable from the other categories yet may also overlap, especially with offenders' motivations and psychology. Within these five categories, offenders may engage in different combinations of behaviors, extreme activities, experimental pornography use, and compulsive behaviors. Offenders' behaviors and interests may flow along a spectrum.

Child Pornographers

Child pornographers share some *modus operandi* (USSC, 2012). Authorities have identified similarities in pornographers' collecting behaviors, involvement in online communities or marketplaces, and hands-on offenses. Online offenders may be identified by four main *modus operandi*: (1) those who access child pornography impulsively or curiously, but without intent to satisfy sexual desires; (2) viewers who experience sexual fantasies about children, but abstain from hands-on offending; (3) solicitors who use the Internet to make contact with children; and (4) content providers who commit production offenses and then distribute pornography exclusively for commercial gain (Babchishin, Hanson, & Hermann, 2011). Among production offenders, there are six main *modus operandi*: (1) offenders who memorialize contact offenses and collect depictions; (2) offenders who memorialize depictions, but do not collect child pornography; (3) offenders who commit hands-on offenses or aid others to do so, but only sometimes memorialize abuse; (4) offenders who memorize abuse of children and collect child pornography, but do not share memorializations with others; (5) offenders who do not sexually contact children, but depict victims who voluntarily participate in pornography production; and (6) offenders who participate in online communities in any of the other five capacities (USSC, 2012).

Internet offending does not necessarily correlate with hands-on offending (Burgess, Carretta, & Burgess, 2012). Scientific findings vary about whether viewing child pornography creates or increases risk for hands-on offenses. Production offenses usually garner longer sentences because it may not be fair to punish producers and viewers equally. Some members of the criminal justice system argue that immobilizing nonproduction offenders with long prison sentences may not necessarily increase child safety. However, production offenses comprise a small portion of all pornography offenses. Prosecution of 207 production offenses in 2010 accounted for less than 0.25% of the federal offender population and only about 11% of federal child pornography cases (USSC, 2012).

Though prosecution of production has risen, for example, only 10 cases were prosecuted in 1992, the government mainly incarcerates viewers. In one study of 101 male federal offenders who had only viewed images online, researchers found that more than half of the men posed an otherwise low risk to society (Figure 8.1) (Burgess et al., 2012). At the time of arrest, offenders were employed parents who had experience with emotionally committed adult relationships. They were also first-time offenders who did not pose a general threat to society or children. An argument against increased lenience for possession offenses is that viewers create demand for production offenses (Figure 8.1). Thus, many judges find mandatory sentencing minimums for pornography viewers to be appropriate (USSC, 2012).

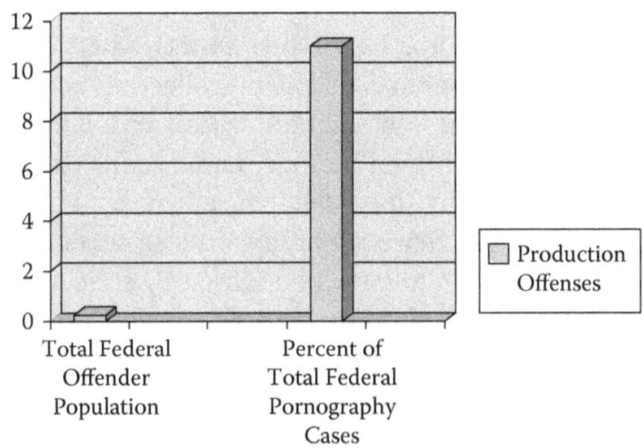

Figure 8.1 Federal offenders.

Pornographers commit production offenses with and without victims' knowledge; some pornography production is voluntary, but some is involuntary (USSC, 2012). Victims are typically groomed before abuse. Offenders may supply victims with drugs, money, gifts, or alcohol. Many victims are convinced that they have consented and voluntarily participate (Murdock, 2014). Some victims will voluntarily take nude pictures when solicited. Pornographers may erroneously believe that production laws are circumvented if children self-produce pornography (e.g., sext). Many victims are also coerced to participate. Offenders may pressure victims and use threats. Threats can include self-harm, harm to the victim or loved ones, exposure, and escalation of abuse. Offenders may also promise to disengage abusive behaviors if victims comply.

Offenders may lure victims in a number of ways (USSC, 2012). Some offenders use one child to bait or recruit other children. Siblings, cousins, friends, or strangers may be recruited. Children who participate in recruitment are often reluctant to report offenders because they feel ashamed or believe that they will be charged with production crimes. Producers may use peer-pressure tactics, and they may also threaten to expose children who do not help them recruit. Images of abuse may glamorize abuse or portray pleasure, which may entice new participants. Violent depictions may be excluded from images used to recruit new victims. Violent depictions include forcible penetration, pain, crying, or distress. Most still-photo child pornography depicts compliance, willingness, happiness, and enjoyment. However, videos sometimes include evidence that producers prompt and command children to smile and look happy.

The National Center for Missing and Exploited Children (NCMEC) has documented more than 57 million photos and videos of child pornography (USSC, 2012). Many victims are unidentified. Offenders may target infants and toddlers because this age group is preverbal and often unaware of abuse or production. Victims' identities may be known, but they may resist disclosing abuse for a number of reasons. Even when confronted by authorities with evidence of abuse, some youth may deny that images exist or that abuse occurred. Most depictions of child sex abuse are duplicate images that have been renamed by members of online pornography communities. This is a common evasion tactic among child pornography reposters. This tactic is discussed in greater detail in Chapter 10. Law enforcement agencies have identified more than 4,000 victims of child pornography, which is merely a fraction of individual pornography victims (USSC, 2012). Estimates suggest that more than 5 million children have been victims of child pornography that currently circulates on the Internet. Some offenders possess thousands or millions of images (USSC, 2012).

Most pornography producers primarily engage in nonpenetrative sexual behaviors with minors (USSC, 2012). Yet, most depicted victims have been penetrated at least once. The NCMEC reported that 84% of pornography victims were featured in at least one image of oral penetration. Slightly more than three-quarters, 76%, were depicted in anal and/or vaginal penetration. Just more than half of pornography victims, 52%, were penetrated by objects or devices. A large number of victims were involved in obscenity. Forty-four percent were involved in bondage or sadism, and 20% of victims were depicted in images involving urine or feces. Bestiality is the least common form of obscenity in child pornography. It reportedly appeared in only 4% of child pornography images. Perhaps this attests more to offenders' disinterest in harming or sexualizing animals rather than their unwillingness to debase children to the most depraved extremes.

Online communities that disseminate child pornography validate deviant interests in child pornography and reduce a sense of remorse. These environments may provide encouragement, support, and ideas. Community involvement may increase viewers' interest and access to pornography, yet it does not necessarily increase dangerousness or risk of child abuse. Communities may be hierarchical and praise members in proportion to members' degree of knowledge and contribution to the community. Praise contributes to members' distorted attitudes about pornography activities, deviant interests, and victims. Within communities, producers are most valued. Producers are more dangerous when community members praise their efforts because they are encouraged to produce and trade new images. People who post new images or prolifically re-post collections also are highly valued participants. Members may demonstrate their value by educating others about technology and where to acquire types of images. Collection size, file organization, and file-sharing capabilities also generate status among community members. Large collections that can be searched according to gender, age, kind of abuse, race, and fetish are valued among community members. Group approval or trusted reputations may be useful to members who wish to access secret or obscure collections requiring permission or vetting. These groups sometimes rely on specific rules for entrance and may moderate content and member interaction. Pertaining to these groups requires involvement, commitment, and time investment.

Child Pornography and Molestation

Research has sought to definitively establish a relationship between child pornography, nonconsensual child sex, and statutory rape. Though correlations exist, no causal relationship has been discovered. Researchers piece together reports from convicted sex offenders, self-identified sexual deviants in the general population, law enforcement, and exploitation experts to understand correlations between hands-on offending and pornography.

Little information is known about most of pornography victims other than generalizable knowledge about the sex industry (USSC, 2012). Infants, toddlers, prepubescent minors, and postpubescent adolescents are victims of battery, sexual battery, rape, forcible sodomy, and numerous other crimes that are depicted in pornography. Postpubescent victims compose one-quarter of images, whereas 76% are prepubescent and pubescent. Prepubescent and pubescent minors are targeted because they typically do not ask for profit sharing or commission (Sotomayor, 2013). Older teens are more likely to ask for money in exchange for participation in pornography production. Of the prepubescent victims, approximately 10% are infants or toddlers (USSC, 2012).

The National Drug Intelligence Center (NDIC) reviewed 495 federal case summaries between 2005 and 2009 (Department of Justice [DOJ], 2010). Of these, 186 defendants, which is 38%, had prior offenses against children, and 301 defendants, 61%, were charged with possessing child pornography after committing hands-on offenses. Some of these included online enticement where offenders used child pornography to entice children to engage in sex or exchange pornography. In many enticement scenarios, the ultimate goal is contact, not acquiring child pornography. In 29% of cases, 145 defendants who were charged with pornography offenses had prior contact convictions or admitted to hands-on offenses. In a few cases, law enforcement were unsure about whether contact offenses or pornography offenses were precedent. Sometimes, images demonstrated multiple victims, which further compounded some confusion about whether viewing or production offenses were precedent.

Among experts interviewed through NDIC, 93% reported that new hands-on offenses occur to meet market demands for child pornography (DOJ, 2010). Market demand explains why abuse has become more violent and images have become more graphic. The great majority of expert respondents, 83%, reported that pornographers commit offenses after becoming stimulated by child pornography. Sixty-four percent of respondents said that curiosity and desire increased among offenders with exposure to pornography. Viewers become desensitized to violence and are more likely to commit hands-on offenses. However, only one-third of NDIC experts stated a definitive belief in a causal relationship between hands-on offenses and pornography.

Bourke and Hernandez (2009) analyzed 155 male sex offenders who were divided into two cohorts and treated over 18 months. Each group viewed and transmitted child pornography. Offenders in the first group were not known to be abusers at the time of sentencing. The second group acknowledged at least one hands-on offense, or evidence demonstrated that offenders in the second group had committed at least one contact offense. Researchers discovered that a reciprocal relationship likely exists between contact offenses and child pornography.

Most contact sex offenders began viewing child pornography after having committed at least one contact offense. Viewing child pornography online correlated with decreased likelihood to sexually abuse multiple victims.

Several researchers have attempted to measure the risk of hands-on offending in terms of levels of severity depicted by indecent images of children (IIOC; Long, Alison, & McManus, 2013). Within a sample of 120 adult males who were found guilty of crimes involving IIOC, 60 had prior hands-on offenses. No evidence existed that the remaining half, 60 men, had ever sexually contact children. Within these two groups, 50% of cases were analyzed to determine any relationships between the quantity of images, levels of images, history of physically abusing children, production offenses, online behavior, and victim selection. Researchers based their hypotheses on studies showing that 12% of pornography offenders had been arrested for sexually contacting children, but 55% of pornography offenders self-reported histories of hands-on offending. In the past, this spread has been as wide-ranging as 1% and 84.5% in various studies. It also has been reported that those who have committed hands-on offenses and pornography offenses (i.e., dual offenders) are much more likely to possess larger collections, participate in victim grooming, and attempt to distribute adult pornography to minors. Researchers also noted that in another study that analyzed how many hands-on offenders produced child pornography, 20% were reported to commit production offenses or persuade minors to self-produce images or images of their friends. These offenders first developed desires to contact children sexually, then viewed child pornography, and finally committed production offenses.

Fantasy plays a role in hands-on offending, but it is not solely to blame. Many offenders wish to immortalize children at ages when abuse occurred or when children are most appealing to the offender. In addition to fantasies about specific sexual activity, offenders may be motivated by specific gender and age factors. In Long et al.'s (2013) study of two groups of offenders, researchers found that noncontact offenders possessed much larger collections of child pornography than dual offenders. Offenders who primarily owned images featuring posing, but not sexual contact, were less likely to engage in abuse even if they owned large collections. Collection size was not as indicative of abuse as much as images that depict penetration or worse crimes.

Noncontact offenders were less likely to produce images, and they were more likely to pay for images (Long et al., 2013). In 69% of noncontact cases, offenders paid for pornography. Far fewer dual offenders, approximately 14%, paid for images. Noncontact offenders were more than 13 times as likely to pay for child pornography. Committing production offenses, including hands-on and hands-off production, made offenders much more likely to commit hands-on offenses. Notably, 80% of hands-off offenders in this study did not engage in production, yet more than 53% of dual offenders produced child pornography. Committing pornography production offenses and committing hands-on offenses were closely related.

Grooming activities correlated with dual offending more than noncontact offending at the rate of 26:1 (Long et al., 2013). The primary purpose of most grooming seems to be to make contact, not to solicit images or record real-time streaming of child nudity. These grooming behaviors were typically offline. Hands-on offenders were more likely to have access to children, especially neighborhood children. They were more likely to groom them and produce images through sexual contact. This means that their intent to contact children and contacting children was precedent to production of pornography. Almost half, 48%, of hands-off offenders admitted to experiencing pedophilic attraction to children. Dual offenders were significantly less likely to confess to police, and 27% possessed distorted views of their offenses. Offenders who committed hands-on offenses were less prone than hands-off offenders to experience cognitive distortions about culpability. Approximately 24% of hands-off offenders provided positive justifications for their actions. However, hands-on offenders may also receive greater feedback from online communities, which contributes to cognitive distortions. Dual offenders were more careful to evade certain risks, like talking to police or paying for pornography. They may be more criminogenic, opportunistic, predatory, or savvy.

Child Pornography: Age, Race, and Gender

Men mostly transmit and view child pornography (USSC, 2012). Though a few women produce pornography and entice minors, the great majority of offenders worldwide are male. Alarmingly there has been an increase of female teachers involved in solicitation and sexting in conjunction with hands-on offenses in recent years, and an escalation of mothers involving their children in pornography to receive money, drugs, or affection from love interests. In some cases, mothers cannot be convicted for giving pornography to minors if parental relationships are an affirmative defense to disseminating harmful materials to minors (Mass. Gen. Laws Ann. 272 § 28, 2013).

Worldwide, most victims of pornography are female. Numbers of female and male victims vary according to age. In one study, pornographers who committed hands-on offenses against male children mostly possessed pornography of male children (Long et al., 2013). This study found that dual offenders tended to possess images of children in the same age group as children with whom they had committed hands-on offenses. However, causal or precedent relationships have not definitively been proved. In 92% of cases, the same was true of female pornography subjects and victims. When images of females and males were about equal, offenders sexually contacted females 57% of the time. They contacted male victims in 14% of cases, and offenders committed hands-on offenses against both genders in 29% of cases. In 75% of cases, dual offenders' pornography interests matched their sexual victims.

A few studies find that male and female victims are nearly as likely to have been victims of abuse; however, the great majority of data demonstrates that females are more often victims of sex abuse and pornography offenses worldwide (Bourke & Hernandez, 2009). The Child Exploitation and Online Protection Centre (CEOP) in the United Kingdom collects all images of abuse seized by law enforcement in the United Kingdom (USSC, 2012). Between 2005 and 2009, a 10% sample of CEOP's 247,950 images featured mainly female victims. Eighty-one percent of victims were female. However, male victims were likely to be younger than female victims. Almost three-fourths of male victims, 73%, were prepubescent. One-quarter of male victims were pubescent or postpubescent. A small fraction of male victims, approximately 2%, were younger than two years old. CEOP analyses reported that 51% of female victims were prepubescent. Fewer than half of the images of females, 48%, were pubescent or postpubescent (Figure 8.2). Less than 1% of images, 0.7%, were of children younger than 2 years old. Offenders typically possess a variety of images, yet identifiable children younger than 3 years old appeared in approximately 28% of offenders' collections; victims between the ages of 3 and 5 years appeared in approximately 46% of offenders' collections; and victims between the ages of 6 and 12 years appeared in approximately 86% of offenders' collections. Children older than the age of 12 years were featured in 67% of offenders' collections (Figure 8.2).

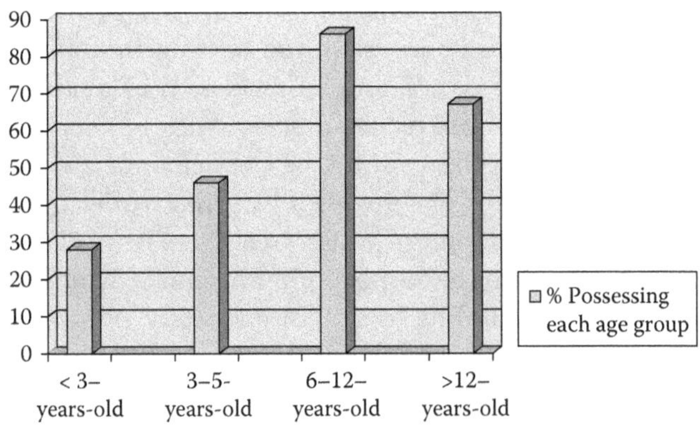

Figure 8.2 Percentage of offenders whose collections included depictions of each age group.

In the United States, NCMEC identifies slightly more female victims than male victims of pornographic exploitation (USSC, 2012). Females compose 57% and males compose 43% of victims. Prepubescent children compose 76% of female and male victims, and 10% were younger than 2 years old. Only 24% of victims were pubescent or postpubescent. A report to Congress stated that based on when abuse began, one-quarter of pornography victims were younger than 5 years old, and 7% were 2 years old or younger. These findings are consistent with NCMEC's findings. The Online Victimization Survey of 2,500 U.S. law enforcement agencies in the years 2000 and 2006 found that most child pornography viewers possess images of children in different age groups. In 2006, 28% of offenders possessed more than one depiction of a toddler or baby. In both years, female victims were featured more prevalently. Prepubescent males are more likely to be victims of production offenses. Pubescent and postpubescent females are featured in greater numbers of commercial pornographic depictions.

Twenty-eight percent of experts at NDIC reported that prostitution is more common among African American children (DOJ, 2010). African American children are at greater risk for domestic instability, drug use, delinquency, inadequate home supervision, poverty, and encounters with Child Protective Services. These factors may increase children's desires to run away from home or ability to be lured from home. A quarter of NDIC respondents, 24%, reported that child sex traffickers are usually African American males, though they may be any ethnicity, including European American, Latin American, Asian, and Eastern European. Violent crime may be part of pimping, production offenses, and trafficking. Criminologists often agree that minorities are at significantly increased risk for perpetration of violent crimes, victimization, and arrest. Thus, minorities may encounter the criminal justice system more often.

One-fifth of NDIC experts reported that child prostitutes are usually between 14 and 17 years old (DOJ, 2010). Online solicitors are reported to be Caucasian males by 65% of NDIC respondents. Yet, strangers soliciting children through online media represent only around 7% of production offenses (USSC, 2012). In one study, 97% of federal production offenders were white, and the great majority, 86%, was U.S. citizens (DOJ, 2010). Thus, while foreign or ethnic traffickers may supply children in the United States, white offenders may likely have produced pornography. Another argument is that foreign traffickers are less likely to be arrested for a number of reasons, as discussed in Chapter 20 and Chapter 22. Therefore, white Americans account for many of the federal charges in the United States. Consistent with other studies and other federal pornography offenders, typical federal pornography production offenders were in their forties (DOJ, 2010; USSC, 2012). Consistent with findings that production offenders may seek status in online communities or may solely be motivated by money, only 47% had completed some college (USSC, 2012). Though 76% were employed, 56% had negative net worth. This population may be distinguishable from nonproduction offenders who pay for pornography. Only 47% of nonproduction offenders had a negative net worth.

Findings about gender, race, and age have been inconsistent. Some NDIC respondents said that online solicitors are so varied that no single profile typifies them, though one unifying feature is that many online offenders have no prior records (DOJ, 2010). In one study, slightly more than 8% of online offenders were racial minorities in one study, but approximately 35% of offline offenders were racial minorities (Babchishin et al., 2011). Online offenders tended to be younger than the average male in the general population, averaging about 38 to 39 years old. Offline offenders averaged between 43 and 44 years old.

Juveniles composed 16% of sexual offenders in 2009 (Fanniff & Kolko, 2012). Juveniles commit more than one-third of sex offenses against children. One study subdivided sex offenders into groups with respect to victims' ages. A sample of 176 male juveniles indicated that 65% of juveniles offended against child victims. They were more likely to offend against biological relatives and male victims. Juveniles who perpetrated sexual crimes against peers or adults composed 28% of the sample. They likely experienced poor monitoring by guardians (e.g., parents). Juveniles who victimized both children and adults composed only 7% of the sample. Only 2 of 176 juveniles sampled in this study were females, which limits the generalizability of these findings. Juvenile female sex offenders may be more rare or less understood because of gendered understandings of culture, society, and criminology.

Convicted sex offenders between the ages of 10 years and 18 years have used coercive sexual tactics, committed rape, engaged in exhibitionism, sexually harassed victims, distributed pornography, and possessed child pornography or obscenity. One study examined this population between the years 2000 and 2008 (Aebi, Vogt, Plattner, Steinhausen, & Bessler, 2012). All victims were younger than 12 years old. In each case, victims were no fewer than 3 years younger than each of the 419 offenders studied. Aebi et al. (2012) analyzed six levels of offenses: (1) noncontact offenses including voyeurism and obscene communications; (2) sexual touching above clothing; (3) nude sexual contact, masturbation, and digital penetration; (4) oral sodomy; (5) vaginal penetration, whether attempted or performed; and (6) anal sodomy, whether attempted or performed. Multiple offenses were analyzed at the highest level of offense if the offender had not separated from the victim for at least one hour between acts. For example, clothed touching and nude touching in the same incident could be scored as the same sex act if they occurred in close proximity. An average offender was between 13 and

14 years old during the first reported sexual offense. Of the juvenile offenders studied by Aebi et al. (2012), 28% (i.e., 119 juveniles), had been convicted only of pornography offenses. Only nine of these were females. Consistent with developmental theories of crime, 41% of offenders came from broken homes or single-parent homes. Only 14 juveniles had been sexually victimized, and only 7 juveniles recidivated sexually. This finding does not support theories about high incidence of cycles of sex abuse among sex offenders. However, findings support theories about deviant and criminogenic behavior patterns, because 37 juveniles committed nonsexual, violent crimes following their convictions for sex offenses. Ninety reoffended nonviolently and nonsexually. More commonly, juveniles committed nonsexual crimes against peers or adults. Crimes against adults or peers were more likely to involve groups (e.g., gangs). Sexual offending against young children, including production offenses, typically involved lone perpetrators, possibly exhibiting antisocial personality traits.

Nonviolent Sex Crimes and Child Pornography

Nonviolent paraphilia, like public exhibitionism and peeping, may correlate with child pornography offenses. Some researchers have suggested that voyeuristic desires and interests develop in relation to viewing child pornography (Babchishin et al., 2011; Seto & Eke, 2008). Surreptitious pornography production may be a nonviolent sex offense. Depictions produced without consent account for significant amounts of pornographic material, even though these depictions do not compose a large percentage of all pornography available online. One study found that voyeuristic materials were present in nearly one-third of offenders' collections. However, fewer than 10% of these offenders may be diagnosed with voyeurism (Babchishin et al., 2011; Galbreath, Berlin, & Sawyer, 2002). This may be because possessing a few voyeuristic depictions alone does not indicate paraphilia or because some authorities and therapists may not differentiate between voyeuristic depictions and other materials when they pertain to large pornography collections.

Cognitive distortions correlate with nonviolent pornography offenses. Viewing hard-core pornography and child pornography may correlate with cognitive distortions and voyeuristic production offenses. Offenders may justify undercover or surreptitious production if they feel that pornographication of sex is normal. They may also believe that voyeurism allows them to abstain from contact offenses. Producers may record contact offenses when children are sleeping because they believe that children are not being harmed. They may believe that conscious children are unharmed if contact is not sadistic and children are unaware that sexual contact was memorialized. Generally, offenders who believe that viewing pornography allows them to relinquish some desire to contact children are typically less remorseful for viewing pornography. Despite the prevalence of online solicitation and attempts to use video equipment to engage in video sex acts with children, in 2006, only 5% of offenders had viewed real-time videos of children being abused by other adults (USSC, 2012).

Pornography offenses may include nonviolent behaviors like probation violations. Offenders may use cell phones, jump drives, or laptops to hide pornography from probation officers. For example, offenders may easily use and stash thumb drives in cluttered or covert areas of the home (USSC, 2012). Unless probation officers know where to look for such small items and intend to look for this kind of contraband, then probation officers would not likely notice them during home verification checks. Pornography addiction can also lead to theft from spouses. Offenders may steal to pay for pornography, abscond with family electronics, purchase and conceal new electronic devices, or dispose of electronics in an attempt to avoid detection. Nonviolent behavior perpetrated against spouses is discussed further in Chapter 12.

Police have offered anecdotal evidence that many offenders begin with child erotica, then progress to pornography and enticement. Some estimates claim that 20% of pornography available online depicts children (Wethal, 2010). The demand of child pornography is high, and some estimates claim that 20,000 images are posted weekly. Offenders' thirst develops through fantasy, and then they may attempt to quench their thirst for deviant sexual experiences or children with nonviolent offenses. Offenders may progress to public masturbation, adultery, exhibitionism, public intercourse, and sadomasochistic, and explicit literature about child molestation. Obscenity may include stories about adult–child sexual relationships, drawings of child sex abuse, or depictions of clothed children that focus on groins and appeal to prurient interests. In one study, 11% of abusers possessed stories, letters, texts, or other forms of written material about sexual abuse (Rellahan, 2014; USSC, 2012). Twenty-one percent of offenders possessed legal or innocuous images of male and female children within their pornography collections. One study found that dual offenders who molest and groom children and view child pornography may also view child "modeling" websites that contain lawful content (USSC, 2012). Compulsive masturbators may relive offenses or rehearse future crimes by masturbating to prior communications with children. Compulsive masturbation does not necessarily increase future risk of reoffending (USSC, 2012). However, pornography viewers who are at high risk of committing hands-on or hands-off offenses in the future are at increased risk for offending with more frequent viewing of children pornography or sadomasochistic obscenity.

Exhibitionism may relate to compulsive masturbation, viewing child pornography, and other paraphilias. Main motives for exhibitionism include

(1) courtship disorders in which offenders exhibit their genitals in an unsolicited manner in an attempt to attract mates, (2) thrill-seeking and frightening victims, and (3) a desire to be viewed while masturbating. A study of 485 male juveniles accused of sex offenses concluded that 60% of respondents self-reported hands-on offending (Zolondek, Abel, Northey, William, & Jordan, 2001). More than 30% self-reported involvement in child pornography. Between 10% and 30% of male juveniles self-reported participation in exhibitionism, fetishism, frotteurism, voyeurism, and obscene phone calls and phone sex. Yet, exhibitionism is diagnosed in fewer than 5% of cases.

Violent Crimes and Child Pornography

Viewing child pornography and sadistic child pornography or reading obscene fantasies about these activities can correlate with violence. Domestic violence, random violence, predatory violence, violence against animals, rape, and sexual assault are some examples of comorbid behaviors.

Compulsive Internet use has been associated with escalating demands for and supply of violent material overall, but especially in video form. Among 1,913 Swedish respondents, Internet addiction was associated with feelings of dysphoria, lack of control, feelings of addiction, and perceived need for professional help (Ross, Månsson, & Daneback, 2012). Men who viewed and shared pornography online experienced the greatest problems. Interests in sadomasochism and fetishes also related to Internet addiction symptoms.

The relationships between violence, Internet addiction, and child pornography are correlative, and they may be reciprocal. Addicts amass thousands, hundreds of thousands, or millions of photos and videos. Collections usually contain a range of violent and nonviolent images, but those who suffer from low impulse control and experience fantasies that have escalated in violence may be most likely to possess large amounts of explicit, penetrative depictions and images of sadomasochism and bondage. NCMEC found that 84% of child pornography victims were penetrated orally at least once (USSC, 2012). Child victims were penetrated anally or vaginally at least once in 76% of cases. Object rape was committed against 52% of victims, and 44% of victims suffered from bondage or sadism. Twenty percent of child pornography victims were battered by or subjected to activities involving urine or feces. Only 4% of victims were subjected to sex acts (e.g., penetration) involving animals. Those who view nonviolent content may not be as likely to commit violent crimes as those who compulsively fantasize about violence while participating in pathological Internet use.

One key symptom of Internet addiction is consumption of numerous videos online. Explicit violence, graphic sexual content, and depictions of penetration increased from the year 2000 to the year 2006 (USSC, 2012). Still photos of these activities are common, yet by 2006, 58% of offenders possessed one or more videos of sexual violence. Individuals who are prone to problematic Internet use and addiction suffer from a lack of impulse control, antisocial tendencies, social inadequacy, career problems, depression, emotional dysfunction, isolation, and deviant sexual interests, attitudes, and beliefs. These traits may relate to loneliness, unhappiness, negative moods, and desires to alter self-perceptions. Unlike hands-on offenders, who tend to be married, pathological online offenders may have no physical sex life with peers or adults. In the *Diagnostic and Statistical Manual of Mental Disorders* (American Psychiatric Association, 2000), the diagnostic criterion for antisocial personality disorder (Section 301.7) includes "deceitfulness, as indicated by repeated lying ... conning others for personal profit or pleasure ... reckless disregard for safety of self or others ... lack of remorse, as indicated by being indifferent to or rationalizing having hurt ... another." Internet addiction may be a doorway to other uncontrollable, pathological, and antisocial personality features like ritualistically cataloging images and backing up images on multiple hard drives or devices. All of these factors heighten risk for violence. When problematic Internet use combines with violent fantasies about children, Internet addicts become more likely to commit violent crimes and sexually violent crimes (e.g., penetration of prepubescent children).

Addiction and antisocial attitudes about sex, fueled by unchecked use of violent pornography online, may very well relate to violent contact with children or adults (*State v. Spargo*, 1982; USSC, 2012). Internet addicts, like hands-on offenders, are likely to masturbate to violent and nonviolent images. One study that reported this also reported that approximately 50% of contact offenders possessed collections with more than 750 images. Noncontact offenders had smaller collections with fewer than approximately 250 images. This suggests that Internet addicts may be more likely to possess larger collections, possess more violent material, and physically contact children.

Violent offenders may evade authorities if evidence of abuse is not memorialized within their pornography collections and crimes are nonviolent. A sample of 4,697 online offenders was surveyed to determine rates of previous contact offenses and recidivism (Seto, Hanson, & Babchishin, 2011). Official records reported lower offending than self-reports and identified previous offenders as composing approximately 12% of the sample. However, self-reports identified 55% of the sample as having committed hands-on offenses. After 1.5 to 6 years, only a small percentage, 4.6%, of the total sample had recidivated. The degree of violence in each offense is unknown, because approximately three-quarters of recidivists' records failed to report the kinds of offenses committed. If victims are not injured, then they may be less likely to report crimes to authorities. Online offenses were recidivated with a hands-on offense in approximately 2% of cases, and slightly more than 3% recidivated with child pornography according to official records. Violent crimes were the most common kinds of recidivism committed, with 4% of instances of recidivism. Accurate self-reporting of recidivism likely would have been much higher.

Offenders as Victims

Offenders' history of abuse is a risk factor for abuse of child victims. The federal government reported to Congress that 30% of production offenders and 18% of nonproduction offenders possibly have histories of sexual abuse (USSC, 2012). At trial, abuse may enter as evidence or be used as a mitigating factor. Trauma may cause child pornography offenders who were victims of sexual abuse to experience differences from the general population in cognition, behavior, socialization, learned behavior, and coping skills. Many sex offenders have reported that pornography is a maladaptive strategy for coping with difficulty or stress (Babchishin et al., 2011; Elliott, Beech, & Mandeville-Norden, 2013).

In one study, 41% of nononline offenders reported histories of physical abuse (Babchishin et al., 2011). Slightly more than 24% of online offenders reported histories of physical abuse. Online and nononline offenders reported similar histories of sexual abuse. Online and nononline offenders' history of sexual and physical abuse was significantly greater than that for nonoffending males. Sex offenders often report poor family histories. Trauma, lack of direction, and poor authoritative oversight are relevant to theories of deviance (e.g., routine activity theory, strain theory, and environmental criminology). Contrary to some studies, nononline offenders experienced greater cognitive distortions. Online offenders expressed victim empathy at higher rates than nononline offenders. Consistent with other studies, online offenders in this study were found to be more sympathetic toward children than were nononline offenders, who may not attempt to repress or divert urges to commit hands-on offenses or who may molest children for profit. However, nononline offenders are capable of identifying emotionally with children. Nononline offenders may identify with children, possibly because of a history of abuse, and, therefore, not identify themselves as adult offenders or identify children as victims.

Social learning theory states that deviant behavior may be learned. Criminal attitudes and activities are adopted during social interaction. Peer groups, relatives, neighbors, classmates, mentors, and others may impart criminal behavior. Child pornographers may learn or accept criminal behavior after being victimized. They may also mirror parents' or mentors' behaviors or attitudes. Pornographers without personal histories of abuse may have learned abusive behaviors and attitudes from authority figures who abused other children. Online communities that support and inform offenders are major influences. Offenders who have been victims of sexual, physical, or psychological abuse may feel traumatized, rejected, and resentful. Peers online may have maladaptive strategies relating to histories of abuse and influence offenders who have no histories of abuse. Camaraderie in online communities may make offenders feel a sense of belonging, acceptance, and approval (USSC, 2012). Viewers who suffered abuse may feel a sense of relief, comfort, or validation. Community members can create new identities, feel popular, and escape from the real world. Communities may condone hands-on offenses. Preexisting pedophilic urges may be exacerbated by exploitative community relationships that encourage members to participate in new crimes. Availability of images may motivate nonpedophilic viewers to participate. Cognitive distortions may develop among many community members because some deny that harm is inflicted on children or that children suffer. Communities extol benefits experienced by children. Some members may identify pedophiles as a politically oppressed group condemned for creating harmless, albeit deviant, expressions of pleasure. Past victims may feel convinced that they were sexually glorified as children or have been selected to participate in a sexual liberation movement. They may be persuaded to appreciate their sexual histories and may even seek civil rights and privacy rights for pedophiles. Simultaneously, as positive connections to online communities develop, bonds to normative society and anchoring relationships may erode.

Some estimates suggest that between 10% and 15% of boys and 20% and 33% of girls have been sexually abused, though official crimes reports indicate that the rate is much closer to 0.1%. Many victims do not report abuse. Former victims who helped to lure other children may fail to report abuse. They may experience a sense of absolution by commiserating with others who have similar histories. By discussing and believing that children enjoyed sex acts, they do not have to confront questions about whether their own behavior was indeed illegal. They may pacify their fears or hide from the justice system by becoming involved in online communities.

Unresolved sexual abuse from childhood may create patterns in adults' consciousness and behavior, compulsive behavior, and addiction (Hunter, 1995). The federal government reported that 43% of production offenders and 36% of nonproduction offenders had histories of substance abuse, which may indicate trauma and self-medicating (USSC, 2012). In one study that compared dual offenders with hands-off pornography offenders, researchers found that a criminal history of sex offense and drug abuse made offenders as statistically prone to commit hands-on offenses as pedophiles (USSC, 2012).

Offenders with histories of abuse and compulsive disorders who have nonsexual interests in child pornography may be drawn to it because they can compulsively collect depictions (Hunter, 1995). Sometimes, offenders who have been abused initially view child pornography because they are curious about other victims of abuse, even though they are not sexually attracted to children.

Victim and nonvictim male offenders commonly experience social inadequacy and isolation (Hunter, 1995). Viewers may indulge in deviance to avoid stress and personal dissatisfaction with life (Elliott et al., 2013). Offenders may substitute deviance for real intimacy and sex. Some offenders with histories of abuse may engage in compulsive masturbation and pornography viewing, voyeurism, exhibitionism, sadomasochism, bestiality, bondage, adultery, sexting and telephone sex, anonymous sex, public indecency, frotteurism, and transvestism.

Among juvenile sex offenders who abused adults, peers, and children, similar histories of physical and sexual abuse were reported (Fanniff & Kolko, 2012). However, when juveniles perpetrated abuses on other minors, juvenile offenders' parents were more likely to disclose possible abuse inflicted on their children. Perhaps parents' roles in doubting or ignoring children's abuse correlates with juveniles acting out or failing to develop coping skills. It may also correlate with some juveniles' resistance to disclose abuse. Only one-third of parents who suspected that juvenile offenders had been sexually abused were certain about abuse. Two-thirds believed that their children may possibly have a history of sexual abuse. Perhaps false claims of abuse by juvenile offenders contribute to juveniles' distorted attitudes toward underage sexual activity, children, or sexual abuse. Hands-on offenders or their parents may attempt to mitigate crimes by alleging abuse or victimization by pornographers. Though mandatory sentencing schemes do not permit excessive lenience, especially for repeat offenders, courts may consider defendants' history of abuse. However, evidence of abuse must be valid. Critics have claimed that offenders forge histories of abuse *ex post facto* for sympathy and that history of sex abuse plays only a marginal role in sex offenses.

Conclusion

Offenders' characteristics, behaviors, and interests may flow along a spectrum. Researchers and criminal justice officials attempt to understand possible relationships between offenders' and victims' behavior, race, gender, violence, history of abuse, and other variables. Data may be predictive of recidivism. Pornography offenders' interests, motives, physicality and violence, sexual attraction to children, use of technology, and compulsive behaviors are studied to improve risk assessment and treatment.

References

Aebi, M., Vogt, G., Plattner, B., Steinhausen, H., & Bessler, C. (2012). Offender types and criminality dimensions in male juveniles convicted of sexual offenses. *Sex Abuse, 24*(3), 265–288.

American Psychiatric Association. (2000). *Diagnostic and statistical manual of mental disorders* (4th ed., text rev.). Washington, D.C.: APA.

Babchishin, K. M., Hanson, R. K., & Hermann, C. A. (2011). The characteristics of online sex offenders: A meta-analysis. *Sex Abuse, 23*(1), 92–123.

Bourke, M. L., & Hernandez, A. E. (2009). The "Butner study" redux: A report of the incidence of hands-on child victimization by child pornography offenders. *Journal of Family Violence, 24*(3), 183–191.

Burgess, A. W., Carretta, C. M., & Burgess, A. G. (2012). Patterns of federal Internet offenders: A pilot study. *Journal of Forensic Nursing, 8*(3), 112–121.

Department of Justice. (2010, August). The national strategy for child exploitation prevention and interdiction. Retrieved from http://www.justice.gov/psc/docs/natstrategyreport.pdf

Elliott, I. A., Beech, A. R., & Mandeville-Norden, R. (2013). The psychological profiles of Internet, contact, and mixed Internet/contact sex offenders. *Sex Abuse, 25*(1), 3–20.

Fanniff, A. F., & Kolko, D. J. (2012). Comparisons across domains in an outpatient sample victim age-based subtypes of juveniles adjudicated for sexual offenses. *Sex Abuse, 24*(3), 224–264.

Galbreath, N. W., Berlin, F. S., & Sawyer, D. (2002). Paraphilias and the Internet. In A. Cooper (Ed.), *Sex and the Internet: A guidebook for clinicians* (pp. 187–205). Philadelphia: Brunner-Routledge.

Hunter, M. (1995). Uncovering the relationship between a client's adult compulsive sexual behavior and childhood sexual abuse. In M. Hunter (Ed.), *Adult survivors of sexual abuse: Treatment innovations* (pp. 56–79). Thousand Oaks, CA: Sage.

Long, M. L., Alison, L. A., & McManus, M. A. (2013). Between contact child sexual offenders and noncontact offenders child pornography and likelihood of contact abuse: A comparison. *Sex Abuse, 25*(4), 370–395.

Mass. Gen. Laws Ann. 272, § 28 (2013).

Murdock, S. (2014, January 27). Erica Ann Ginnetti, teacher, had sex with student: Cops. *The Huffington Post.* Retrieved from http://www.huffingtonpost.com/2014/01/27/erica-ann-ginnetti-student-sex_n_4673660.html?icid=maing-grid7%7Cmain5%7Cdl11%7Csec3_lnk4%26pLid%3D435345

Rellahan, M. P. (2014, February 14). Family man sentenced in child porn case. *Daily Local News.* Retrieved from http://www.dailylocal.com/general-news/20140214/family-man-sentenced-in-child-porn-case

Ross, M. W., Månsson, S., & Daneback, K. (2012). Prevalence, severity, and correlates of problematic sexual Internet use in Swedish men and women. *Archives of Sexual Behavior, 41*(2), 459–466.

Seto, M. C., & Eke, A. W. (2008, October). *Predicting new offenses committed by child pornography offenders.* Paper presented at the 27th Annual Conference of the Association for the Treatment of Sexual Abusers, Atlanta, GA.

Seto, M. C., Hanson, R. K., & Babchishin, K. M. (2011). Contact sexual offending by men with online sexual offenses. *Sex Abuse, 23*(1), 124–145.

Sotomayor, S. (2013). *My beloved world.* New York: Vintage.

State v. Spargo, 103 Ill. App. 3d 280 (1982).

United States Sentencing Commission. (2012). Report to the Congress: Federal child pornography offenses. Retrieved from http://www.ussc.gov/Legislative_and_Public_Affairs/Congressional_Testimony_and_Reports/Sex_Offense_Topics/201212_Federal_Child_Pornography_Offenses/

Wethal, T. (2010). The problem with porn. *Law Enforcement Technology, 37*(2), 18–25.

Zolondek, S. C., Abel, G. G., Northey, W. F., Jr., & Jordan, A. D. (2001). The self-reported behaviors of juvenile sexual offenders. *Journal of Interpersonal Violence, 16*(1), 73–85.

Prosecution

9

Overview

Prosecution of unprotected speech may be complex and costly. For example, prosecution may require interagency collaboration, expert witnesses, and subpoenas for international witnesses. Prosecution of pornography may be more prevalent in districts with higher income, but not if they have higher crime rates overall (Buzzell, 2007). Data show that complexity and cost make prosecution of obscenity crimes less likely if offenders are not involved with child pornography or other commercial sex enterprises. The National Drug Intelligence Center (NDIC) has reported significant difficulty in surreptitious investigation of obscene and pornographic images of children online because offenders use wireless Internet connections, online image storage, external hard drives, wireless storage devices, USB drives, CDs, secure password technology, proxy servers, encryption, and Internet protocol (IP) spoofing (Department of Justice [DOJ], 2010). Investigators often rely on human connections involving social media, peer-to-peer (P2P) file sharing, and tip lines to gather evidence. Internet monitoring, sting operations, and mandatory reporting may produce sufficient evidence to result in prosecution. Stings are not costly, but forensic analysis and expert testimony, extradition, and other aspects of trying the accused may be more costly. On occasion, false accusations have resulted in investigation, prosecution, or conviction; however, use of recorded technological evidence aids the state in meeting its burden of proof. Technological evidence may also aid defendants.

Monitoring

By and large, the Internet is unregulated and unmonitored. Though laymen may believe that all Internet activity is recorded and traceable, sophisticated pornography dealers, buyers, traders, and viewers understand how to evade detection and justice. Attempting to monitor the Internet is especially challenging because the number of computers or hard drives used to traffic illegal depictions or file share is unknown (DOJ, 2010). Similarly, the number and location of individuals facilitating online distribution are unknown because no surveillance mechanism exists that is capable of determining the quantity.

Internet monitoring efforts are proactive yet insufficient to eliminate transmission of child pornography. NDIC reports that a lack of Internet service provider (ISP) regulations requiring retention of IP addresses and subscriber information significantly facilitates the presence of unprotected material online (*Blumenthal v. Drudge*, 1998; DOJ, 2010). Authorities record traceable IP addresses suspected of file-sharing illegal material, but the Wiretap Statute prevents law enforcement from intercepting international electronic communications without warrants, even if authorities suspect that communications contain unprotected speech. In the past decade, more than 20 million distinct IP addresses trafficking child pornography have been identified. Though most of these IP addresses traffic the same images, hundreds of thousands of images are unique. Authorities catalog repeat images to better understand the volume of this material and trafficking patterns. Cataloging involves multiple agencies. For example, child pornography is cataloged by Operation Fairplay in Wyoming, the Palm Beach County State's Attorney Office in Florida, and Operation RoundUp in Massachusetts. Monitoring is also challenged each minute of the day because names of child pornography files constantly change. Countless images have yet to be discovered. Undetected and uncataloged images are traded by e-mail, in chat rooms, or through direct download (*Doe v. America Online*, 2001).

Nonproduction offenders in the United States have rarely been sentenced to federal prison for commercial child pornography crimes, yet the United Nations Children's Fund (UNICEF) estimates that four million commercial websites offer child pornography generating between $3 billion and $20 billion each year (DOJ, 2010; [United States Sentencing Commission] USSC, 2012). Commercial producers generally work in networks using technological protection that provides total anonymity. Most federal convictions have involved production and free file sharing (USSC, 2012). It is extremely difficult to monitor and prevent child pornography production because it is typically produced offline in safe environments, for example, homes, doctors' offices, or day cares (DOJ, 2010). For example, in a recent bust of an international child pornography ring involving abuse of 400 children by 348 adults, those arrested included 6 law enforcement personnel, 9 doctors and nurses, 9 pastors and priests, 3 foster parents, and 40 schoolteachers (Silva, 2013). However, UNICEF approximates that there are almost 1 million online predators attempting to contact children to produce sexual images and engage in hands-on offenses. Overall, predators attempting to initiate contact through the Internet are thought to work alone and be far less sophisticated than commercial pornography dealers and consumers. Law enforcement monitor social media to prevent, intercept, and interrupt online production offenses. Stings that monitor online solicitors are relatively easy and successful, though they may be time-consuming and, therefore, can be costly.

Sting Operations

In 2010, 90% of nonsolicitation online pornography cases were discovered by law enforcement using three investigation methods: (1) tracing offenders' identities following online purchases of child pornography, (2) receiving pornography by e-mail or instant message during undercover online "chats" with offenders, or (3) retrieving files directly from offenders' computers using P2P file-sharing programs (USSC, 2012).

To conduct sting operations, the government may obtain pornography distributors' mailing lists (*U.S. v. LaChapelle*, 1992). Mailing lists may contain hundreds, thousands, or millions of names of active customers. Customers who are interested in child pornography may represent a large percentage of some pornography distributors' revenue base. These customers will be targeted for sting operations. In one case, agents developed a sting list and mailed a flyer pretending to advertise "extremely hard to obtain erotica" provided by a Belgium company to 5,700 customers. One-third of the targeted clients requested more information. Of those who responded, 300 customers inquired about child pornography. Faux catalogs were distributed to these customers. Orders for child pornography were placed by 160 individuals. Defenses of entrapment were raised, but the court found that agents had not entrapped offenders.

The great majority of NDIC personnel report that undercover stings in which government personnel pose as children are the most successful method for investigating and prosecuting online solicitors seeking child pornography, obscenity, and live videoconferencing with minors (DOJ, 2010). All NDIC experts reported that investigations normally involve only one suspect. About one-quarter of experts reported that investigations occasionally or rarely involve two suspects. Frequently, local police or members of federal agencies, for example, the Internet Crimes against Children Task Force Program (ICAC), initiate online stings in chat rooms or social media sites (*Doe v. MySpace*, 2008; DOJ, 2010). Enticement investigations may also commence pursuant to tips made by concerned parents or anonymous citizens placed with local or federal agencies, a tip line for Child Protective Services (CPS), or CyberTipline managed by the National Center for Missing and Exploited Children (NCMEC); (DOJ, 2010). From the time that a tip is placed and the sting concludes with prosecution and conviction, agencies may have spent between one and six months gathering information.

First, offenders make contact with agents in chat rooms designed for teens. Agents pretend to be minors so that predators will attempt to groom them. Once contact has been made or conversations about sex have been initiated, predators will persuade agents to relocate conversations to instant message or private chat rooms. Then, predators will solicit agents for personal information and photographs. A predator may attempt to use information to probe an undercover officer's vulnerabilities and to build trust. At this point, predators may disengage if they believe that children are inappropriate targets (e.g., are undercover police). However, if a predator believes that the intended victim is vulnerable, then a predator may attempt to blackmail or coerce a child for pornography or obscenity or an offender may request for the child to voluntarily engage in live sexual conversation or image sharing (Seto, 2013). If a victim seems vulnerable immediately, then predators may attempt a "quick hookup" (DOJ, 2010). Predators may attempt to meet in person to photograph victims. Immediate attempts to coerce or obtain sexual images result in significantly shorter investigations. Novice predators usually move more quickly, whereas experts spend greater time grooming and minimizing their perceived risk of dealing with law enforcement. Predators may delay one week to several months before asking to meet a child in person to produce pornography. Law enforcement usually attempt to expeditiously investigate, yet they are cautious to avoid accusations of entrapment. Experienced predators may need time to attempt to groom victims by building friendships and confidence, delivering gifts, and feigning sympathy for victims' emotional problems; only then will some request to video chat using webcams, cell phones, or smartphones. Sometimes predators can locate victims or agents using cell phone GPS capabilities. Sophisticated predators may ask to video chat following the initial exchange of information about age, sex, and location in an attempt to detect the sting. Many predators provide agents with sexually explicit photos sooner in the sting and ask for a *quid pro quo* later. Irrespective of whether they provide pornography or request it, their intent to communicate with a minor for immoral purposes is illegal (Rev. Code Wash. § 9.68A.090, 2013).

Law enforcement agents use P2P to collect evidence. They pose as members of online communities and access pornography directly from other members' computers using file-sharing programs. P2P programs and file sharing are discussed in greater detail in Chapter 10.

Police Investigation: Obscenity

Police may investigate publicly accessible pornography online (e.g., tease reels and Youporn.com), and they may investigate sites requiring membership. In alleged obscenity cases, agents often use reverse stings. They will frequently pose as customers by establishing accounts and ordering films. Films may arrive through the mail, become visible on a website, or be available for download. Police investigate obscenity violations by watching films and independently determining whether they believe that depictions are obscene. They refer suspected obscenity cases for prosecution to the state's attorney's office. Some jurisdictions do not specifically criminalize certain kinds of depictions, thus police discretion may be influential. The *Miller* test, discussed in Chapter 3, allows police and prosecutors to preemptively evaluate obscenity. Government agents may apply their personal standards, ad hoc interpret *stare decisis*, or infer community standards before putting alleged obscenity before a jury. If charges are brought but defendants settle with the state, then a judge and jury never have the opportunity to decide. Essentially, a defendant's speech acts may be prosecuted according to police officers' and prosecutors' opinions of a work.

Pornography producers and distributors work from personal home computers because homes have greater privacy rights. When police investigate inside homes, they are restricted by search and seizure rules pertaining to homes unless the area to be searched is used as a public place or inhabitants have a lower expectation for privacy in that particular area (*State v. Johnson*, 1992). When police investigate and search businesses, they have greater latitude in seizing property than when they search homes. In one case, an anonymous tip received by Florida police alleged that a defendant produced obscenity in his home and sold videos to customers in other states using federal mail. After ordering and watching certain videos, police obtained a search warrant. The warrant was issued to search the defendant's home for those videotapes. Unlike a search of a business, which can include all possessions possibly related to the crime, a search of a home must be restricted to those items listed in the warrant. Officers brought VCRs and televisions to the defendant's home and watched videos. They decided whether videos listed in the warrant were obscene and seized those materials consistent with the warrant. However, officers also seized every videotape that they deemed to be obscene, not solely those listed in the warrant. They seized office equipment, including blank cassettes, a bookstand, blank paper, pamphlets, files, photos, advertisements, clear video cases, shipping envelopes, a typewriter, a clock, a file cabinet, notebooks and address books, card files, clothing, video cameras and accessories, a sound boom, lights and tripods, cameras, chairs, power cords, a mirror, a CD player, a stereo, a TV/VCR stand, and the defendant's mail. The search was ruled to be outside the scope of the warrant. Because police violated the defendant's constitutional rights, a motion to suppress evidence was granted, and illegally obtained evidence was ruled inadmissible against the defendant.

Police Investigation: Child Pornography

Most victims of child pornography are unidentified or unidentifiable because images provide no clues (DOJ, 2010). Of countless images available online, fewer than 2,000 victims' identities are known to the DOJ. To identify children in pornography, police will often analyze photos for objects that can be traced to locations, manufacturers, or owners. A list of possible locations will be compiled, and potential exact locations will be narrowed. The Federal Bureau of Investigation (FBI) and NCMEC began analyzing victims' identities in 2006 when a certain female victim was featured in several widely circulated images. The number of images involving the victim and the severity of the crimes against the victim increased steadily over a four-year period beginning in 2005. One of the images depicted a commemorative plate decoration. The decorative plate bore the victim's name and birthdate. Pursuant to a court order, the Social Security Administration and Internal Revenue Service supplied all possible identity matches. Twenty-nine local government offices received censored images of the victim along with identification requests. In 2009, the victim's identity was verified. Authorities interviewed the victim, and she disclosed the abuse and abuser's identity. Police seized items from the victim's home that were visible in the photos. The offender lived in a different jurisdiction; however, local authorities in that jurisdiction conducted surveillance and issued a warrant for his arrest. A search of his property yielded jewelry that was visible in the photo. The offender confessed to the crime.

U.S. Immigration and Customs Enforcement's (ICE's) Operation Predator relies on forensic analyses shared between federal agencies and state agencies to identify obscenity and pornography victims and predators (ICE, n.d.; 2013). Operation Predator grew from Operation Sunflower. The first case was the Sunflower Case, a famous case that prevented an 11-year-old victim of child pornography from being raped by a 16-year-old boy. In the Sunflower Case, U.S. ICE's Victim Identification Program worked with Danish law enforcement after they discovered that the offender posted on a pedophile chat board materials, plans, and requests for advice about how to rape the victim. One image of abuse posted in the chat room was taken in a moving vehicle. A yellow road sign was discovered by ICE to contain a sunflower graphic used by the state of Kansas (Figure 9.1). By patrolling highways in Kansas for two weeks and comparing forensic analyses of the photos, special agents and local law enforcement located the target residence before the child was raped.

Mandatory Reporting and Protective Responses

The Providing Resources, Officers, and Technology to Eradicate Cyber Threats to Our Children Act of 2008 (PROTECT Our Children Act) requires ISPs to report online storage of child pornography. Reports may be made through CyberTipline. Though U.S. ISPs are not required to block child pornography, many block it. Child pornography is blocked by ISPs throughout the world.

Figure 9.1 Kansas highway markers.

In the United Kingdom, one ISP reported blocking 20,000 daily attempts to access child pornography in 2004 (USSC, 2012).

NCMCE maintains the CyberTipline, an online system that can be used to place anonymous tips (DOJ, 2010). ISPs and concerned citizens can report the presence of child pornography online. Most investigations into allegations of online pornography begin with tips to NCMCE's CyberTipline. Authorities may investigate P2P file sharing or conduct undercover or reverse stings (DOJ, 2010). Many allegations of sexual abuse are reported to CPS tip lines or directly to authorities.

Some professionals are required to report when they suspect that a child has been a victim of pornography production or has been exposed to pornography. Depending on jurisdictional requirements and professional policies, teachers, caretakers, healthcare providers, counselors, and others who work with children may be required to report suspicions of abuse directly to authorities, to superiors, or through tip lines. State responses to reports can range from investigation to removal and prosecution (English, Wingard, Marshall, Orme, & Orme, 2000). For example, a report that a postpubescent teen viewed soft-core pornography on a parent's computer could initiate contact with a family. However, a report that a parent produced child pornography may result in immediate removal.

Professionals who work with children and who are required to report play a significant role in the type of response created because their observations qualify the allegations. Many states utilize a three-tier response to allegations of abuse. Tips are referred to specific state services according to the amount of evidence presented, whether allegations can be substantiated, and the seriousness of the allegations. A third-tier response includes making contact with families and offering services. This means that abuse has not been substantiated. Contact between officials and a possible victim could lead to an investigation if abuse is disclosed or signs of abuse are observed. However, without additional suspicious details, an investigation will not be initiated. A second-tier response would result within a few days if evidence indicates that a child may be in danger of abuse. Police or CPS investigations may involve speaking with the tipster, if the person's identity is known. Professionals who are required to report suspicions of abuse would likely disclose as much detail as possible. Investigators may speak to members of the community, relatives, and the suspected child victim, who may not be as forthcoming with details. Investigators may focus on a person of interest by researching criminal records or online presence in social media. A state agent may ask to enter a home and observe a person of interest interacting with a suspected child victim. Depending on investigation findings, police could obtain search warrants. Searches may substantiate abuse; for example, a cache of pornography or obscenity could be discovered. A first-tier response to allegations would likely occur within one day if allegations of abuse are founded. Reports of contact or production offenses, for example, could result in immediate police investigation, searches, arrest, and removal of the child or a suspect from the home.

False Accusations

Unfortunately, innocent people are arrested, prosecuted, convicted, and incarcerated. People have been falsely accused or wrongly prosecuted by the state under a variety of circumstances. Some child pornography and obscenity may be self-downloading, a virus may download pornography, people may accidentally or incidentally deal in obscenity or child pornography, individuals may be framed by hackers or by others who have access to their computers, and child witnesses may be subject to error or memory manipulation. When spouses or employers discover illegal material and report it to authorities, the accused rarely escape prosecution by claiming that they had no knowledge of the pornography. This excuse rarely exonerates the accused because those who knowingly transmit child pornography commonly use it (*U.S. v. Caldwell*, 2009). It is known as the "Some Other Dude Did It" (SODDI) defense.

Innocent people are prosecuted and may spend thousands of dollars proving their innocence to the government. In one case, an employee of the state of Massachusetts was arrested for possession of child pornography (Robertson, 2009). He spent $250,000 on his legal defense to prove that a virus on his computer caused his computer to visit up to 40 child pornography websites every minute for 90 minutes. It was discovered that a hacker had remotely logged into his computer when the defendant was not home. It is estimated that at any moment 20 million computers are susceptible to this sort of takeover or can be transformed into data storage lockers for anonymous remote users. People who possess P2P file-sharing capabilities are more at risk for accidentally downloading illegal images in the course of downloading legal images. Defenses and claims of innocence may be harder to prove or in greater doubt when defendants voluntarily use P2P file sharing.

Viruses can cause child pornography or obscenity to pop up on computers at any moment. Ransomware is a virus that prevents users from using the Internet (Horejsi, 2013). A locked screen appears containing logos from law enforcement agencies (e.g., FBI). The screen contains images of sexually abused children, their supposed birthdates, and names. The virus claims that the user visited inappropriate sites and must pay to unlock the computer or pay a fine.

Illegal material can be placed on computers in person. In Pennsylvania, a woman placed child pornography on her estranged husband's home computer (Pennsylvania Woman Tries to Frame Hubby, 2013). She reported the presence of child pornography to police. The estranged wife alleged that her husband had committed hands-on offenses with children prior to photographing them. Police investigation determined that the husband became estranged from the home prior to the date that child pornography appeared on the computer. The estranged husband did not have access to the computer on the date when child pornography first appeared on the computer. The woman was charged with dozens of counts of lying to police and with felony possession of child pornography.

Witness credibility is at the heart of the U.S. criminal justice system (*Pennsylvania v. Walker*; see American Psychological Association [APA], 2010). In a situation where depictions of children could be considered to be obscenity because of the circumstances surrounding production, juries may be asked to rely on child witnesses' perceptions or memories of events. Children's memories may offer evidence of whether depictions ought to be interpreted to be obscenity (Belli & Loftus, 1994). For example, a mother reports that a family portrait photographer took numerous photos of her child's partially clothed groin while the child was alone in a photo studio. Neither the parent nor the photographers employed by the portrait studio know which of five photographers took the photos, but one photographer proved that he experienced a technical error with his camera that could have caused his camera to erroneously focus on the child's groin. The state continues to investigate allegations of obscenity and interviews the child. The child may remember one of the other four photographers as having taken her photo, but that memory may be false. The child's perception or memory may stem from a dream or fantasy or result from confusion. Though research has repeatedly demonstrated that eyewitness identification is faulty, investigators and jurors may be unaware that child witnesses may be less credible than adult witnesses and possess poorer face recognition than adults (Karpel, Hoyer, & Toglia, 2001; Leippe & Romanczyk, 1989). Depending on the level of authority and pressure involved and the children's age, maturity, stress, history of trauma, and racial bias, children's memories can be fabricated, embellished, or altered (APA, 2010). Contamination of eyewitness identification testimony is not uncommon, but it is especially prevalent among child witnesses. Children can be convinced that obscenity was produced at any stage of memory formulation, including (1) the acquisition stage, when events occur; (2) the retention stage, which occurs before any attempt to recall the memory; or (3) the retrieval stage (APA, 2010). Parents, police, therapists, judges, forensic experts, and jury members could persecute an innocent individual in an attempt to protect a child, who lacks recognition skills or has suffered from memory manipulation.

Conclusion

The criminal justice system relies on countless operations, strategies, agents, and procedures to investigate, prosecute, and convict pornography offenders. Though law does not comprehensively regulate the Internet, police presence online has produced results. In response, offenders have increased their evasiveness and the sophistication of their tactics. The law attempts to uniformly exact justice, yet many variables may affect the achievement of justice. For example, the quality and acuity of police and prosecutor participation, tip line report substantiation, witnesses' credibility, and other factors may impact procedures and the outcomes of cases.

References

American Psychological Association. (2010, August 23). Amicus briefs *Pennsylvania v. Walker*. Retrieved from http://www.apa.org/about/offices/ogc/amicus/walker.pdf

Belli, R. F., & Loftus, E. F. (1994). *Recovered memories of childhood abuse: A source monitoring perspective*. New York: Guilford Press.

Blumenthal v. Drudge, 992 F. Supp. 44, 51 (D.D.C. 1998).

Buzzell, T. (2007). The effects of organizational and community context on local prosecution of computer child pornography cases. *Criminal Justice Studies: A Critical Journal of Crime, Law and Society*, *20*(4), 391–405.

Department of Justice. (2010, August). The national strategy for child exploitation prevention and interdiction. Retrieved from http://www.justice.gov/psc/docs/natstrategyreport.pdf

Doe v. America Online, 783 So. 2d 1010, 1013-1017 (Fl. 2001).

Doe v. MySpace, 528 F.3d 413 (5th Cir. 2008).

English, D. J., Wingard, T., Marshall, D., Orme, M., & Orme, A. (2000). Alternative responses to Child Protective Services: Emerging issues and concerns. *Child Abuse and Neglect, 24*(3), 375–388.

Horejsi, J. (2013, November 21). Ransomware shocks its victims by displaying child pornography pictures. Avast. Retrieved from http://blog.avast.com/2013/11/21/ransomware-annoys-its-victims-by-displaying-child-pornography-pictures/

Karpel, M. E., Hoyer, W. J., & Toglia, M. P. (2001). Accuracy and qualities of real and suggested memories: Nonspecific age differences. *Journal of Gerontology: Psychological Sciences, 56B*, 103–110.

Leippe, M. R., & Romanczyk, A. (1989). Reactions to child (versus adult) eyewitnesses: The influence of jurors' preconceptions and witness behavior. *Law and Human Behavior, 13*(2), 103–132.

Miller v. California, 413 U.S. 15 (1973).

Pennsylvania woman tries to frame hubby with child porn, police say. (2013, December 23). *Fox News*. Retrieved from http://www.foxnews.com/us/2013/12/23/pennsylvania-woman-tried-to-frame-hubby-with-child-porn/

Rev. Code Wash. (ARCW) § 9.68A.090 (2013).

Robertson, J. (2009, November 9). Internet virus frames users for child porn. *Huffington Post*. Retrieved from http://www.huffingtonpost.com/2009/11/09/internet-virus-frames-use_n_350426.html

Seto, M. C. (2013). Solicitation (pp. 71–115). Washington, D.C.: American Psychological Association.

Silva, D. (2013, November 14). Nearly 400 children rescued and 348 adults arrested in Canadian child pornography bust. *NBC News*. Retrieved from http://worldnews.nbcnews.com/_news/2013/11/14/21462256-nearly-400-children-rescued-and-348-adults-arrested-in-canadian-child-pornography-bust?lite =

State v. Johnson, 605 So. 2d 545 (Fla. 1992)

United States Sentencing Commission. (2012). Report to the Congress: Federal child pornography offenses: Technology and investigation by law enforcement in child pornography cases. Retrieved from http://www.ussc.gov/news/congressional-testimony-and-reports/sex-offense-topics/report-congress-federal-child-pornography-offenses

U.S. Immigration and Customs Enforcement (ICE). (n.d.). Child Exploitation/Operation Predator. Retrieved January 17, 2014, from http://www.ice.gov/predator/

U.S. Immigration and Customs Enforcement (ICE). (2013, January 3). 123 sexually exploited children identified by HSI during "Operation Sunflower." Retrieved from http://www.ice.gov/news/releases/1301/130103washingtondc.htm

U.S. v. Caldwell, 586 F.3d 338 (2009).

U.S. v. LaChapelle, 969 F.2d 632 (1992).

Illegal Pornography, Cyberspace, and Technology

10

Overview

Interviews were conducted with 168 child exploitation experts within 26 local, state, and federal task forces, law enforcement, and private victim-oriented organizations (United States Sentencing Commission [USSC], 2012). Among respondents, 96% reported an increased threat over the past 10 years caused by child pornography; approximately half of those attributed the increase to growing technological sophistication. Two-thirds of responding child exploitation experts reported that the Internet has increased the quantity of and ease of access to child pornography. Half of respondents also credited larger collections of exploitative material to increased data storage capability and Internet speed. However, renewed attention is being paid to traditional distribution methods that cannot be detected by technology.

The Dark Net

Much of the Internet is a vast, uncharted area, like outer space. Only a small percentage of websites can be found by using search engines. The majority of accessible content online requires visitors to be "in the know" to locate sites. People are able to transmit illegal pornography without being detected by police, the public, or search engine crawlers. In 2002, Microsoft® programmers coined the term "Dark Net" (USSC, 2012). This term is synonymous with "Deep Web." These terms describe a process whereby users share content anonymously using undetectable Internet protocol (IP) addresses and The Onion Router (TOR) (Figure 10.1). Several companies legally offer this technology to the public, though companies know that users may transmit illegal pornography. Freenet and TOR are two corporations that claim to prioritize anonymity and freedom of speech by offering anonymity to users. A few trusted users volunteer to route data for these companies. TOR anonymizes data by bouncing transmissions around between anonymous relays. This effectively eliminates records of how data were transmitted between end points. It creates an underground, untraceable Internet.

Volunteers route data through their IP addresses without recording content or IP routers' addresses. It would be difficult, if not impossible, for law

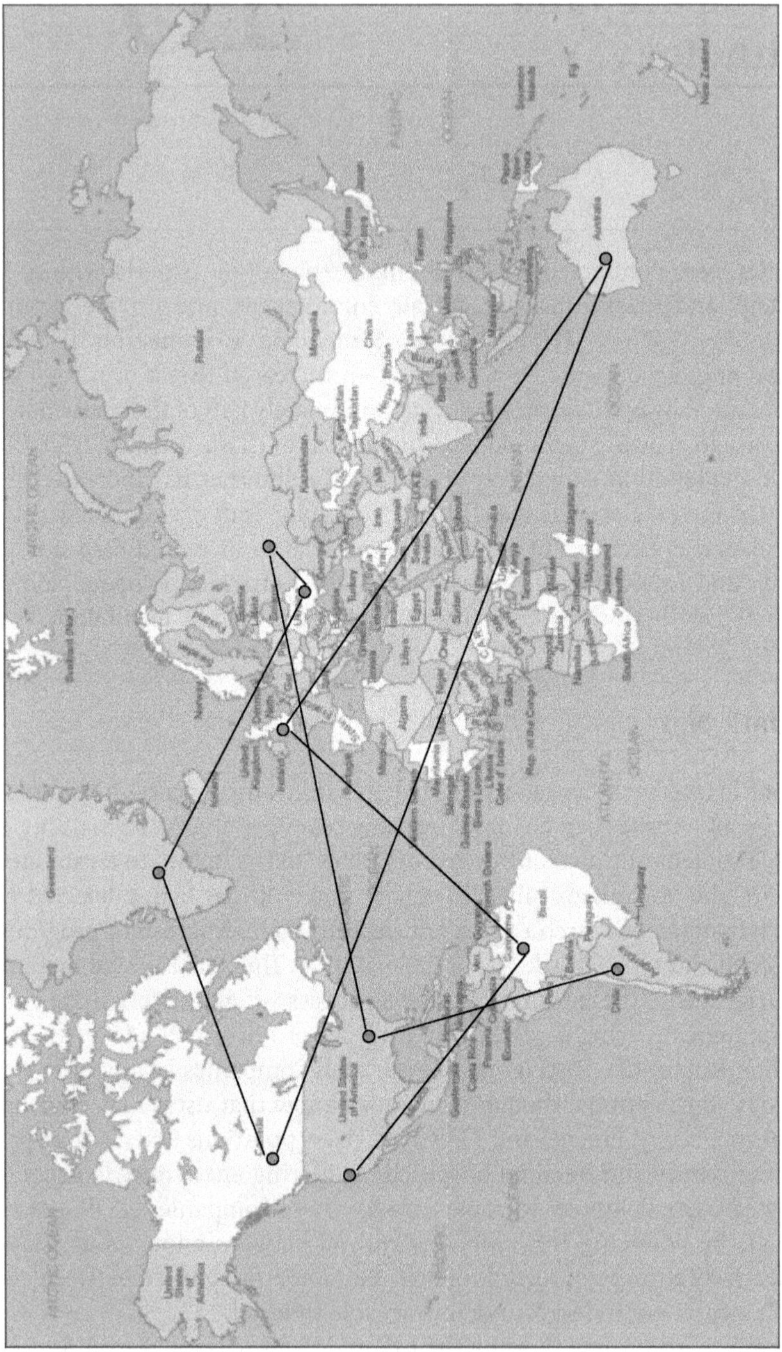

Figure 10.1 The Onion Router (TOR).

enforcement to pose as a volunteer IP router to conduct a sting operation on TOR (USSC, 2012). This parallel web cannot be accessed by the outside world and requires all users to access it through certain companies' browsers. Users quickly suss out routers that record information or cannot be trusted. However, law enforcement conduct stings and gathers intelligence on the Dark Web by posing as users. The success of this strategy has been limited.

Technology

In research submitted to Congress in 2012, two-fifths of field experts reported that increased child pornography is attributable to greater options for anonymity, untraceable public wireless Internet connections, and encryption (USSC, 2012). A number of technological advancements facilitate transmission of unprotected depictions. Governmental interventions have failed to respond quickly enough to technological developments. For example, public libraries may restrict access to pornography at government facilities, but laptop users may download pornography using Wi-Fi at countless hotspots, such as airports, coffee shops, nearby private residences, hotels, and businesses. Proxy servers used by web administrators can cause websites to appear to be located abroad. Complications associated with international investigations dissuade local law enforcement from investigating. Offenders may use remailers to anonymize their e-mail messages. Remailers forward e-mails without recording a sender's identity. New, free e-mail accounts may be opened without limitation and disposed of after each use. Hushmail.com and other services offer encrypted e-mails. People dealing in obscenity and child pornography may use encrypted pay sites that accept Bitcoin or stolen credit cards. Bitcoin is an untraceable Internet currency that facilitates sale of contraband, like state secrets, assassination services, slaves, nuclear weapons, and commercial child pornography. Famously, a virtual marketplace, the Silk Road, was busted for massive online contraband sales in 2013 when the operator, Ross Ulbricht, was arrested by the FBI for facilitating the sales of drugs, weapons, illegal identification, hacking software, and other contraband (Grossman & Newton-Small, 2013).

Authorities are challenged by shifting trends in file-sharing techniques. Among National Drug Intelligence Center (NDIC) personnel participating in research about online child pornography, 29% said that offenders had increased their uses of chat rooms and peer-to-peer (P2P) file sharing on the Dark Net and tapered their use of e-mail and instant messaging services (Department of Justice [DOJ], 2010). Local law enforcement agencies reported that in 2006, only 20% of child pornography offenders used technology to obscure their activities. However, commercial activities have become more sophisticated in recent years and more difficult to detect because of P2P (USSC, 2012). Professional pornography dealers sometimes return to instant messaging, chats, and face-to-face meetings with other pornographers when investigations of high-tech techniques become prevalent. Because law enforcement consistently monitor chat rooms for unprofessional enticement operations, professional pornography dealers sometimes evade detection there (USSC, 2012).

P2P networks no longer require centralized servers, which means that no single company or person is responsible for or can disclose the content (USSC, 2012). P2P networks maintain no records of which files are shared or the types of digital content transmitted (e.g., software, films, photos, or text). Rather than logging into a network, users may download file-sharing program software (e.g., LimeWire). Before downloading any files, new users may opt in to share files already in that user's possession. P2P software independently creates an "incomplete" folder on a new user's computer to store files that are in the process of downloading. A second file, containing completed downloads, is also created. Completed file downloads are stored in a "shared" folder. "Shared" files are accessible to all other program users. Users may search other program users' folders using keyword searches. Because of rampant, unmonitored copyright infringement, like those that occurred using Napster, one of the most popular P2P programs, LimeWire, was closed in 2010 (*Arista Records LLC v. LimeWire LLC*, 2010). However, pirated editions of LimeWire still operate, and many other P2P programs continue to surge in popularity.

FrostWire, KaZaA, and eDonkey are pegged by federal agencies as programs through which people heavily traffic child pornography. LimeWire was used by a sizable percentage of federal offenders who transmitted child pornography. Federal agents identified more than 20 million unique IP addresses using LimeWire to transmit child pornography. Federal agents believe that isoHunt has become the most popular P2P program for distribution and receipt of child pornography. In 2011, more than half of worldwide Internet use, 57%, occurred through P2P traffic (USSC, 2012). Small numbers of users post most of the depictions available in communities. Other members are usually "leechers" who fail to actively post images, discussions, or technological information. The economy of P2P depends on sharing, not only using. To stimulate sharing, P2P networks may provide faster downloading to sharers. Some networks require sharing.

Some programs (e.g., Gigatribe) allow users to establish private networks, invite "friends," remove "friends," share files with certain "friends," and search "friends'" files (USSC, 2012). This kind of sharing is called friend-to-friend (F2F). Users may also chat with each other using encrypted technology. F2F requires users to specify which users may view certain types of files. F2F reduces accidental access to child pornography. Using F2F decreases defendants' ability to claim that they did not knowingly download or distribute pornography.

Numerous technological advancements aid law enforcement to detect and reduce child pornography. Spam blockers, content filters, IM chat channels, application signatures, and numerous other technological implementations have helped resist child pornography's infiltration into mainstream web use. MacForensicsLab Field Agent software allows U.S. Customs agents to swiftly flag child pornography present on computers entering the United States (Wethal, 2010). Use of this software by agents does not require technological skill. Hashing technologies were previously ineffective because changes to photos impeded signature identification, but the government now possesses technology that is far more effective at detecting duplicate images online. Microsoft® donated PhotoDNA to the National Center for Missing and Exploited Children (NCMEC). Microsoft PhotoDNA improves basic hashing detection technology. Distinct features of digital images may be calculated to match images online using PhotoDNA. PhotoDNA searches for digital image signatures that survive image alteration, compression, color change, textual changes, and resizing. Law enforcement may be able to better detect re-posted images, and they are able obscure images to help shield agents from viewing explicit details of abuse depicted in pornography. SurfRecon Inc. is a program placed on jump drives used by corrections and parole departments to rapidly crawl through sex offenders' hard drives. Probation terms and home verification checks are discussed further in Chapter 18.

Regulating the Internet

Harmful materials cannot always be controlled by the law, either because they do not meet legal standards or because they are available through international distributors. Internet filters may be overinclusive and thus bound to fail strict scrutiny. Strict scrutiny of constitutional impingements requires restrictions on speech to limit no more speech than is necessary to effectuate compelling goals (i.e., child protection). Internet regulations mostly aim to protect minors from exploitation and corruption. In some cases, courts have considered whether pornography websites depicting corruptive material should be enjoined. Courts consider whether graphic material is protected by passwords or adult verification technology. Answering these questions helps courts to determine whether a privacy right is concerned, whether material violates local standards, and whether material is within the scope of the First Amendment (Nunziato, 2007; *U.S. v. Extreme Associates, Inc.*, 2005). In other cases, courts have held that attempts to restrict the Internet impinge on constitutional rights.

The Child Online Protection Act (COPA) Commission analyzed specific methods and tools for limiting minors' access to harmful material (Cybertelcom Federal Internet Law and Policy, 2013). COPA legislation attempted to filter and segregate harmful materials, but COPA was stricken for overbreadth (*Ashcroft v. American Civil Liberties Union*, 2004). The commission analyzed numerous methods for regulating the Internet. It considered parental controls, blocking and filtering software or services, labeling systems or ratings, age verification systems, and .xxx domains. The COPA Commission also analyzed cost and impact, utility by law enforcement, privacy issues, accessibility to parents, and whether minors worldwide were accessing harmful materials. The commission found that family education and parental involvement superseded the effectiveness of law and technology. For example, special domains, like .xxx, may help steer minors from pornography, but .xxx may also become an attractive nuisance. Furthermore, .xxx domains have been alleged to engage in trust practices that gouge pornographers. These domains will likely face many hurdles before they can fully benefit society. Yet, the commission extolled kid-friendly domains (e.g., .kids). Chat rooms, Usenet, and videoconferencing applications and sites may be monitored in .kids sites.

The Prosecutorial Remedies and Other Tools to End the Exploitation of Children Today Act of 2003 (PROTECT Act) prohibits misleading domain names in Section 2252B. The government criminalizes intent to trick minors into viewing pornography. Pornography includes depictions of mere nudity that meet the *Miller* test. Masturbation, intercourse, contact with genitals, and sexual arousal are specifically listed in the PROTECT Act. Depictions of "arousal" include adults' genitals and children's genitals. The PROTECT Act does not limit definitions of material that is "harmful to minors" to depictions of actual humans. The definition includes simulations. The PROTECT Act threatens violators with fines and imprisonment.

Under the Children's Internet Protection Act (CIPA), the Federal Communication Commission (FCC) regulates technology in schools and libraries (FCC, n.d.). Regulation of technology in libraries also is discussed in Chapter 13. Libraries that receive certain federal funding must adequately provide safety to minors who communicate online at libraries. Libraries must secure e-mail, chat rooms, and computers to prevent hacking, and they must prevent disclosure and dissemination of minors' personal information. However, they may not track Internet usage by any patrons. Schools subject to CIPA must meet the same requirements as libraries, that is, preventing minors from engaging in harmful activities or accessing harmful material, like obscenity. Schools must monitor minors' online activities. The Protecting Children in the 21st Century Act requires schools to educate minors about online safety, cyberbullying, social networking, and chat rooms (USSC, 2012). To some extent, CIPA materializes goals relating to the COPA Commission's findings (FCC, n.d.). CIPA's constitutionality may be challenged if filtering software is too broad, and its effectiveness may be questioned if blocking software is underinclusive (Nunziato, 2007). To avoid some challenges, schools and libraries are not required to block adults and may unblock content for adults upon request (FCC, n.d.; *U.S. v. American Library Assn., Inc.*, 2003).

Some pornography storage sites may illegally store copyrighted content. This transforms their purpose from being pornography servers to web-storage operations. In some cases, virtual pornography storage lockers have been attacked civilly for storing, distributing, and downloading copyrighted material (*Disney Enterprises, Inc., et al. vs. Hotfile Corp., et al.*, 2013). This benefits antipornography efforts because storage sites may be shut down or severely limited through civil litigation. Civil litigation also threatens to expose users' identities. In one case, an attorney wrongfully acquired contact information for Internet users who illegally stored copyrighted pornography on servers (*Mick Haig Prods. E.K. v. Does*, 2012). The attorney sent letters to users shaming them and threatening to sue them unless they paid for copyrighted material. This tactic violated the law, but demonstrated that anonymity in online pornography storage may be illusory. To reduce civil and criminal violations, technology should be designed so that it is governable (Mopas, 2009). In keeping with the adage that an ounce of prevention is worth a pound of cure, regulations also ought to focus on how technology should be developed to avoid violations rather than concentrate on ending violations after they occur.

Physical "File Sharing"

Customs and Border Protection, Immigration and Customs Enforcement, and the U.S. Postal Inspection Service (USPIS) attempt to detect physical pornography sharing (USSC, 2012). Between 1997 and 2008, USPIS arrested 2,893 child pornographers. Of these arrestees, 931, approximately 32%, had committed hands-on offenses. International advertisers and customers may conduct business online, but depictions may be transmitted using the mail. Among NDIC experts, 60% reported decreased physical transportation of child pornography through the use of U.S. mail and an increase in technological transmission (USSC, 2012). Experts claim that virtual capabilities have exacerbated and promoted child pornography, anonymity, and demand for production offenses. Authorities are challenged by shifting trends in file-sharing techniques. At NDIC, 86% of experts typically encounter individuals, not organized groups. Individuals may meet in person to physically share flash drives, VHS cassettes, DVDs, cell phones, Polaroids, and other tools. Items shared in person are more difficult to detect and may contain depictions that are not widely circulated. More than half of NDIC experts reported that gaming sites attract solicitors, and games, programs, and consoles may be hacked for use in P2P file sharing or in-person file sharing (USSC, 2012). In-person meetings usually come to authorities' attention only if (1) plans are made online, (2) undercover agents are involved, or (3) confidential informants working for the government set up offenders in sting operations (Sotomayor, 2013).

Conclusion

Anonymous, encrypted, and undetectable technologies shield child pornographers. Investigators have been unable to deeply infiltrate online networks and technologies that fully anonymize file transmission. Certain technology aids the criminal justice system at various levels of intervention. Spam blockers, hashing, content filters, application signatures, and forensic programs aid in crime deterrence, investigation, evidence collection, and prosecution. Law enforcement agencies have responded to the resurgence of low-tech operations with increased stings and use of confidential informants.

References

Arista Records LLC v. LimeWire, LLC, No. 06-Civ-05936 (KMW) (S.D.N.Y. Oct. 27, 2010).

Ashcroft v. American Civil Liberties Union, 542 U.S. 656 (2004).

Cybertelecom Federal Internet Law and Policy: An Educational Project. (2013, December 12). Reports: Online safety. Retrieved from http://www.cybertelecom.org/cda/reports.htm#cop

Department of Justice. (2010, August). The national strategy for child exploitation prevention and interdiction. Retrieved from http://www.justice.gov/psc/docs/natstrategyreport.pdf

Disney Enterprises, Inc., et al. vs. Hotfile Corp., et. al., 2013 U.S. Dist. LEXIS 172339 (2013).

Federal Communication Commission (FCC). (n.d.). Children's Internet Protection Act (CIPA). Retrieved February 6, 2014, from http://www.fcc.gov/guides/childrens-internet-protection-act

Grossman, L., & Newton-Small, J. (2013, November 11). The secret web: Where drugs, porn and murder live online. *Time*. Retrieved from http://content.time.com/time/magazine/article/0,9171,2156271,00.html#ixzz2rSuNCY7V

Mick Haig Prods. E.K. v. Does, 687 F.3d 649 (2012).

Mopas, M. S. (2009). Imagining the Internet and making it governable: Canadian law and regulation. *Dissertation Abstracts International: Section A. Humanities and Social Sciences*, 1426.

Nunziato, D. C. (2007). Technology and pornography. *Brigham Young University Law Review, 2007*(6), 1535–1584.

Prosecutorial Remedies and Other Tools to End the Exploitation of Children Today Act of 2003 (PROTECT Act) §§2252B (2003).

Sotomayor, S. (2013). *My beloved world.* New York: Vintage.

United States Sentencing Commission. (2012). Report to the Congress: Federal child pornography offenses: Technology and investigation by law enforcement in child pornography cases. Retrieved from http://www.ussc.gov/Legislative_and_Public_Affairs/Congressional_Testimony_and_Reports/Sex_Offense_Topics/201212_Federal_Child_Pornography_Offenses/Chapter_03.pdf

U.S. v. American Library Assn., Inc., 539 U.S. 194 (2003).

U.S. v. Extreme Associates, Inc., 431 F.3d 150 (3d Cir. 2005).

Wethal, T. (2010). The problem with porn. *Law Enforcement Technology*, *37*(2), 18–25.

The Pornography Business and Crime

11

Overview

The pornography industry has been described as unsavory and unscrupulous. The government's perception that pornography relates to gangs, prostitution, and human trafficking is plainly evident in statutory language found in several states, for example, Illinois, Delaware, Iowa, and Mississippi (respectively, 740 Ill. Comp. Stat. § 147/10(2), 2013; 79 Del. C. § 107, 2013; Iowa Code §§ 710A.1, 725.1, 2013; Miss. Code Ann. § 97-44-3 (d) (iii), 2013). In addition to those crimes, pornography producers' and actors' involvement with drugs, violence, tax evasion, and fraud also has been raised in courts and in the media.

Drugs

Abundant anecdotal evidence attests to drug use in the pornography industry. Politically oriented research articles frequently claim that pornography actors and producers are involved in selling, taking, using, and pushing illegal drugs. Stories about forced drug use support claims that pornography involves prostitution and sex trafficking. However, some scholars and numerous participants in pornography have asserted that drug abuse is not an underbelly of the pornography industry (Murphy, 1987). They reject rumors that drugs are part of the pornography profession, which requires tremendous physical exertion, long hours, and healthy appearance. They distinguish between licensed pornography production and amateur or illegal production. Industry productions are said to be regulated, professional, and rigorous, but nonindustry productions could be vulnerable to illegal activity, including drug use.

Rob Black, a famous pornographer, claims that pundits, the government, and industry insiders will allege that industry people use drugs to discredit free speech freedom fighters (Abowitz, 2013). Black feels that detractors use this tactic to limit freedom of expression and equality in the marketplace of ideas. When pornographers depict controversial images or push the envelope, Black claims that people will accuse them of being on drugs. This logic could explain why objective and definitive knowledge is lacking about drug abuse in the pornography industry. Most research is anecdotal, philosophical, political, or based on studies about human trafficking and prostitution.

Individual pornography actors have discussed heavy drug and alcohol use or abuse. For example, an actor in pornographic films required hospitalization after watching pornography with actor Charlie Sheen throughout a night of heavy cocaine use (Boyle, 2011). Another pornography actor, who started stripping in college, went on to be nominated for several pornography awards (Jalsevac, 2013). She converted to Christianity and discussed how she abused drugs while working in the pornography industry. She discussed that she felt drained by the monotony of pornography, and she consumed cocaine and heroin to numb her pain and sustain her interest in her work. Allegedly, pornography industry employees at all levels ranging from drivers to vendors consume or deal drugs (McCarthy, 2008; Porn Stars Speak Out, 2013; Sex, Drugs and Beards, 2013). Of illegal drugs, marijuana is allegedly the most liberally consumed. It should be noted that personal possession of marijuana is noncriminal in California, where most pornography is produced. Nevertheless, Ecstasy, Xanax, Valium, and other hard drugs are also supposedly prevalent (Porn Stars Speak Out, 2013). Some actors illegally use Viagra to enhance performance (Huffstutter & Frammolino, 2001). Many male actors consume it at twice the recommend dosage, even though they do not suffer from erectile dysfunction. They use it to work 10- to 14-hour days. Directors are allegedly delighted by Viagra use because it significantly reduces delays in filming and production costs. Because of their increased performance skills, male actors can earn additional money, though they typically make less than female actors.

Young women compose the majority of pornography actors (Porn Stars Speak Out, 2013). Youth in the general population are most likely to consume drugs between the ages of 12 and 25 years. When people with tendencies for addiction, risk taking, poor coping skills, and impulsivity enter the pornography industry at young ages, they increase their risks for drug addiction. They also reduce their opportunities for acquiring marketable skills while they are young (North, 2012). Performers' limited abilities to earn income in the real world may relate to continued drug use or involvement in commercial pornography and sex work.

Production of child pornography may involve drug abuse. For example, children have been traded into child pornography to help parents and grandparents fuel drug habits (Charged, 2013). More troubling is the fact that major drug trafficking from Mexico and production of child pornography are related. Mexico, a major drug dealer to the United States and the world, is also the world's second-largest producer of child pornography (McLaughlin, 2012). In the past five years, Texas Hold 'Em Initiative has stopped hundreds of trucks smuggling humans from Mexico (Wilson, 2013). Many of these people become involved in prostitution and pornography. Drivers also smuggle drugs. Drugs are the largest black market worldwide, and human traffic is the second largest (Tanagho, 2007). Mexican smugglers have little incentive to stop because they only pay fines or serve brief prison sentences. The problem is not isolated to Mexican trafficking. A study found that drugs and alcohol were involved in 70% of cases of sex trafficking across five countries (MacKinnon, 2011).

In the United States, police sweeps of Internet chat rooms have uncovered a surge of runaway children involved in pornography, prostitution, drugs, and alcohol (Birkhead, 2011). The government acknowledges that gangs participate in drug markets, pornography, obscenity, human trafficking, and prostitution (740 Ill. Comp. Stat. § 147/10(2), 2013; Miss. Code Ann. § 97-44-3 (d) (iii), 2013). Among National Drug Intelligence Center (NDIC) interviewees, 14% reported correlations between gangs and child sex abuse (Department of Justice [DOJ], 2010). Some independent criminals and criminal enterprises have shifted from street-level drug dealing to child sex trafficking and pornography production for a few reasons: (1) drug dealing requires capital investments, (2) street-level drug dealing requires greater risks, and (3) child sex trafficking offers pimps greater insulation from police encounters. The government reports that in online enticement scenarios, only 34% of agents rarely uncover drugs (DOJ, 2010). Nineteen percent of agents report that alcohol is rarely encountered in online enticement stings. One-quarter of government respondents report that alcohol is commonly present in online enticement. Marijuana was encountered by 16% of government respondents. Solicitors may ply children with drugs, yet children may voluntarily become involved with drugs. Children involved with child pornography may become traumatized and self-medicate, they may sell drugs to build income without parents, or they may become intoxicated to continue performing in pornography. Similar experiences occur among adults who participate in pornography through prostitution (i.e., films with johns). In one study, 41% of respondents used drugs to tolerate sex work (Farley, 2006). Forcible involvement in pornography by pimps may cause trauma and symptoms of post-traumatic stress disorder to increase substantially, even after women end sex work. Commemoration of a victim's humiliation may contribute significantly to a victim's suffering long term.

Violence

Relationships between prostitution, pimping, violence, and pornography are well documented. However, within mainstream pornography production, violence seems to be uncommon. There are very few famous pornographers who claim to be victims of violence due to their involvement in pornography. Some mainstream pornographers experience violence in their private lives, but it is not likely at a rate greater than that experienced by members of the general population. Mainstream pornography never involves children, yet violence may be more prevalent in child pornography.

Linda Boreman, known as Linda Lovelace, allegedly pierced the veil of the hard-core pornography industry by accusing her manager and husband, Chuck Traynor, of severe abuse. She rose to fame after her film *Deep Throat* crossed from hard-core pornography into mainstream media. That film's title likely inspired the pseudonym given to a secret tipster who provided to the press information about the Watergate break-in, which demonstrates that the film was known within mainstream media. After the success of *Deep Throat*, but prior to her allegations of abuse, Boreman traveled throughout the United States in a self-promotional tour with another man, but she failed to maintain the public's interest. She retired from pornography years after her peak in the industry and then became a national spokesperson against pornography. Her main platform was domestic violence and forced performance. Boreman claimed that prior to *Deep Throat*, her husband sadistically beat her and forced her to perform at gunpoint in the bestiality film *Dog Fucker*. She reportedly experienced trauma, shame, and remorse about her involvement. Many people involved in filming her scenes and industry insiders doubt her rendition of the truth. During that time, Boreman alleges that she was abused and was addicted to drugs. Drug addiction could be a factor in her memory of abuse. Jenna Jameson, a well-known pornographic actor, has called Boreman a liar (Jenna Jameson, 2013; Page, 2013). Jameson, who always worked as a contract girl, claims that work in pornography leads to wealth. However, Boreman performed small gonzo scenes before becoming famous, and she alleges that abuse occurred then. Distinctions between the treatment of contract girls and the treatment of gonzo actors or independent contractors was discussed further in Chapter 7.

John Holmes experienced fame in the pornography industry, which is unusual for male actors. Then, he devolved into a life of drug addiction, violent crime, and disease. After rising to fame, Holmes lived at a flophouse and orchestrated a home invasion. The robbery victim later killed four robbers in revenge. Those murders are known as "the Wonderland murders." Holmes, who was present during the murders, was charged for all four deaths, but he was acquitted. Interestingly, Holmes's trial was the first to allegedly admit into evidence a video made by police depicting a crime scene.

Joe Francis, creator of the *Girls Gone Wild* film franchise, has been accused of violence by several women. In 2009, at a nightclub he grabbed pornography actor Jayde Nicole by her hair and threw her to the ground (Jenner/Francis, 2009). A video of the scene shows that Francis was walking by Nicole in a crowd when she intentionally pushes the back of his head. He turned around and dragged her by the hair to the ground in retaliation. In another incident in 2011, Francis deprived three women of liberty to leave his house following a night of partying (Fernandez, 2013). During the incident of false imprisonment, he smashed one woman's head on the floor. He was convicted of aggravated assault and three counts of false imprisonment. He was sentenced to three years of probation, counseling, and anger management.

Child pornography often involves violence. The government reports that in online enticement scenarios, only 34% of agents rarely uncover violence or guns (DOJ, 2010). More than two-thirds of agents sometimes or commonly encounter violence or guns. Pimping, prostitution, and gangs may involve children in violent crimes. Legislatures believe that gangs participating in criminal markets for arson for hire, stolen credit cards, robbery, burglary, armed robbery, theft, and stolen property also are involved in human trafficking, prostitution, obscenity, or pornography (740 Ill. Comp. Stat. § 147/10(2), 2013; Miss. Code Ann. § 97-44-3 (d) (iii), 2013).

Tax Evasion

Major companies have been alleged to evade taxes while transmitting pornography. The owner of YouPorn.com and PornHub.com, the world's largest pornography sites and some of the most trafficked sites on the Internet, was extradited from Belgium to Germany in 2012 for tax evasion (Kerr, 2012). The People's Republic of China has accused Apple® of distributing pornography illegally, circumventing customs duties, and evading taxes with Apple's online store (Boehler, 2013). The Internet Entertainment Group (IEG) became wealthy by exposing and exploiting celebrities (Waxman, 2000). The Internal Revenue Service (IRS) and Federal Bureau of Investigation (FBI) began examining whether profits were obtained illegally after it was rumored that the founder, a media mogul, charged viewers double or triple for a single service. The mogul, Seth Warshavsky, fled to Thailand, and IEG crumbled afterward. *Girls Gone Wild* founder, Joe Francis, was charged with felony tax evasion, but pleaded to two misdemeanor charges for filing false tax returns (Holmes, 2009). He was ordered to pay the IRS approximately $250,000 in restitution for withholding $500,000 in interest income.

Pornography stars are alleged to have lifestyles that open the door to tax problems. For example, Sandra Bullock's ex-husband, Jesse James, was once married to Janine Lindemulder (Caron, 2009). James reportedly informed the IRS that Lindemulder withheld money from the IRS that she was granted in their divorce settlement; the money was supposed to be used to settle a tax debt. Lindemulder owed $200,000 to the IRS, but she spent her income and the divorce settlement lavishly. Lindemulder claims that James reported her to the IRS to gain leverage in a custody battle for a child who was yet unborn when James left Lindemulder and married Bullock. Lindemulder was sentenced to prison. This behavior is alleged frequently in family court, thus it also occurs in family disputes involving pornography actors. Pamela Anderson, a famous pornography film star and Playboy Playmate, became entangled with the IRS, though charges were never filed (Dillon, 2012). For several years, Anderson owed the IRS unpaid taxes. She has claimed that she has poor financial management skills. Lack of management skills could relate to foregone opportunity costs of developing business acumen while in the pornography industry. This problem may affect other actors in pornography.

Fraud

Pornography companies have committed fraud against consumers and shareholders. Tens of thousands of consumers complained to the government about Crescent Publishing, which operates PlayGirl.com and numerous other pornography websites (Enos, 2000). Crescent Publishing took credit card information from consumers under the pretense that the information would be used for age verification. Consumers were charged almost $200 million for an online peep show that the company claimed could be seen for free. Other consumers who had never visited pornography sites were charged. Because of various obstacles created by the company, many customers were unable to cancel reoccurring charges. Once the company was prohibited by Visa from doing business in the United States, it moved to Guatemala to make governmental prosecution more difficult. In another scam, a web advertiser took money from major corporations, but intentionally failed to deliver the promised product (Steel, 2011). The advertising company bundled pop-up ads and embedded them into pornography websites. When users viewed pornography, the links opened, but viewers could not see the ads. The ads were intentionally hidden from viewers. To advertisers it seemed as if the public had been clicking on or viewing ads, but they had not. The FBI began to investigate after Google blocked the scam.

Online currency companies, like Bitcoin, have been used by pornographers to transmit child pornography (Krebs, 2007). One company, E-Gold, was prosecuted for credit fraud; the federal government alleged it intentionally allowed users to convert cash into the value of precious metals to pay for child pornography. In addition to E-Gold's other suspicious activity, the government pointed to the fact that E-Gold failed to require users to acknowledge a user agreement stating that they would not use E-Gold for criminal activity.

In an alleged attempted fraud against shareholders, Playboy asked its corporate controller to separate discretionary bonuses that had not been approved by the board of directors (Playboy Must Pay $6 million, 2014). When the corporate controller was fired, she alleged that her termination violated whistle-blower laws (e.g., Sarbanes-Oxley Act). A jury agreed and awarded her $6 million.

Individual actors have attempted to defraud the government while performing in films. Nadya Suleman, known as "Octomom," first used *in vitro* fertilization to conceive octuplets, and then she subsisted with her 14 children using government assistance (Romero, 2014). She applied for government healthcare while working in the adult film industry. After it was discovered that she did not legally qualify for those benefits because of her income, she was prosecuted.

Conclusion

The pornography industry is associated with crime. Labeling the entire industry may be unjust because a mere fraction of industry members are convicted of crimes, like battery, fraud, or tax evasion. However, relationships between organized crime and pornography cause the government to group the pornography industry with serious drug and trafficking crimes. In that sense, labeling may benefit victims of abuse. Performers who feel pressured to perform may be most vulnerable to abuse and addiction.

References

740 Ill. Comp. Stat. § 147/10(2) (2013).

79 Del. C. § 107 (2013).

Abowitz, R. (2013, April 21). Rob Black, porn's dirty whistlebower, spills trade secrets. *The Daily Beast*. Retrieved from http://www.thedailybeast.com/articles/2013/04/21/rob-black-porn-s-dirty-whistlebower-spills-trade-secrets.html

Birkhead, T. R. (2011). The "youngest profession": Consent, autonomy, and prostituted children. *Washington University Law Review, 88*(5), 1055–1155.

Boehler, P. (2013, May 10). Apple accused of tax evasion and spreading pornography by mainland legal group. *South China Morning Post*. Retrieved from http://www.scmp.com/news/china/article/1234616/apple-accused-tax-evasion-and-spreading-pornography-mainland-legal-group

Boyle, S. (2011, January 29). Charlie Sheen's 36-hour drink and drugs bender with adult film star. *Daily Record*. Retrieved from http://www.dailyrecord.co.uk/entertainment/celebrity/charlie-sheens-36-hour-drink-and-drugs-1093458

Caron, P. (2009, January 1). Porn star sentenced on tax evasion charges. Law Professor Blogs Network. Retrieved from http://taxprof.typepad.com/taxprof_blog/2009/01/porn-star-sentenced.html

Charged: Tennessee couple sells their 6 year-old daughter and three others to pornographers. (2013, October 20). FreakOut Nation. Retrieved from http://freakoutnation.com/2013/10/20/charged-tennessee-couple-sells-their-6-year-old-daughter-and-three-others-to-pornographers/

Department of Justice. (2010, August). The national strategy for child exploitation prevention and interdiction. Retrieved from http://www.justice.gov/psc/docs/natstrategyreport.pdf

Dillon, N. (2012, December 10). Pamela Anderson owes over $370,000 in taxes: "Baywatch" babe has long history of money woes. *NY Daily News*. Retrieved from http://www.nydailynews.com/entertainment/gossip/pam-anderson-sizable-bills-article-1.1216986

Enos, L. (2000, August 24). U.S. cracks down on net porn fraud. *Ecommerce Times*. Retrieved from http://www.ecommercetimes.com/story/4110.html

Farley, M. (2006). Prostitution, trafficking, and cultural amnesia: What we must not know in order to keep the business of sexual exploitation running smoothly. *Yale Journal of Law and Feminism*, *18*, 109–144.

Fernandez, M. E. (2013, August 27). "Girl Gone Wild" creator Joe Francis sentenced to 270 days in jail. *NBC News*. Retrieved from http://www.nbcnews.com/entertainment/girl-gone-wild-creator-joe-francis-sentenced-270-days-jail-8C11015303

Holmes, B. (2009, November 6). "Girls Gone Wild" founder Joe Francis sentenced in tax evasion and jail bribery case. *Los Angeles Times*. Retrieved from http://latimesblogs.latimes.com/lanow/2009/11/girls-gone-wild-founder-sentenced-for-filing-false-tax-returns-and-bribing-jail-workers.html

Huffstutter, P. J., & Frammolino, R. (2001, July 20). Viagra gives adult entertainment industry a boost/Drug eliminates filming delays, directors say. *SF Gate*. Retrieved from http://www.sfgate.com/news/article/Viagra-gives-adult-entertainment-industry-a-boost-2897185.php#page-

Iowa Code §§ 710A.1, 725.1 (2013).

Jalsevac, J. (2013, July 26). "I made it": Top porn star quits business after 7 years of drugs, suicide attempts, misery. Life Site News. Retrieved from http://www.lifesitenews.com/news/i-made-it-top-porn-star-quits-business-after-7-years-of-drugs-suicide-attem

Jenna Jameson interview cut short on GDNY (10-21-13). (2013, October 21). Youtube.com. Retrieved from http://www.youtube.com/watch?v=RF-kXwtzGlM

Jenner/Francis in knock down bar fight, tased. (2009, August 28). TMZ. Retrieved from http://www.tmz.com/2009/08/28/brody-jenner-in-known-down-bar-fight-tased-joe-francis/#ixzz2rW3igWMQ

Kerr, D. (2012, December 16). Porn bigwig extradited to Germany for tax evasion. CNet. Retrieved from http://news.cnet.com/8301-1023_3-57559480-93/porn-bigwig-extradited-to-germany-for-tax-evasion/

Krebs, B. (2007, May 1). U.S.: Online payment network abetted fraud, child pornography. *The Washington Post*. Retrieved from http://www.washingtonpost.com/wp-dyn/content/article/2007/05/01/AR2007050101291.html

MacKinnon, C. A. (2011). Trafficking, prostitution, and inequality. *Harvard Civil Rights-Civil Liberties Law Review*, *46*, 271–309.

McCarthy, M. (2008, November 10). Police bust "sex fest" in Campbell County. Local 8. Retrieved from http://www.local8now.com/home/headlines/34157974.html

McLaughlin, K. A. (2012). Securing the U.S. Mexico border: Case of child pornography. *Women Lawyers Journal*, *97*(1–2), 31–32.

Miss. Code Ann. § 97-44-3 (d) (iii) (2013).

Murphy, M. E. (1987). A question of procurement: Not prostitution. *Working women: The subterranean world of street prostitution* by Arlene Carmen and Howard Moody [Book review]. *Columbia Law Review*, *87*(5), 1075–1092.

North, A. (2012, July 4). Ex-porn star speaks out about sex addiction in porn. Buzz Feed. Retrieved from http://www.buzzfeed.com/annanorth/ex-porn-star-speaks-out-about-sex-addiction-in-porn

Page, M. (2013, October 22). Jenna Jameson "battling addiction to pills": Friends urging her to go to rehab. Pop Dust. Retrieved from http://popdust.com/2013/10/22/jenna-jameson-drug-addiction-oxycontin-rehab/

Playboy must pay $6 million to fired whistleblower. (2014, March 6). *NBC News*. Retrieved from http://www.nbcnews.com/news/us-news/playboy-must-pay-6-million-fired-whistleblower-n46466

Porn stars speak out: STDs, drugs and abuse. (2013). Pink Cross. Retrieved from https://www.thepinkcross.org/pinkcross-articles/june-2009/porn-stars-speak-out-stds-drugs-and-abuse

Romero, D. (2014, January 13). Octomom charged with welfare fraud over porn income. *LA Weekly*. Retrieved from http://www.laweekly.com/informer/2014/01/13/octomom-charged-with-welfare-fraud-over-porn-income

Sex, drugs and beards: An afternoon in a Pakistani porn cinema. (2013, December 23). Channel 24. Retrieved from http://www.channel24.co.za/Movies/News/Sex-drugs-and-beards-an-afternoon-in-a-Pakistani-porn-cinema-20131223

Steel, E. (2011, March 16). Porn sites trick advertisers. *The Wall Street Journal*. Retrieved from http://online.wsj.com/news/articles/SB20001424052748704893604576200383793893712

Tanagho, J. (2007). New Illinois legislation combats modern-day slavery: A comparative analysis of Illinois anti-trafficking law with its federal and state counterparts. *Loyola University Chicago Law Journal*, *38*(4), 895–962.

Waxman, S. (2000, July 7). Online porn exec is alleged target of investigation into fraud, tax evasion. *The Washington Post*. Retrieved from http://articles.latimes.com/2000/jul/07/business/fi-48893

Wilson, A. (2013). Using commercial driver licensing authority to combat human trafficking related crimes on America's highways. *University of Memphis Law Review*, *43*(4), 969–1012.

Family Law and Pornography

12

Overview

Family law and criminal law overlap when crimes are committed between relatives, or sometimes, crimes influence family relationships. Inside a home, children or intimate partners may discover child pornography, obscenity, or erotica. Discovery could provoke confrontation or instigate governmental intervention. Viewing pornography or convictions for pornography offenses could reflect poorly on personal character and parenting abilities.

Domestic Violence and Pornography

Behavioral science studies demonstrate how pornography may correlate with intimate partner violence. Sexual offenders are mostly married or committed men. Many use websites, like Craigslist, to increase their chances of going undetected (Farley, 2006). On Craigslist, Erotic Services is a subcategory of postings. At its height, 25,000 new ads listed erotic services each week on Craigslist. Intimate partners have responded violently after uncovering evidence of solicitation on Craigslist.

Pornography is not considered to be mainstream in the United States. For some people, viewing pornography is akin to adultery or promiscuity. Understandings of pornography, definitions of pornography, and the seriousness of viewing pornography vary between adults and marriages. Much like other crimes of passion at common law, the presence of pornography in the home has incited partners to violence. In one strange case, a wife was charged with domestic violence after finding in the trunk of her husband's car the satirical periodical *The Onion* (Petrie, 2012). She said that she considered *The Onion* to be pornography. It is possible that she may have been confused about *The Onion*'s content; she may have misperceived a relationship between *The Onion* and The Onion Router (TOR) and pornography, or she may have felt that *The Onion* is salacious. She quarreled with her husband and eventually threw an object, which led to the charges.

TOR is a web browser and router system that allows users to anonymize their activity by randomly scattering data through various Internet protocol (IP) addresses that fail to record activity. Illegal pornography can be shared without detection on TOR (Lawrence, 2014). TOR was explained further in Chapter 10. TOR employees advocate for privacy and believe that neither the government nor corporations ought to be able to track all Internet use in spite of users' desires to remain anonymous. TOR is headquartered in the YWCA in Cambridge, Massachusetts. One of its pitch points is that victims of domestic violence, stalking, and cyberstalking who desire anonymity may use TOR to evade detection. Several employees at TOR, which employs only a couple dozen people, have been victims of stalking. Relationships between pornography and stalking were also discussed in Chapter 6. Next door to TOR in Cambridge is Transition House. Transition House offers assistance to domestic violence survivors. Together, these two organizations partner to teach women living at the shelter how to safely use the Internet, anonymize their online activity, and avoid dangerous people.

In the United Kingdom, Keir Starmer, director of public prosecutions, stated that he fears that rising rates of intimate partner violence among teens could relate to teens' increased exposure to pornography (Hope, 2012). More than ever before, abused women have reported that their intimate partners watch pornography. Some battered women have claimed that their partners become dissatisfied with marriage and insult them because they cannot compare to pornography actors (Park, 2009). Verbal abuse may escalate to physical and sexual abuse. This cycle may affect teens' relationships as well. Though incidents of adult domestic violence have not risen with increased pornography viewing among adults, several distinctions between teens and adults could partially support theories about escalating domestic violence among teens. Teens' morality is less solid, they may be more immoderate, they may be more emotionally sensitive, and they likely do not have well-developed coping skills.

In relationships that experience violence, or where one party has been the victim of violence in the past, trauma may be present. The presence of trauma may trigger violence. Excessive anger or emotionalism in response to pornography could correlate with past abuse, especially past sexual abuse. Seeing sexually degrading images may trigger memories or sentiments that relate to untreated or unretrieved memories of abuse. Pornography use may also relate to viewers' physical or sexual trauma. Being confronted about viewing pornography may cause viewers to experience deep shame or defensiveness, especially if viewers also perpetrated sex crimes.

Lethal domestic violence has resulted from the discovery of pornography. In Brooklyn, a woman murdered her husband in front of their child during a fight about money and a pornography DVD (Lysiak & Lemire, 2010). It is unclear whether the husband was watching pornography in front of their child, but he threatened to stab his wife with a kitchen knife. In response, she fatally stabbed him with scissors. Another highly publicized case involving child pornography and murder arose in Pennsylvania (Moran, 2013). A wife discovered that her husband possessed child pornography and stabbed him to death using two different knives as he slept. Her reasoning for murdering her husband was distinguishable from other crimes of passion. She said that she was acting as an avenger. She felt that she was compelled to kill her husband for participating in child abuse because she loves children. In another case, a woman verbally confronted her husband about a charge on her bank statement for pornography (Siahoma Man Kills Wife, 2011). After she struck her husband in the head, he stabbed her to death. These cases demonstrate variability between violent results. In Alabama, a brother, a sister, an ex-husband, and a roommate were involved in a murder-suicide pact after being charged with child pornography following an investigation by the FBI (Gates, 2013). Two former spouses and their roommate volunteered to be murdered by the ex-wife's brother, who then killed himself. All four parties, who co-habited, left suicide notes declaring that they neither exploited a child sexually nor transmitted child pornography. This case highlights the role that socialization and home environment plays in family violence.

The law provides few legal avenues for members of the family who feel violated by legal pornography present in a home or marriage. For instance, in one case, grounds for divorce were insufficiently established after the petitioner failed to show on appeal that her husband's use of pornography amounted to "habitual cruel and inhuman treatment" (Divorce Grounds, 2003). This mismatch between traditional values and lawful recourse could be one reason that people resort to domestic violence. Pornography use is typically private and often secretive. Clandestine use of pornography may surprise and incite those who discover it. Perhaps domestic violence relates to instability and insecurity; however, it likely also relates to poor coping skills, shame, and conscience, especially when pornography depicts obscenity or abuse.

Child Custody and Pornography

Pornography offenses may impact child custody in a few ways. A study analyzed consequences of sex offenses in families (Levenson & Tewksbury, 2009). Of 584 participants who were in familial relationships with sex offenders, 9% of sex offenders exclusively offended with child pornography, and 6% committed other Internet sex offenses. Most offenders were white males, and most respondents were middle-aged females. More than half were married, and 15% were estranged, divorced, or separated. Almost half of respondents were college educated. More than half of respondents reportedly shared a home with a registered sex offender. Approximately one-third indicated that they co-parented with a sex offender. Sixty-three percent of children reportedly were allowed unsupervised or unrestricted contact with parents who had committed sex offenses. Almost one-quarter of children, 23%, required supervised contact. Some children, 14%, were not permitted to have any contact with sex-offending parents.

Family courts may use certain factors to decide custody cases. Best interest of the child factors vary between jurisdictions. Yet, jurisdictions generally share several of the same considerations. Restrictions imposed on sex offenders by the state and fetishistic lifestyles could result in negative analysis of these factors. Courts may consider (1) love and affection between family members; (2) capacity of parents to nurture children in religion; (3) ability of parents to provide necessities and medical care; (4) environmental stability and time spent in the environment; (5) family cohesion and siblings' preferences; (6) morality; (7) family members' mental and physical status; (8) school and community; (9) children's reasonable preferences; (10) domestic violence, including use of obscene language; and (11) any other relevant factors (*Booth v. Booth*, 2004; Cal. Fam. Code § 3040-3049, 2013; Child Custody Act of 1970, 2009; Fla. Stat. § 61.13 (3)(d)(3), 2013). A custodial parent seeking to limit an offender's or fetishist's access to children could argue that offense history or lifestyle demonstrate that custody is not in the best interest of the children.

In at least 30 states, sex offender registries may limit proximity between offenders and children, schools, parks, bus stops, day care centers, and other places where children may be unaccompanied by parents. Though sex offenders tend to victimize children known to them, the policy rationale behind these laws is that some offenders victimize children who are unattended or accessible publicly. Offenders may be subject to housing buffers that place them outside school districts. The residential location may limit their usefulness as a co-parent or exceed the limit of the court's jurisdiction required by custody agreements.

Pornography offenses may make co-parenting impracticable or undesirable. Among respondents in Levenson and Tewksbury's (2009) study, 66% of sex offenders reported that shame due to notification had kept them from engaging in community activities. Pornography offenders may not be able to provide lifestyles that are in the best interest of children. Respondents living with sex offenders reported that children were embarrassed or ostracized in the community and at school because of notifications. Many community members, though not all, were hesitant to let children visit in the same home with a sex offender. More than three-quarters of respondents reported that sex offender parents were unable to attend some of their children's activities (e.g., birthday parties, school plays, or sporting events). All of these limitations resulted in psychological side effects: 80% of sex offenders expressed anger, depression was experienced by 77%, 73% experienced anxiety, and 63% suffered from fear. Though researchers reported that these correlated with registration and notification, researchers did not measure how many of these symptoms were experienced by sex offenders prior to offending or how many of these symptoms correlated with sex offenses (e.g., poor coping skills, impulsiveness, antisocial behavior, etc.). Offenders' moods may influence analyses of the best interest factors. Approximately 13% of sex offenders' children reported suicidal tendencies. This may relate to sex offense registration, as well as biology or learned behavior. These secondary effects may be inferred by the court as not being in the best interest of the child.

To establish mental health issues, co-parents may allege that former partners suffer from paraphilia irrespective of whether they are convicted sex offenders. The American Psychiatric Association has questioned whether it is appropriate to use the *Diagnostic and Statistical Manual of Mental Disorders* (4th and 5th ed.) to label paraphilias in family cases (Krueger, 2010). In some cases, therapists have expressed concerns that behaviors that do not directly target children are being misrepresented to persuade the court. For example, offenders who suffer from sadomasochistic interest in adult pornography may be unfairly targeted in child custody proceedings. They may be characterized in proceedings as dangerous to children without any type of risk assessment or scientific support.

Perhaps paraphilias ought to be flagged as a precaution because they may relate to larger or riskier problems. One researcher recalls from childhood:

> Family behavior [is a sign] of our inner problems. I understood how my father's own childhood experiences directly contributed to his becoming a perpetrator of sexual abuse, how my mother's upbringing got in the way of her protecting her daughters from abuse, and how my family's dynamics allowed that abuse to go on for so long undetected. I realized … that sexual abuse is only one symptom of a dysfunctional family, that my abuse was not an isolated incident but grew out of my family's overall problems with personal boundaries, appearance, and control. (Reddington & Kreisel, 2009, p. 205)

Paraphilias may be biological, neurological, or learned; result from trauma; relate to addiction; or have numerous other causes or correlatives that may merit consideration by family court. Perhaps evaluations of parents who suffer from pornography addiction or other paraphilia behaviors ought to be conducted by the court.

A survey was conducted of 94 adults involved in intimate partnerships with offenders who had committed sexual activity online. Respondents found cybersex activities to be problematic continuations of compulsive sexual behaviors that existed before online sex activity (United States Sentencing Commission, 2012). Raising sexual dysfunction in custody cases may seem to disadvantage deviants, but perhaps it might deter deviants from progressing along a continuum or implement necessary oversight. Though it may be somewhat invasive of parents' privacy, court-ordered evaluations may definitively establish that paraphilics do not suffer from the sort of mental health issues that pose severe risks to children or place parents at risk for sex offending.

Consent to Search

Searches of private property must be constitutional. Public policy denies police and the state the benefit of unlawful searches by excluding evidence obtained during searches that violate the Constitution. Police can only legally search under a few conditions: exigent circumstances, impounding a vehicle, search incident to arrest, with consent, and with a warrant. Searches for pornography usually occur when police have warrants. However, searches may occur when parties grant consent for searches. Parties' relationships, location of the objects to be searched, presence or absence of the parties at the time of the search, and other factors would influence whether a party can legally consent to search of a common area or another's personal property. Some rules governing consent to search apply to all jurisdictions, but other searches may be limited by jurisdictional case law.

In *Georgia v. Randolph* (2006), the U.S. Supreme Court held that a warrant is required to search a house when one resident consents to a search, but another resident objects. This rule is in line with the co-occupant consent rule set forth in *U.S. v. Matlock* (1974). The co-occupant consent rule permits police to search when consent is granted by one resident if the co-occupant is absent. This may occur when a suspected pornographer is not present in the home when the search occurs, or it may occur when a pornographer who opposes the search is lawfully arrested and, consequently, is not present in the home. Though prior objection to search is not normally vitiated if an occupant leaves the home, under this limited circumstance, the absence of an arrested party permits the present occupant to consent to search well after arrest, but only if removal of the arrested party was reasonable (*Fernandez v. California*, 2014; *U.S. v. Murphy*, 2008).

A third party who possesses common authority over the area to be searched can consent. The basic tenets of this rule are (1) authority over the premises and (2) the absence of the co-occupant. If any occupants object, then the rule reverts to *Randolph*'s rule. If a third party does not have authority to consent to a search, then consent is valid only if police reasonably believe that the person granting consent has common authority over the property (*Illinois v. Rodriguez*, 1990). A guest may have a reasonable expectation of privacy within the home if the guest has a sufficient relationship with the place or objects to be searched. A guest may exclusively have a reasonable expectation of privacy in an area if that area is not in common use (*U.S. v. Taylor*, 2010). Yet, *Randolph*, *Matlock*, and *Rodriguez* still apply, for the most part. Mutual use of an area sufficiently demonstrates joint control. Joint control does not extend to areas not under the third party's control or where the third party has no reasonable expectation of privacy (*U.S. v. Dearing*, 1993). Parties who do not have joint control, but use a property, assume the risk that those who control the property will grant consent to search.

Jurisdictional rules can vary constitutional interpretations. In the 4th Circuit, a wife was held to have apparent authority to consent to search her husband's computer files, which were password protected (*U.S. v. Buckner*, 2007). The files were on a home computer, which was already booted when officers arrived. The computer was leased in the wife's name and was located in a common area. If a girlfriend has possession of a hard drive that the owner keeps in her home for safekeeping, the owner of the hard drive is periodically present in the girlfriend's home, and the owner has never granted the girlfriend permission to review the contents of the hard drive, then the girlfriend's consent to search would not suffice in the 10th District (*U.S. v. Salinas-Cano*, 1992). In the 1st, 7th, and 8th Districts, a third party could grant consent to search without mutual use of the object or area if control over the object or area creates express or implied agency or a reasonable belief of agency (*U.S. v. Baswell*, 1986; *U.S. v. Gonzalez*, 2010; *U.S. v. Miller*, 1986). In the 7th Circuit, a property owner may not grant consent if the owner does not have keys, keeps no belongings in the home, and does not pay rent (*U.S. v. Brown*, 2003).

The scope of a warrantless search must be limited by consent granted. When the scope of consent is debated, the reasonable-person standard is used to gauge scope. If consent is withdrawn prior to the conclusion of the search, then police may not continue searching. If elicit objects are in plain view, then consent is not necessary to search and seize the contraband. The plain-view doctrine may apply to digital files (Dodovich, 2011). For example, if a printout specifies that the suspect digitally purchased child pornography, or police find a secret camera used to record girls in a bathroom, then the contraband is considered to be in plain view even though depictions are digital.

Conclusion

Child custody, domestic violence, and home searches may intersect pornography, domestic life, and criminal justice. Family law and criminal justice may also intersect where agents of the law are required to consider particular relationships between parties. Viewing legal pornography may be controversial, and viewing illegal pornography may be detestable. Strong reactions to pornography offenses could provoke domestic violence. Courts may hold that it is not in the best interest of children to live with pornography offenders. However, viewing pornography may not alone be grounds for divorce or other proceedings in family court.

References

Booth v. Booth (2004, 4th Dept) 8 App Div 3d 1104, 778 NYS2d 643.

Cal. Fam. Code § 3040-3049 (2013).

Child Custody Act of 1970, 91 § 722.23 (2009).

Cusack, C. M. (In press). *Criminal Justice Handbook on Masculinity, Male Aggression, and Sexuality*. Springfield, IL: Charles C. Thomas.

Divorce grounds—cruel and inhuman treatment—interest in pornography—medication. (2003). *Family Law Reporter, 29*(16), 1188.

Dodovich, M. (2011). The plain view doctrine strikes out in digital file searches. *I/S: A Journal of Law and Policy for the Information Society, 6*, 659.

Farley, M. (2006). Prostitution, trafficking, and cultural amnesia: What we must not know in order to keep the business of sexual exploitation running smoothly. *Yale Journal of Law and Feminism, 18*, 109–144.

Fernandez v. California, U.S. Supreme Court, 12-7822 (2014).

Fla. Stat. § 61.13 (3)(d)(3) (2013).

Gates, V. (2013, October 8). Child pornography suspects found dead in Alabama murder-suicide. Yahoo. Retrieved from http://news.yahoo.com/child-pornography-suspects-found-dead-alabama-murder-suicide-171514298.html

Georgia v. Randolph, 547 U.S. 103 (2006).

Hope, C. (2012, July 5). Keir Starmer suggests teenager relationship violence link to Internet pornography. *Telegraph*. Retrieved from http://www.telegraph.co.uk/news/politics/9379401/Teenager-relationship-violence-link-to-internet-pornography-admits-Keir-Starmer.html

Illinois v. Rodriguez, 497 U.S. 177 (1990).

Krueger, R. B. (2010). The DSM diagnostic criteria for sexual masochism. *Archives of Sexual Behavior, 39*(2), 346–356. doi:10.1007/s10508-010-9613-4

Lawrence, D. (2014, January 23). The inside story of TOR, the best Internet anonymity tool the government ever built. *Bloomberg Businessweek*. Retrieved from http://www.businessweek.com/articles/2014-01-23/tor-anonymity-software-vs-dot-the-national-security-agency

Levenson, J. S., & Tewksbury, R. (2009). Collateral damage: Family members of registered sex offenders. *American Journal of Criminal Justice, 34*(1–2), 54–68. Retrieved from http://dx.doi.org/10.1007/s12103-008-9055-x

Lysiak, M., & Lemire, J. (2010, September 10). Porn and money woes push Brooklyn mom over edge, she plunges scissors in husband's chest. *New York Daily News*. Retrieved from www.nydailynews.com/news/crime/porn-money-woes-push-brooklyn-mom-edge-plunges-scissors-husband-chest-article-1.439190

Moran, L. (2013, February 13). Former basketball star allegedly stabbed to death by wife after she caught him looking at child porn. *New York Daily News*. Retrieved from http://www.nydailynews.com/news/crime/wife-arrested-killing-husband-child-porn-article-1.1262937

Park, L. (2009, September 19). Pornography at root of more and more domestic violence incidents. *Standard Examiner*. Retrieved from http://www.standard.net/topics/news/2009/09/19/pornography-root-more-and-more-domestic-violence-incidents

Petrie, J. (2012, June 20). Wife attacks husband after finding copies of *The Onion* in car. *Menomoneefalls Patch*. Retrieved from http://menomoneefalls.patch.com/groups/police-and-fire/p/woman-attacks-husband-for-having-the-shepherd-express0d0f69fe27

Reddington, F. P., & Kreisel, B. W. (Eds.). (2009). *Sexual assault*. Durham, NC: Carolina Academic Press.

Siahoma man kills wife of 30 years after she catches him watching porn, stages scene to look like a rape/murder. Then goes to basketball game [video]. (2011, January 15). ThisIs50.com. Retrieved from http://www.thisis50.com/profiles/blogs/sicko-oklahoma-man-kills-wife

United States Sentencing Commission. (2012). Report to the Congress: Federal child pornography offenses. Retrieved from http://www.ussc.gov/Legislative_and_Public_Affairs/Congressional_Testimony_and_Reports/Sex_Offense_Topics/201212_Federal_Child_Pornography_Offenses/

U.S. v. Baswell, 792 F.2d 755, 759 (8th Cir. 1986).

U.S. v. Brown, 328 F.3d 352, 356 (7th Cir. 2003).

U.S. v. Buckner, 473 F.3d 551, 555 (4th Cir. 2007).

U.S. v. Dearing, 9 F.3d 1428, 1429 (9th Cir. 1993).

U.S. v. Gonzalez, 609 F.3d 13, 18-19 (1st Cir. 2010).

U.S. v. Matlock, 415 U.S. 164 (1974).

U.S. v. Miller, 800 F.2d 129, 134-35 (7th Cir. 1986).

U.S. v. Murphy, 516 F.3d 1117, 1122 (9th Cir. 2008).

U.S. v. Salinas-Cano, 959 F.2d 861, 864-65 (10th Cir. 1992).

U.S. v. Taylor, 600 F.3d 678, 681-82 (6th Cir. 2010).

Public Pornography 13

Overview

Pornographic depictions and sexual activities may be criminalized or protected based on location. Privacy is a fundamental right that protects private, nonharmful sexual activity. However, the state can enforce public morality using police power as long as laws are rational. Though private and public realms may seem to be separate, they overlap in many ways. One example is that the government seems to possess some power to regulate some private morality. Another example is that the government seems to protect and regulate public explicit depictions of sex. Public speech can be regulated according to time, place, and manner if the state demonstrates an important reason.

Public versus Private Distinctions

Public and private speech receives different protections under the Constitution (Figure 13.1). Pornography is protected speech under the First Amendment. Yet, some protection to view obscenity exists under a due process right to privacy. The bright line rule is that obscene content may not be depicted or made visible to the public. However, legal variability arises from jurisdictional fluctuations in morality; interpretations of art; definitions of "public," "private," and "obscene"; and utilization of new technology (Albright, 2012). Nuanced distinctions influence when and where legal pornography can or cannot be shown publicly.

Sharing obscenity with others is a crime. Reaching the public through the mail is a public activity. Use of the U.S. Postal Service or electronic mail to deal in obscenity and child pornography is criminal. One key fact of *Miller v. California* (1973) is that the defendant mailed pornography to unsolicitous members of the community. However, courts apply *Miller* to direct online file sharing of obscenity even when the public may be incapable of viewing the transmissions. When statutes are silent or material approaches the bright line, some seeking to publicize depictions may err on the side of caution and strictly follow *Miller*. Yet, others may take risks in the public sphere. Defining the public sphere is a somewhat unsettled area of law that relates to the kind of content depicted. Just as storefronts may not knowingly display

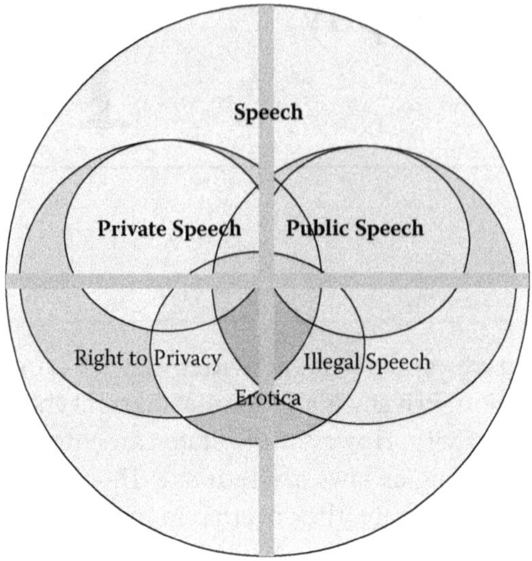

Figure 13.1 Context and content. A schematic diagram of First Amendment rights.

risqué material that corrupts minors, operators of computer services may not knowingly allow users to publicize obscenity or sexual content if the operator believes that minors may be able to witness it (Fla. Stat. § 847.0135, 2013). Such statutes reach outside the scope of the local community originally contemplated by *Miller*, but contemporary understandings of *Miller* include publicly visible depictions on the Internet.

The U.S.-based company Google was ordered by a German court to delete content depicting an orgy hosted by a former Formula One boss (ten Wolde & Rotscheroth, 2014). Google was held to be responsible for the images because it distributed the content. This reasoning seems in line with U.S. jurisprudence; however, in the United States, service providers are exempted from some pornography laws because they do not actively distribute images. The German court held that Google participated in privacy violations. A French court also ordered Google to remove the photos. The case was civil even though images depicted sadomasochistic sex with the plaintiff and five prostitutes. The photos, which could potentially violate the law in some U.S. jurisdictions, can be viewed in the United States using a Google search. Depicted sex acts are not explicit, but could be considered to be offensive and appealing to prurient interests. Google defended its position by claiming that it cannot prevent re-posting of the images and that the role of service providers is not to police photos. However, Google does help people to remove content that violates the law. This situation highlights the expansive spectrum stretching between international law, civil law, criminal law, private speech, protected speech, public speech, and unprotected speech.

Mainstream advertisements and artistic images have undergone "pornification" to garner greater public response (Albright, 2012). Inexplicit depictions of bondage, nude dancing, group sex, and interracial sexual relations may be alluded to in mainstream media. Depictions insinuating nontraditional sex may be less offensive than in years past within some communities. Yet, many communities continue to firmly believe that extremely sexy or nonnormative themes ought to remain private. These debates play out in the public eye, but rarely do through the criminal justice system. Almost half of all advertisements include images of minors (Bristol, 2007). Pedophiles routinely collect images of topless or partially clothed minors wearing bathing suits, shorts, undergarments, diapers, and other revealing clothing. Companies, like Calvin Klein and Abercrombie & Fitch, have been accused of promoting pedophilia in their advertisements to the public. Perhaps in response, other companies have intentionally attempted to promote "real" women. American Apparel, a competitor of Abercrombie & Fitch, decorated mannequins' pubic regions with pubic-hair-like wigs (Boone, 2014). As long as advertisements are legal, then uproar, celebration, or rejection is a matter for public debate. It is not a governmental issue.

Libraries

Profanity, obscenity, pornography, and child pornography are legally distinguishable, though they are all typically taboo in public. Many public libraries block profanity and lewd material, while others do not. Legally, books ought to be treated similarly to films, but practically, books are quite distinguishable from films. Perhaps one historical difference is that several books that were once banned subsequently became protected. This topic was discussed in Chapter 3. Another distinction may lie in how children obtain explicit material (Reddington & Kreisel, 2009). Private bookstores may not sell pornography to children; however, they rarely ask customers for proof of age unless bookstores cater to adults or the material is produced by the pornography industry. Public libraries, which are part of the government, may elect to keep erotica off their shelves. They may not provide children with erotic materials. However, most libraries do not discriminate between patrons' ages. Libraries may not be strictly liable for granting access to minors, thus jurisdictions may hold libraries responsible only if they intentionally give harmful materials minors (Fla. Stat. § 847.0125, 2012). "Harmful" may be defined by each jurisdiction and sometimes by context. Thus, some texts may not be considered harmful to minors even if they depict material that may obscene if it were shown to minors in a film, photo, or drawing. Some statutes that proscribe dissemination of harmful materials to minors may exempt agents and employees of bona fide retail stores, museums, libraries, or schools serving an educational purpose (Mass. Gen. Laws Ann. 272 § 28, 2013). Cases may turn on definitions of "bona fide" or "educational purpose."

A great deal of controversy exists over the fact that some public libraries may be used to view pornography even if images on the monitor offend other patrons. Washington and New York were pioneers in this area. In some jurisdictions, viewing pornography at public libraries has been protected under the First Amendment. Though, in many jurisdictions, library policies prohibit it, and violators could be arrested. People have been arrested in Florida, Pennsylvania, and other states. Arrest is almost certain to occur if violators are recidivists who have been warned previously, are engaged in other lewd conduct (e.g., masturbation), or appear to be viewing hard-core pornography or child pornography.

The Federal Communications Commission (n.d.) developed the Children's Internet Protection Act (CIPA). Libraries will not receive federal discounts through the E-rate program if they do not abide by specific Internet safety policies. Under *South Dakota v. Dole* (1987), the federal government may deny states federal funds if states fail to accept certain conditions. To receive federal funds, state libraries must certify that technology protection measures block or filter patrons' access to online obscenity, child pornography, and material that is harmful to minors. Content needs to be blocked only if it can be accessed by children. Before adopting this policy, libraries are required to provide notice to the public and hold one or more public hearings or meetings to discuss the proposed certification of CIPA policies. Definitions of "harm," "access," "obscenity," and "child pornography" may open the door to future challenges to CIPA. CIPA avoids some challenges by providing that authorized library personnel may disable safety filters and blocks to allow adults to lawfully access certain material. For example, researchers may access pornography. The meaning of adults' "lawful" activities at libraries remains open for interpretation. Libraries and CIPA also were discussed in Chapter 10 and Chapter 5.

Public Masturbation

Public masturbation is a crime involving self-exposure. Indecent exposure may overlap with exhibitionism, or it may be incidental to public masturbation. Public masturbation is discussed further in Chapter 21, and exhibitionism was discussed throughout Chapter 8. Public masturbation often occurs at public theaters where pornographic films are shown or during online video chats. Exposing one's genitals in a lewd or lascivious manner is a crime that may be aggravated when children may witness it (Fla. Stat. § 847.0135,

2013). Children are at greater risk of viewing an offender's genitals when public masturbation is committed outside an adult entertainment venue. However, adult theaters may attract more attention from the criminal justice system because public masturbation is more likely to occur there. Even when offenders do not wish to be viewed masturbating inside adult theaters and go to some trouble to cover their groin, circumstantial evidence, such as hand motions and unbuttoned pants, may sufficiently create probable cause (*Washington v. Diaz-Flores*, 2009).

Patrons may masturbate in restrooms at adult theaters or in booths that play pornography at adult stores (Guillen, 2012; *Ward v. State*, 1994). Society recognizes that people have a reasonable expectation of privacy in public restrooms. Private masturbation is legal, thus masturbating in a public restroom is likely to be legal as long as others do not witness it. What another person may witness by peering through the crack of a bathroom door does not transform masturbation into public lewdness or exhibition; rather, the act of peering violates an occupant's privacy. However, society does not recognize an expectation of privacy in booths that exhibit pornography. If booths are used as dressing rooms, then privacy expectations may be reasonable. However, masturbation may not be lawful inside pornography booths unless jurisdictional laws permit people to undress inside the booths.

Sex Films and Theaters

Free speech protects some public depictions of erotic content, for example, seminude dancing, adult bookstores, and adult theaters (*City of Erie v. Pap's A.M.*, 2000; Cusack, 2012). Zoning laws, criminal decency laws, and obscenity laws overlap to regulate theaters playing pornographic films. Permitted adult entertainment establishments are forbidden in certain areas and are always prohibited from promoting, displaying, distributing, or selling harmful materials to minors (*City of Renton et al. v. Playtime Theatres, Inc.*, 1986; Farley, 2006; Fee, 2009; Fla. Stat. § 847.0134, 2012; Lasker, 2002; *Los Angeles v. Alameda Books, Inc.*, 2002; Wis. Adm. Code SFP 2.03, 2013; *Young v. American Mini Theatres, Inc.*, 1976). Zoning laws may proscribe adult businesses within a certain distance of schools, fairgrounds, residential areas, religious establishments, or other regulated areas. Zoning ordinances are designed to preserve community character and control secondary effects correlating with the presence of adult entertainment venues. Secondary effects include increased crime in the community, increased vices, and reduced property value.

Laws restricting adult establishments to certain zones discriminate against content, but courts do not strictly scrutinize these laws. Critics claim that morality, class warfare, racism, preferences for traditional families, gender prejudice, and maintenance of sexual status quos undergird these content-restrictive zoning laws. Yet, the government's goal is not to impinge on the message or on speakers, but to reduce secondary effects created. Restrictions are content neutral because secondary effects correlate with the presence of adult businesses in the community. Thus, restrictions are scrutinized at an intermediate level because laws are substantially related to important governmental interests in reducing secondary effects. Zoning laws effectively regulate time, place, and manner to reduce the effects of a particular kind of business. Zoning regulations do not affect how many or which pornographic depictions may be played. Speech contained within depictions and acts of exhibiting pornography is not chilled by zoning laws.

Live Performance

Recorded depictions of live sex acts may be pornographic or artistic. Theater productions involving sex acts are sometimes, albeit rarely, considered to be art. Typically, theater productions depict sex in an inexplicit manner. Recorded depictions of these shows are not likely to be considered pornography. However, public sex shows are often considered to be indecent, and films of such shows could potentially be considered pornographic or possibly obscene.

Patrons and vendors could be charged with obscenity, pandering, or pimping in relation to live sexual performances. Knowing promotion, performance, or participation in live public obscenity may be a misdemeanor or a felony depending on the jurisdiction and the circumstances (Fla. Stat. § 847.011 (4), 2012). Variables may include whether money was charged for the performance, the degree of sexual conduct, audience members, and whether performers recidivated after receiving a warning or being charged. In *People v. Maita* (1984), a proprietor was convicted of charges relating to providing live nude entertainment. Entertainers were hired by the theater to interact sexually with audience members. The appellate court affirmed convictions for pandering and pimping. However, the proprietor was acquitted of charges for obscene live conduct. In that case, the court specified that pimping laws and pandering laws do not necessarily criminalize live adult entertainment or nudity in entertainment. However, entertainers and patrons may not engage in sexual relations. Production offenses arising from depictions of live public obscenity may relate to the content of the depictions irrespective of whether performers were pandering or pimping.

Conclusion

Governmental policies intend to protect speech and the public. Laws may seem inconsistent, but they are designed to protect as much speech as possible while fulfilling necessary government functions. The government is interested in protecting community values. Some forms of public speech damage communities' moral and economic values. Sexual speech may be regulated using strict scrutiny or intermediate scrutiny, that is, time, place, and manner restrictions. Other forms of speech (e.g., masturbation) are protected under privacy laws even though they occur outside the home. In most jurisdictions, minors may not access pornographic depictions in private or public. Case law and separation of powers permits a patchwork of jurisprudence and legislation.

References

Albright, J. M. (2012). Porn 2.0: The libidinal economy and the consumption of desire in the digital age. In D. G. Mick, S. Pettigrew, C. Pechmann, & J. L. Ozanne (Eds.), *Transformative consumer research for personal and collective well-being* (pp. 499–522). New York: Routledge/Taylor & Francis Group.

Boone, J. (2014, January 17). American Apparel's mannequins have pubic hair! Company says they're celebrating "natural beauty." EOnline. Retrieved from http://www.eonline.com/news/500811/american-apparel-s-mannequins-have-pubic-hair-company-says-they-re-celebrating-natural-beauty

Bristol, J. E. (2007). Free expression in motion pictures: Childhood sexuality and a satisfied society. *Cardozo Arts and Entertainment Law Journal, 25*(1), 333–365.

City of Erie v. Pap's A.M., 529 U.S. 277 (2000).

City of Renton et al. v. Playtime Theatres, Inc., 475 U.S. 41 (1986).

Cusack, C. M. (2012). Boob laws: An analysis of social deviance with in gender, family, or the home (etudes 2). *Women's Rights Law Reporter, 33*, 197.

Farley, M. (2006). Prostitution, trafficking, and cultural amnesia: What we must not know in order to keep the business of sexual exploitation running smoothly. *Yale Journal of Law and Feminism, 18*, 109–144.

Federal Communication Commission. (n.d.). Children's Internet Protection Act (CIPA). Retrieved February 6, 2014, from http://www.fcc.gov/guides/childrens-internet-protection-act

Fee, J. (2009). The pornographic secondary effects doctrine. *Alabama Law Review, 60*(2), 291–338.

Fla. Stat. § 847.011 (4) (2012).

Fla. Stat. § 847.0125(1)(a)(b) (2012).

Fla. Stat. § 847.0134 (2012).

Fla. Stat. § 847.0135 (2013).

Guillen, R. (2012). Pushing Alice down the rabbit hole: How Florida's video voyeurism laws protect victims. *University of Florida Journal of Law and Public Policy, 23*(1), 103–144.

Lasker, S. (2002). Sex and the city: Zoning "pornography peddlers and live nude shows." *UCLA Law Review, 49*, 1139–1185.

Los Angeles v. Alameda Books, Inc., 535 U.S. 425 (2002).
Mass. Gen. Laws Ann. 272 § 28 (2013).
Miller v. California, 413 U.S. 15 (1973).
People v. Maita (1984) 157 Cal.App.3d 309 (203 Cal.Rptr. 685).
Reddington, F. P., & Kreisel, B. W. (Eds.). (2009). *Sexual assault.* Durham, NC: Carolina Academic Press.
South Dakota v. Dole, 483 U.S. 203 (1987).
ten Wolde, H., & Rotscheroth, N. (2014, January 25). Google appeals German courts orgy photos ruling. *NBC News.* Retrieved from http://www.nbcnews.com/technology/google-appeal-german-courts-orgy-photos-ruling-2D11988265
Ward v. State, 636 So. 2d 68 (1994).
Washington v. Diaz-Flores, 148 Wn. App. 911 (2009).
Wis. Adm. Code SFP 2.03 (2013).
Young v. American Mini Theatres, Inc. 427 U.S. 50 (1976).

Unintended Pornography

14

Overview

Some adults and children unknowingly participate in pornography. Parents may innocently depict children while nude. Nude sunbathers may be photographed without their knowledge. Voyeurs may photograph beneath the clothing of unaware members of the public. Treacherous lovers and sexual assailants may produce or distribute pornography without consent (Iowa Code § 709.1, 2013).

Childhood Photos

In recent years, some parents have been prosecuted under child pornography statutes for photographing their children while nude. Often, children appear nude because they are bathing. Parents who attempt to develop film are reported at film processing labs. Authorities must decide whether allegedly innocent photos are actually child pornography.

One case in Texas demonstrates the difficulty in regulating depictions of nude children (Breast Is Best, 2003; Korosec, 2003). A mother, Jacqueline Mercado, was reunited after a year with the father of one of her children. Soon after the reunion, the couple posed for several naked photos in bed, took numerous nude photos of Mercado bathing with both her children, depicted one of her children from a previous relationship touching his genitals, and took pictures of Mercado on her knees while the couple's naked toddler—who had already been weaned from breast-feeding—sucked on one of her nipples. In some photos, Mercado modestly covered her chest with her arm, but police characterized Mercado as fondling her breasts in the shower. They also characterized the photo of breast-feeding as sexual performance of a child because the child had already desisted breast-feeding. The couple's photos came to the attention of Texas law enforcement pursuant to mandatory reporting requirements for photo lab technicians who encounter questionable material. Many states have similar laws (*Oregon v. Porter*, 2010). The couple was charged for producing the depiction of breast-feeding. The government thought that the case was weak, yet the couple agreed to undergo sex therapy. They also underwent risk assessments and evaluations before Child Protective Services agreed to return their children.

Once innocently produced images of children are processed at photo labs, depictions could be published to the Internet and used as child pornography. These photo labs are an important checkpoint, but digital cameras circumnavigate technicians. Experts at the National Drug Intelligence Center (NDIC) reported that technology potentially interrupts the important checkpoint that photo labs once created (United States Sentencing Commission [USSC], 2012). Among NDIC experts, 73% reported that digital technology and the Internet have made acquisition and distribution of child pornography easier. Twenty-four percent reported digital cameras as a factor facilitating child pornography because photo labs and print shops are bypassed. Photos are uploaded online directly from cameras. Nearly one-quarter, 22%, reported that the Internet prompted individuals to commit situational offenses based on previously unavailable ease. While some critics would argue that prosecution of innocent parents misappropriates the use of photo labs as checkpoints, others would point out that most children are victimized by acquaintances and relatives. More specific legislation and education about exploitation and the law could help avoid prosecution of innocent depictions.

Public Photography of Nude People

First Amendment protections for free speech include the right to photograph others in public places. The law often permits publication of photos depicting nude bodies in public irrespective of whether subjects consented to be photographed. Jacqueline Kennedy Onassis and other famous people have been photographed while nude. Onassis was photographed while nude sunbathing and doing yoga on Skorpios Island in 1971 (Jackie O. Nude Photos, 2010). Capturing the photos involved a matter of seconds, not minutes or hours. Images of her nude body were distributed as pornography. Depictions of her breasts and "million dollar muff" appeared in Italy's *Playmen* in 1972, and, in 1975, the photos appeared in *Hustler* magazine in the United States (Tarihi, 2009). When subjects engage in public nudity, photographers cannot typically be prosecuted unless a photographer has trespassed or committed another crime (e.g., peeping). The paparazzo who captured Onassis, Settimio Garritano, frequently photographed the former First Lady. In this instance, he posed as a gardener to take the photos. However, that crime did not occur in the United States, and it may not trump First Amendment rights to publish the photos unless a court ordered that paparazzo not to profit from that invasion and enjoined publication. Even when crimes occur in the United States (e.g., home videos were stolen), the criminal justice rarely intervenes.

> It's creepy and it's not fair and one can debate whether it's even legal in some cases, but you can't pretend to be shocked when it does happen. The same goes for the seemingly endless parade of stories about leaked videos and/or photos, whether the leaking was done by the subject as a publicity stunt or it's a legitimate case of someone's privacy violated. [It has happened to] Paris Hilton. Blake Lively. Vanessa Hudgens. Jessica Alba. Scarlett Johansson. Olivia Munn. Kristin Davis. Britney Spears. Madonna. Vanna White. Dr. Laura Schlessinger. Rihanna. Leighton Meester. Ashley Greene. Kat Dennings. Miley Cyrus. Christina Aguilera. Christina Hendricks. That's just a partial roster. (Roeper, 2012)

Some jurisdictions have attempted to refine broad interpretations of the First Amendment. For example, the state of Texas has grappled with application of improper photography laws. Improper photography occurs when defendants possess specific intent to gratify or arouse sexual desire; improper photography laws complement other laws prohibiting depiction of people who are in dressing rooms or bathrooms (Murphy, 2008; Tex. Penal Code § 21.15, 2013). The statute requires sexual intent or intent to invade another's privacy. Thus, specific criminal intent and the victim's nonconsent to be photographed are two keys to prosecution. Nonconsent may require the victim to hold a reasonable expectation of privacy. Courts may flexibly define "reasonable expectation of privacy." Therefore, this statute may apply to a person hiding in the bushes who photographs publicly nude sunbathers if (1) specific sexual intent can be established, (2) a reasonable expectation of privacy was held by the victim, and (3) society is prepared to recognize that privacy right (*In re Vasquez*, 2007).

Statutes prohibiting improper photography in public are not overbroad because they require specific intent (*Lo v. Texas*, 2011; Tex. Penal Code Ann. § 33.021(b), 2011). In some cases, *Dost* factors, which were discussed in Chapter 5, may be used to evaluate whether publicly produced depictions can be prosecuted as improper photography (*Doe v. Chamberlin*, 2001; *U.S. v. Dost*, 1986). Lascivious exhibition of children's clothed pubic areas may constitute pornography even if children are in public and photography was otherwise lawful. Photos focusing on children's clothed buttocks and groins may constitute improper photography; arrest for improper photography may raise probable cause for a home search for child pornography (*McKissick v. Texas*, 2006).

Typically, naturist magazines containing images of nude children are not pornography. Naturist images are intentionally produced by photographers and parents to depict naturist lifestyles. However, exploitation of children may trigger statutes if photos are used as pornography or intended to be pornographic even if they are inexplicit. Public nudity and naturism may be lewd criminal activities in certain jurisdictions. Under those circumstances, nude depictions of minors may be prosecutable. Naturist materials were discussed in Chapter 5.

"Up-Skirt" Photos

Surreptitious recording beneath females' clothing is generally referred to as "up-skirt" recording (Figure 14.1). This kind of pornographic image is invasive, taboo, and, often, illegal (Guillen, 2012; *Minnesota v. Morris*, 2002). Two defining features of this sort of pornography are that (1) a victim lacks knowledge of a pornographer's intentions and (2) a pornographer lacks a victim's consent (*Washington v. Burk*, 2013). This kind of fetishistic pornography may be re-posted online numerous times. Deviants may hide imaging devices in their hands, on their shoes, or in bags, or they may use other equipment to momentarily place devices under a victim's clothing. Criminal statutes are typically triggered when a photographer's intent is to create amusement, intrusion, profit, or sexual satisfaction (Fla. Stat. § 810.145, 2012; Minn. Stat. § 609.746, 2000; N.J.S.A. § 2C:14-9, 2013). Depending on the jurisdiction, up-skirt photos may constitute voyeurism, disorderly conduct, criminal invasion of privacy, or other charges. Civil remedies may be available for invasion of privacy and other harms if victims and offenders are identified.

Some defendants have argued that people do not hold privacy expectations in public places. Defendants argue that legislatures only forbid cameras in fitting rooms, bathrooms, and places where people are legally permitted to undress. Victims should not expect the public to recognize general privacy

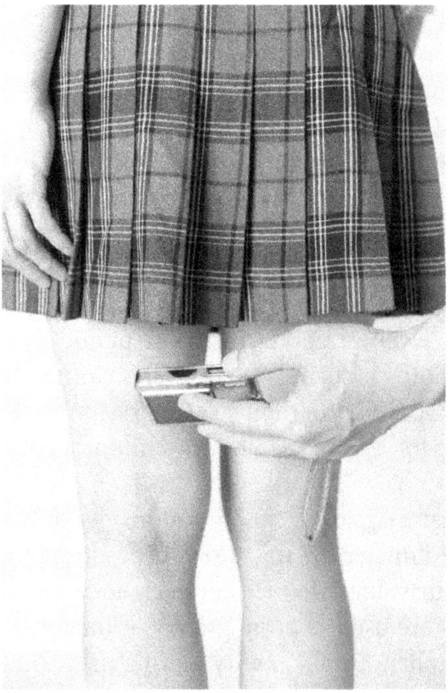

Figure 14.1 Upskirt photography.

rights in public. To avoid exposing themselves, people could wear more modest clothing. Defendants have also argued that nude people in shared public spaces, like locker rooms, have no expectation of privacy. Courts have generally ruled against defendants who make these arguments. Some legislatures have codified these holdings.

Expectation of privacy extends to private areas on one's person even when he or she is in public. First, the reason for criminalizing up-skirt photos is not victims' privacy expectations in public stores, subways, and other public places. Privacy expectations exist under victims' clothing. Second, while people are nude in locker rooms, people expect that they will not be photographed (*Katz v. U.S.*, 1967; *State v. Dennison*, 2012). Their privacy is violated when their expectations are violated. Third, in quasi-public places like nursing homes, residents may have expectations of privacy akin to privacy expectations inside homes (*Washington v. Larson*, 2003). Residents would not expect to be photographed under their clothing. Elders may be protected under sexual exploitation and vulnerable victim statutes (43A Okla. Stat. § 10-103, 2013; HRS § 28-94, 2013; Neb. Rev. Stat. § 28-367.01, 2013).

Not all courts agree that up-skirt photos violate voyeurism laws or unlawful filming laws (*C'Debaca v. Virginia*, 1999; *Tennessee v. Gilliand*, 2010). In *Durant v. State* (2008), the Oklahoma Court of Appeals held that voyeurism statutes must be strictly construed to mean that victims are violated while physically inside places where they hold a reasonable expectation of privacy. The meaning of voyeurism statutes could not be construed to include private places on a victim's body. However, people who take up-skirt photos may be charged with other crimes that do not require expectation of privacy as an element (e.g., disorderly conduct or assault). Massachusetts' Supreme Court ruled that a man who repeatedly recorded up-skirt images had not violated a statute prohibiting recording people in a partial state of undress without consent. The court held that the statute did not protect victims who were recorded in public places. In response to that case law, Massachusetts' legislature statutorily criminalized up-skirt photos punishable by a prison term and a fine (Mass. B.1611, 2014; Mass. H.R. 3924, 2014). In addition, legal analysis may vary when children are victims (*State v. Byrne*, 2009). Generally, up-skirt photos of children could be prosecutable under a variety of statutes designed to protect children irrespective of children's privacy expectations.

Hidden Cameras

People may illegally install cameras in public or private locations. Generally, they do so surreptitiously to produce pornography involving nudity, sexual conduct, and excrement (Minn. Stat. § 609.746, 2013; *Minnesota v. Morris*, 2013). Offenders often create a hole or take advantage of gaps or slits in walls and doors. They may use high-powered lenses or adjust cameras' apertures to capture people through window coverings or in the dark. Sometimes cameras are installed relatively closely to victims (e.g., in school locker rooms). Camera instillation may be a misdemeanor or felony depending on who is recorded. Victims' reasonable expectation of privacy is often required by voyeurism statutes addressing surreptitious recording.

Almost every state forbids undercover filming of people in a state of undress or while wearing undergarments (Reporters Committee for Freedom of Press, 2012). Usually, laws directly target surreptitious filming, but sometimes voyeurism and improper photography laws overlap with up-skirt laws (*Guerrero v. Texas*, 2007). Child pornography laws also overlap with laws targeting hidden cameras. Surreptitious pornography production is somewhat atypical of child pornography offenses (USSC, 2012). Most victims of child pornography are aware that offenses are occurring. Yet, approximately 25% of depictions are produced without victims' knowledge, though some of these victims may be too young to know. Surreptitious filming may involve strangers or known offenders, like roommates, relatives, and teachers (*Guerrero v. Texas*, 2007). In one case, a woman borrowed her landlord's computer and discovered videos of herself undressing in her bedroom, as well as child pornography, on his computer (Kahn, 2013). The landlord was charged with felony video voyeurism and 17 counts of child pornography.

Predators who engage in video voyeurism may suffer from behavioral, sexual, and psychological disorders; these disorders may relate to childhood experiences. In one case, a defendant first experienced pornography as a child (*In Re Commitment of Charles Steven Chapman*, 2013). When he was 10 years old, pornography became a daily habit. The defendant became obsessed with pornography and developed voyeuristic interests. At 26 years old, the defendant recruited a friend with whom he covertly video recorded nude exotic dancers. During his service in the U.S. Air Force, he began secretly video recording consensual sexual contact. He was officially reprimanded for filming sex after an intimate partner reported him. His activity progressed to recording inside dressing rooms and at nude beaches. The defendant's interests became hebephilic, and he became obsessed with secretly filming nude teens. Finally, police investigated the defendant after a sex partner, whom he met online, complained that the defendant attempted to video record her genitals as she slept. Pursuant to a warranted search, police found 18 photographs depicting sleeping or unconscious women with their private areas explicitly displayed; the defendant's body appeared in three of the digital photos. Also in the defendant's possession were numerous undercover videos and videos depicting sexual assault upon each of the defendant's wife's sisters. The defendant possessed more than 100,000 pornographic pictures, including 2,213 pictures of children and 69 child pornography videos. Experts diagnosed the defendant with paraphilia, hebephilia, alcohol abuse, and voyeurism. He was described as displaying strong sexual deviancy and predatory behaviors. The defendant's diagnosed disorders were the underpinnings of sexual violence, which required the defendant to be civilly committed. This case demonstrates potentially serious dangers associated with secret recording.

Revenge Porn

Revenge porn is pornography produced or distributed by intimate partners with the intent of humiliating or harassing victims (Bartow, 2012). Sometimes revenge porn is produced surreptitiously or while victims are intoxicated. Some victims have reportedly been forced to produce revenge porn through threats and violence. Many victims consent to produce pornography with partners, but they have not granted their partners consent to distribute pornography. Often, consent to produce pornography is predicated on the condition that pornography will be kept private. Once revenge porn is placed online, it may be viewed thousands of times within a few days (Flaherty, 2013). Commercial and amateur websites capitalize on revenge porn.

The criminal justice system may become involved when pornographic websites publish revenge pornography. This is especially true if participants depicted are minors or depictions are stolen or hacked. Hunter Moore spearheaded the revenge porn fetish with his website IsAnyoneUp.com (Blankstein, 2014; *U.S. v. Hunter Moore*, 2014). In 2014, Moore was charged with conspiracy to hack computers for pornographic content. To fulfill content demands that generated more than $13,000 each month, Moore paid for pornography from hacked accounts. Along with an associate, Moore allowed people to post revenge porn on his website, but then he hacked victims' e-mail accounts to gather more pornography.

Victims of revenge porn have some recourse through the criminal justice system, though current laws may not fully protect victims. The Communications Decency Act does not require Internet service providers to assist victims of revenge porn; however, if victims are children, then the government may order depictions to be removed from the Internet. If victims are adults, courts could order pornography to be removed and prosecute offenders, though victories may be less certain for adults. Ex-lovers who distribute pornography could be charged with criminal harassment, cyberstalking, criminal invasion of privacy, and other related crimes.

Several legislators have attempted to pass legislation that directly targets revenge porn (Meola, 2014). However, some courts have found that distribution of revenge porn is legal. In New York, a defendant posted nude photos of his girlfriend to Twitter without her consent (*NY v. Barber*, 2014). The defendant also sent nude images to his girlfriend's employer and sister. He was charged with aggravated harassment. The court held that the defendant's "reprehensible" actions were completely legal. The court reasoned that the defendant's speech could not be suppressed because the victim's depiction was not obscene. The court distinguished *Barber* from a prior case in which a New York defendant was prosecuted for criminal harassment (*People v. Kochanowski*, 2000). In *Kochanowski*, the defendant created a website containing provocative photos of his ex-girlfriend along with her contact information. The defendant was convicted of having used a computer to harass the victim. The *Barber* court held that the defendant did not repeatedly contact or encourage others to contact the victim like the defendant in *Kochanowski*. Though the court found that defendant's actions did not meet the statutory definition for aggravated harassment, society does not seem to support such "reprehensible" violations of privacy. Thus, new laws may be created to stop revenge porn distribution.

To avoid injustice and the justice system, some amateur websites have begun requiring video posters to upload expressions of consent (You May Be Surprised, 2014). All people depicted must express consent. Express consent may include a declaration of free will, sobriety, and agreement to the site's user terms. This measure assures viewers that they are not viewing revenge porn. One website with a consent requirement found that more than half of uploaders are women, which is interesting because men are typically involved in pornography and sex crimes at much higher rates than women.

Conclusion

Generally, society has an interest in protecting people from unknowing participation in pornography. Children are well guarded by laws and social policies. Some conscription into production offenses is predicated on guardians' good intentions, but nevertheless triggers systemic responses. Other imposing and violative nonconsensual production may be completely legal. Legislators have recognized numerous harms associated with improper photography. Where existing laws have been insufficient to prosecute defendants, legislators have passed new laws, and are likely to pass additional laws, criminalizing violations facilitated by technological advancements.

References

43A Okla. Stat. § 10-103(A) (2013).

Bartow, A. (2012). Copyright law and pornography. *Oregon Law Review*, *91*(1), 1–55.

Blankstein, A. (2014, January 23). "Revenge porn" site creator, alleged hacker charged with computer crime, ID theft. *NBC News*. Retrieved from http://investigations.nbcnews.com/_news/2014/01/23/22418229-revenge-porn-site-creator-alleged-hacker-charged-with-computer-crime-id-theft?lite

Breast is best. (2003, May 1). *Dallas Observer*. Retrieved from http://www.dallasobserver.com/2003-05-01/news/letters/full/

C'Debaca v. Virginia, 1999 Va. App. LEXIS 72 (1999).

Doe v. Chamberlin, 139 F. Supp. 2d 637 (M.D. Penn. 2001).

Durant v. State, 188 P.3d 192 (2008).

Fla. Stat. § 810.145 (2012).

Flaherty, A. (2013, November 15). "Revenge porn" victims press for new laws. *Wichita Eagle*. Retrieved from http://www.kansas.com/2013/11/15/3119226/revenge-porn-victims-press-for.html#storylink=cpy

Guerrero v. Texas, 2007 Tex. App. LEXIS 3837 (2007).

Guillen, R. (2012). Pushing Alice down the rabbit hole: How Florida's video voyeurism laws protect victims. *University of Florida Journal of Law and Public Policy*, *23*(1), 103–144.

HRS § 28-94 (2013).

In Re Commitment of Charles Steven Chapman, 2013 Tex. App. LEXIS 11404 (2013).

In re Vasquez, 2007 Tex. Crim. App. LEXIS 1324 (Tex. Crim. App., Oct. 3, 2007).

Iowa Code § 709.1 (2013).

Jackie O. nude photos: Paparazzo reveals how he snapped infamous pictures. (2010, March 18). *Huffington Post*. Retrieved from http://www.huffingtonpost.com/2009/11/17/jackie-o-nude-photos-papa_n_360569.html

Kahn, J. D. (2013, September 5). Cops: Woman borrowed landlord's computer … finds naked videos of herself. BreitBart.com. Retrieved from http://www.breitbart.com/InstaBlog/2013/09/05/Cops-Woman-Borrowed-Landlord-s-Computer-Finds-Naked-Videos-of-Herself

Katz v. U.S., 389 U.S. 347 (1967).

Korosec, T. (2003, April 17). 1-hour arrest. *Dallas Observer*. Retrieved from http://www.dallasobserver.com/2003-04-17/news/1-hour-arrest/3/

Lo v. Texas, 393 S.W.3d 290 (2011).

Mass. B.1611, 188th Cong. (2014).

Mass. H.R. 3924, 188th Cong. (2014).

McKissick v. Texas, 209 S.W.3d 205 (2006).

Meola, O. (2014, February 12). Virginia house of delegates votes to outlaw "revenge porn." *Richmond Times-Dispatch*. Retrieved from http://www.huffingtonpost.com/2014/02/12/virginia-revenge-porn_n_4771837.html

Minn. Stat. § 609.746 (2013).

Minnesota v. Morris, 644 N.W.2d 114 (2002).

Murphy, B. (2008, August 16). Photos may have violated topless Austin women's privacy. *Houston Chronicle*. Retrieved from http://www.chron.com/news/houston-texas/article/Photos-may-have-violated-topless-Austin-women-s-1777791.php

Neb. Rev. Stat. § 28-367.01 (2013).

N.J.S.A. § 2C:14-9 (2013).

NY v. Barber, 2014 N.Y. Misc. LEXIS 638 (2014).

Oregon v. Porter, 241 Ore. App. 26 (2010).

People v. Kochanowski, 186 Misc 2d 441 (App Term 2d Dept 2000).

Reporters Committee for Freedom of Press. (2012, August 1). State-by-state guide. Retrieved from http://www.rcfp.org/reporters-recording-guide/state-state-guide

Roeper, R. (2012, September 17). No shock on leaked photos. *Chicago Times*. Retrieved from http://www.suntimes.com/news/roeper/15213108-452/no-shock-on-leaked-photos.html

State v. Byrne, 972 A.2d 633 (2009).

State v. Dennison, 2012 Ohio 1988, 2012 Ohio App. LEXIS 1744 (Ohio Ct. App., Williams County May 4, 2012).

Tarihi, Y. (2009, November 18). Jackie Onassis naked! Italian paparazzi Settimio Garritano took those pictures! HPort. Retrieved from http://www.hport.com.tr/dunya/jackie-onassis-cirilciplak-italyan-paparazzi-settimio-garritano-o-resimleri-anlatti

Tennessee v. Gilliand, 2010 Tenn. Crim. App. LEXIS 501 (2010).

Tex. Penal Code § 21.15 (2013).

Tex. Penal Code Ann. § 33.021(b) (2011).

United States Sentencing Commission. (2012). Victims of child pornography. Retrieved from http://www.ussc.gov/Legislative_and_Public_Affairs/Congressional_Testimony_and_Reports/Sex_Offense_Topics/201212_Federal_Child_Pornography_Offenses/

U.S. v. Dost, 636 F.Supp. 828 (S.D.Cal.1986).

U.S. v. Hunter Moore and Charles "Gary" Evens, Indictment CR13 - 0917(C.D. Cal., 2014). Retrieved from http://cbsla.files.wordpress.com/2014/01/revenge-porn-moore-evens-indictment.pdf

Washington v. Burk, 2013 Wash. App. LEXIS 542 (2013).

Washington v. Larson, 2003 Wash. App. LEXIS 2752 (2003).

You may be surprised by who's filming and uploading amateur porn. (2014, February 12). *Huffington Post*. Retrieved from http://www.huffingtonpost.com/2014/02/12/amateur-porn-filming-uploading-women-bible-belt_n_4776919.html

15 Bestiality

Overview

There are three main kinds of bestiality pornography. The first kind depicts sexual relations with animals or sexual abuse of animals. The second kind depicts animals being tortured and killed. The third kind is synthetic depictions simulating bestiality. Obscenity laws typically focus on offense to the community, thus even when bestiality pornography does not depict harm to animals, it may be banned. Cartoon depictions do not harm animals, yet simulated depictions of bestiality are often held to be obscene. Simulations may be proscribed when depictions are of imaginary animals, not earthly animals (e.g., unicorns). Some critics argue that depictions of animals voluntarily engaging in pleasure are illegal only under morality statutes because of speciesism (Cusack, in press). Speciesism was considered along with racism and sexism in Chapter 3.

Bestiality: Obscenity, Per Se

Laws in certain jurisdictions statutorily criminalize bestiality. Per se exclusion from First Amendment protection seems to be the norm because of widespread taboos against bestiality, but prior restraints on content are not the norm. Bestiality pornography is most commonly criminalized in conjunction with child pornography statutes or corruption of minor statutes. For example, federal law prohibits anyone from providing minors with depictions of bestiality (U.S. 18 § 1466A(i), 2014).

Virginia is one of a few jurisdictions in which possession of more than a couple of images of obscenity, including bestiality, may be unprotected by *Stanley v. Georgia* (1969). In Virginia, possession of a couple of images of bestiality anywhere, including a computer cache storing temporary Internet files, could evidence possession of criminal sexually explicit material for the purpose of child pornography statutes. Aggravated charges may result under some child pornography statutes for depictions of bestiality (Va. Code Ann., 2014). In Virginia, bestiality is not criminalized per se under obscenity statutes, like depictions of excretory functions, which are specifically banned under child pornography and obscenity statutes. Bestiality is not included in statutes proscribing child grooming videos. Though cartoons and animation of children engaged in sex acts are proscribed, the statute only criminalizes depictions of children masturbating or engaging in acts with "another." A plain reading of the statute would not render "another" to be defined to include animals.

Bestiality: Obscenity Under *Miller*

Some depictions of bestiality could ostensibly be legalized in some jurisdictions under a full *Miller* analysis. First, if acts and depictions do not violate the law, then they are nonobscene. The criminal justice system's treatment of sexual encounters between humans and animals may be somewhat uncertain. Moral definitions of bestiality may include all erotic contact between humans and animals, yet numerous behaviors (e.g., tongue kissing) may not be prosecutable under statutes designed to protect animals from cruelty. Thus, definitions of "bestiality" could potentially lead to gray areas in pornography law (*Miller v. California*, 1973). Second, depictions of bestiality may be inoffensive to the community. This is extremely unlikely in the case of actual bestiality pornography, though it is certainly possible in the case of simulated bestiality. However, judges have made independent determinations and courts have abbreviated the three-pronged analysis set forth in *Miller* to find that simulations are obscene (*U.S. v. Whorley*, 2008). Third, bestiality pornography may possess value on a national scale. Prurient material may be offensive, but it will be protected if it possesses nationally recognizable artistic or literary value. Value may be established by expert opinion in court, but paintings, sculpture, literature, and songs depicting bestiality may be subject to public scrutiny, persecution by police, and prosecution prior to receiving full First Amendment protection (Cable, 2011). Protections are not guaranteed merely because depictions are artistic or well-known. Some depictions of classic themes, for example, the raping of Leda by Zeus as a swan, may be prosecuted. Classic works and valuable obscenity were discussed in detail in Chapter 3, and simulated depictions are discussed further in Chapter 16.

Bestiality as Cruelty and Abuse

Bestiality pornography may serve as evidence of animal cruelty (Cusack, in press). Sexual abuse of animals may be evidenced by injury to an animal; however, not all abuse results in physical harm to animals, so bestial pornography may be the only evidence. Some bestial pornography is produced during surveillance. Prurient depictions of sex abuse may not be produced with intent, yet depictions of sex abuse may nevertheless be obscene. Depictions that are produced during surveillance and are promptly surrendered to authorities are not likely to be prosecuted. A farmer in New York noticed that his cows exhibited anxious behavior and had slowed milk production (Moye, 2014). The farmer installed a camera to surveil his cows because he knew that, under extreme stress, animals reduce or discontinue reproductive behaviors. He discovered that two men were raping his cows. The offenders were charged with misdemeanor sexual misconduct. The charge related to the men's sexual behavior, but not to the abuse inflicted on the cows. This may be because the cows did not suffer physical damage. In similar cases, offenders may be charged with cruelty and trespass to property.

In Washington, production of bestiality pornography is criminalized per se under cruelty statutes (Rev. Code Wash., 2013). First-degree animal cruelty includes intentional infliction of substantial pain and negligence resulting in substantial and unjustifiable physical pain and considerable suffering. Washington's laws are quite progressive because first-degree cruelty laws also include knowing engagement in any sexual conduct or contact with an animal. Production offenses and observing any sexual conduct or contact with an animal for commercial or recreational purpose are also first-degree cruelty, which is a Class C felony. In this statute, an "'animal' means every creature, either alive or dead, other than a human being" (Rev. Code Wash., 2013). This includes insects. "'Sexual conduct" means any touching or fondling by a person, either directly or through clothing, of the sex organs or anus of an animal or any transfer or transmission of semen by the person upon any part of the animal, for the purpose of sexual gratification or arousal of the person." The definition of "sexual contact" in Washington's cruelty statute is nearly identical to definitions of "penetration" in sexual assault statutes designed to protect humans (Cusack, 2014).

> "Sexual contact" means any contact, however slight, between the mouth, sex organ, or anus of a person and the sex organ or anus of an animal, or any intrusion, however slight, of any part of the body of the person into the sex organ or anus of an animal, or any intrusion of the sex organ or anus of the person into the mouth of the animal, for the purpose of sexual gratification or arousal of the person. (Rev. Code Wash., 2013)

In addition to retributive punishments, convicted offenders may be banned from owning animals, may be required to pay for and attend counseling, and may be ordered to reimburse any animal care organizations for related expenses.

Crusher Laws

Crushing is a kind of pornographic depiction that is banned by the federal government (Cusack, in press). Crusher films are distinct from other forms of bestial pornography insofar as these films always involve the gruesome demise of a small animal. Federal crusher laws seek to heighten the criminal justice system's response to bestiality and sexual films that depict harm to animals. During Bill Clinton's presidency, crusher laws were first criminalized. Under that legislation, animals were classified as a quasi-protected class (Morrison, 2009). Thus, the legislation was overboard because it could apply to conventional and legal depictions of animals (e.g., hunting films). Thus, subsequent legislation was narrowly tailored to only criminalized animal snuff films. To criminalize speech, the government must demonstrate a compelling interest. The government's compelling interest in criminalizing crusher films is prevention of extreme acts of animal cruelty (Kinsella, 2009; Perdue, 2011).

Pornographers who kill animals may receive sexual pleasure from their acts; however, films do not necessarily depict actors being gratified. Crusher films are designed to appeal to viewers' prurient interests. Though the federal government bans crusher films as obscenity, applicability of state-level cruelty charges may vary. For example, a Florida woman was charged with eight counts of felony animal cruelty for torturing, harassing, mutilating, and murdering rats, chickens, and other animals in crusher films (Blevins & Bickham, 2014). Rats may not be included in definitions of "animal" in all jurisdictions. Thus, some jurisdictions may prosecute actors differently depending on definitions of "animal" and "cruelty" (Cusack, in press).

Videos often feature masked offenders who intentionally disguise the dates and locations of their crimes (Beerworth, 2011). Unlike child pornography forensics that utilize significant budgetary resources, government agencies are often unable to locate animal snuff film participants. The industry garners little money in comparison to child pornography or other forms of obscenity (i.e., around $1 million annually). However, it does glorify cruelty to animals and poses a significant threat to animals and social conscience.

Conclusion

Bestiality is often treated as per se obscene. Statutes, binding precedence, and persuasive sources consistently call for bestiality pornography to be treated as obscenity. Crusher films and bestiality are the least prevalent form of obscenity. Under rare circumstances, sexual depictions of cruelty may be nonobscene. More often than not, they are taboo, offensive, and criminal.

Bestiality pornography and crusher films may result in cruelty charges, in addition to charges for sexual misconduct, production, possession, and transmission. When bestiality is simulated, speciesism may be an underlying rationale for allegedly moral prior restraints. Simulated pornography is discussed in detail in Chapter 16.

References

Beerworth, A. A. (2011). *United States v. Stevens*: A proposal for criminalizing crush videos under current free speech doctrine. *Vermont Law Review, 35*, 901–924.

Blevins, T., & Bickham, T. (2014, April 5). Sara Zamora charged with role in animal torture sex pornography fetish video. Local 10. Retrieved from http://www.local10.com/news/miami-woman-charged-animal-torture-sex-porn-fetish-video/25340632

Cable, S. (2011, August 5). The explicit art that shows bestiality with a goat just yards from the Ritz. *Nigeria Daily News*. Retrieved from http://www.nigeriadailynews.com/uk/25143-the-explicit-art-that-shows-bestiality-with-a-goat-just-yards-from-the-ritz.html#sthash.oHMgkLfy.dpuf

Cusack, C. M. (2014). 50 state survey of prosecutors' willingness to prosecute nonconsensual insemination. *Family and Intimate Partner Violence Quarterly*, 6(3), 7–32.

Cusack, C. M. (2015). *Animals in the criminal justice system* (in press). Piscataway Township, NJ: Transaction Publishers.

Kinsella, E. L. (2009). A crushing blow: *United States v. Stevens* and the freedom to profit from animal cruelty. *UC Davis Law Review, 43*, 347–384.

Miller v. California, 413 U.S. 15 (1973).

Morrison, P. (2009, April 30). Does the First Amendment protect dog snuff films? *Huffington Post*. Retrieved from http://www.huffingtonpost.com/patt-morrison/does-the-first-amendment b 193351.html

Moye, D. (2014, February 23). Reid Fontaine, Michael Jones accused of sexually abusing cows. *The Huffington Post*. Retrieved from http://www.huffingtonpost.com/2014/02/23/reid-fontaine-michael-jon_n_4840560.html

Perdue, A. L. (2011). When bad things happen to good laws: The rise, fall, and future of section 48. *Virginia Journal of Social Policy and the Law, 18*, 469.

Rev. Code Wash. (ARCW) § 16.52.205 (2013).

Stanley v. Georgia, 394 U.S. 557 (1969).

U.S. 18 § 1466A(i) (2014).

U.S. v. Whorley, 550 F.3d 326, 330 (C.A. 4 12/18/08).

Va. Code Ann. §§ 18.2-372-374 (2014).

Simulations 16

Overview

This chapter discusses simulated pornography. One distinguishing feature of pornographic simulations is that they may depict hard-core themes, but they usually do not depict actual people or animals being harmed. Simulations may include cartoon obscenity, Photoshopped depictions, and fake snuff films.

Simulated Child Pornography

Child pornographers have cultivated a variety of images to simulate child pornography (Figure 16.1). Simulations are produced for various reasons. Some pornographers intend to avoid prosecution by simulating child pornography. Others have simulated depictions of specific children when no authentic depictions are available. In some cases, simulations have been produced with intent to avoid harming actual children. Simulated depictions include synthetic computer images, collages of actual nonobscene and obscene images, and Photoshopped depictions. The criminal justice system's response to these images has been definitive in some cases but equivocal in other cases.

Detailed simulations may look eerily similar to actual children. In some cases, the government has used synthetic child pornography to apprehend pedophiles during solicitation stings. Presently, simulated child pornography is legal under child pornography statutes, but it is not legal if pornographers hold a subjective and objective belief that the pornography is of actual children. The U.S. Supreme Court held in *U.S. v. Williams* (2008) that Congress designed child pornography statutes to protect actual children. Applying the Harm Principle to simulated child pornography, the Court held that because actual children are not victims of production offenses and are not humiliated by circulation of their images, child pornography statutes cannot reach synthesized pornography depicting simulated children.

Simulated pornography may fuel or participate in demand for actual child pornography. However, it may also substitute for it in some cases. An expert neuroscientist in the Netherlands, Dr. Dick Swaab, believes that electronic pornographic comic strips may help pedophiles to manage their disorder (April, 2012). Very little literature has discussed studies on simulated

Figure 16.1 Synthetic child.

pornography and pedophilia. Simulated depictions seem to account for a very small percentage of child pornography available on the web (*U.S. v. Williams*, 2008). The effect of simulations on pornographers, pedophiles, and the child pornography market is virtually unknown. A Dutch team advocating for children's rights generated a virtual 10-year-old Filipino child named Sweetie to gather intelligence about online solicitation crimes (The Ten-Year-Old Girl Called 'Sweetie,' 2013). In fewer than 100 days, they collected information from 20,000 predatory solicitors in 71 countries, including 254 solicitors from the United States. Online offenders may not know the difference between simulated and actual child pornography, yet they may not care whether children are actual or simulated.

An evidentiary problem may arise. Many defendants have argued, and courts have held, that prosecutors must prove that victims depicted in pornography are actual children. The government may only be required to prove that children are actual, and not simulations, when defendants claim that depictions are simulated. If prosecutors are unable to identify an actual child victim, then prosecutors may use experts to meet their burden. However, other courts have permitted the inference, though this may not be sound law. In *Rhode Island v. Coriander* (2010), the court held that the state has the burden of proving beyond a reasonable doubt that alleged child pornography involves actual children (R.I. Gen. Laws § 11-9-1.3, 2010). Defendants are not required to prove that child pornography was simulated. If a defendant does not present evidence demonstrating how the depiction could be simulated, then prosecutors need not provide much evidence to meet their burden of proof. However, this does not shift the burden of proof to the defendant.

Simulated child pornography may be prosecutable under obscenity statutes. Under *Miller* (*Miller v. California*, 1973), simulated child pornography likely possesses *de minimis* artistic value. Simulations may be prurient and offensive to an average member of the community. Prosecution for obscene simulations often occurs in conjunction with prosecution of actual child pornography. Courts may find that simulated material depicting adults is protected but simulations depicting children are obscene (*People v. Cochran*, 2002). Ages of actual and simulated victims may be inferred in some instances (i.e., depictions appear to be infants). The fact finder has been permitted to make inferences about ages depicted. In many instances, fact finders will attempt to infer subjects' ages by judging subjects' body types and facial features (*Rhode Island v. Coriander*, 2010). But, stereotypes about normal bodies may unfairly prejudice juries. The Court held in *New York v. Ferber* (1982) that images of young-looking adults did not constitute child pornography even if promoters labeled actors as "teens." This holding referred to adult actors whose ages were known. When simulated ages are unknown, predominance of "normal" standards about the appearance of sexual maturity may permit courts to find that small bodies, small genitals, small breasts, large round eyes, smooth skin, and other features indicate age or sexual immaturity (Cusack, 2011). The effect of norms on interpretation of obscenity was discussed in Chapter 3. A typical pornography actor is a white female from California or Florida who weighs 117 pounds at 5′5″ (The Average Female Porn Star, 2013). She is less physically robust than the average American woman, not only because she weighs less but because her 34B bust size is smaller than average. Nevertheless, many people seem to believe that female pornography stars would have an average cup size of DD, even though more female actors are cup sizes C and D than DD. The average female pornography actor is between the ages of 22 and 25. The shortest pornography stars are around 3'7" for females and 4'3" for males.

In one case, the court found explicit depictions of Power Puff Girls to be obscene (*U.S. v. Whorley*, 2008). Power Puff Girls are cartoons depicted to be like little girls, except that they are not depicted to be human. They are depicted to be laboratory-created superhumans. The girls possess sophisticated fighting skills, unlike vulnerable children. Without applying each prong of *Miller*, the court held that the images, which resembled children, were similar enough to simulated drawings of children to make the drawings obscene. This case is part of a trend to prosecute graphic cartoons depicting children. Though *Stanley* articulated a right to possess obscenity, possessing a large number of cartoons may be evidence of receipt or attempt to distribute, which adds to charges for possessing drawings (*U.S. v. Kutzner*, 2010; *Stanley v. Georgia*, 1969).

Morphed images of children use actual children's photos. Photos are pasted onto advertisements, other photos, computer graphics, cartoons, or images not belonging to the original photos (*U.S. v. Hotaling*, 2011). Depictions may involve a child's face or body. Courts have tended to hold that when an actual, identifiable child's face is depicted in a sexually explicit context, the depiction harms that child, like child pornography. Some courts have held that child pornography results when a child's face is superimposed into adult pornography because people may believe that the child was subjected to those experiences. Other courts have held that the humiliation and harm occur when the child's image is used. Still, at least one court has held that if children are not pornographized during production, then the images do not constitute child pornography. Depending on the content depicted and use of actual children's images, morphed images may be criminalized under child pornography statutes, but if they are not, then they may still qualify as obscenity.

Under federal law, morphing the face of an identifiable child to appear as if the child engaged in sexually explicit conduct is punishable by up to 15 years in prison (United States Sentencing Commission, 2012). Morphed images represent an exception to typical child pornography. The relationship between morphed images and actual pornography may be more immediately dangerous than the relationship between cartoon pornography and child pornography. In one case, a man was arrested for possessing approximately 15,000 child pornography photos and 200 child pornography videos (Little, 2014). U.S. authorities became involved after a foreign agency flagged his posts on a foreign bulletin board. The offender posted more than 1,000 pictures of two specific young female children. He requested for community members to morph those photos into child pornography, and he had received altered photos in exchange for authentic child pornography. Authorities were afraid that predators would attempt to commit production offenses with the two children. Thus, in addition to the harm suffered by children whose photos are in circulation, more serious problems could result from morphed images.

Simulated Bestiality

On several occasions, courts have held that cartoons depicting bestiality are obscene (*People v. Kirkpatrick*, 1970). Synthetic bestiality, compilations, collages, and cartoons may not possess sufficient scientific, political, and artistic value to decriminalize material under *Miller*. One reason that synthetic bestiality may seem so offensive is that defendants are typically arrested and tried for transmission of synthetic bestiality in conjunction with other obscene material, including sexually explicit cartoons depicting child sex, sadomasochism, sodomy, rape, mutilation, ejaculation, profanity, and other graphic themes. In that context, or when works contain several of those themes, explicit bestiality cartoons may seem more offensive, especially when taken as a whole (*Miller v. California*, 1973).

Computer-generated or hand-drawn cartoons may not intrinsically possess artistic value under *Miller* (*U.S. v. Handley*, 2008). In *Handley*, customs agents intercepted seven manga comic books ordered online from Japan. The federal government prosecuted the defendant for dealing in obscenity depicting "graphic bestiality, including sexual intercourse, between human beings and animals, such as pigs, monkeys, and others." The court held that the government was not required to provide expert testimony about *de minimis* artistic value because the judge was able to decide that bestiality manga was obscene (*Paris Adult Theatre I* v. *Slaton*, 1973; *Pinkus v. U.S.*, 1978; *U.S. v. Handley*, 2008). The judge decided that the material met all three prongs of the *Miller* test. However, in that case, the court seemed to conflate community standards evaluated in the first two prongs of *Miller* with national standards evaluated in the last prong. The defendant argued that obscene manga cartoons are legal and culturally celebrated in Japan. Manga production requires artistic skill and is produced by professional artists. The court suggested that irrespective of community standards in Japan, an average member of the community in the Southern District of Iowa would find that the images meet the *Miller* test. Because the judge considered only Iowans' viewpoint, it is questionable whether the *Miller* test was applied properly to consider national standards.

Sexually explicit cartoons depicting people dressed in animal costumes (e.g., Barney and Friends at alt.sex.bestiality.barney) may qualify as obscenity (Cusack, in press; Friedman, 1996; Virtual Sex, 1995). Just as one court held that depictions of superhuman Power Puff Girls are obscene, explicit cartoons depicting Barney the dinosaur may be obscene even if prurient cartoons depict adults wearing costumes. Any sexually explicit cartoons, photos, or films of people dressed as animals, whether living or extinct, may qualify as obscenity. Furries, a sexual fetish in which people dress as animals and mascots, is legal; however, depicting it explicitly may qualify as obscenity depending on community standards. One well-known appellate judge presiding over a controversial obscenity trial was subject to a disciplinary hearing after the public discovered on his personal website that he distributed sexual, albeit inexplicit, images of a woman painted as a cow (Cusack, 2011; 2012). The image was non-obscene, but the fiasco suggests that the public and the justice system may be sensitive to pornographic depictions in which humans portray animals.

Simulated Violence

Snuff films allegedly use cinematographic tricks to illegally depict murder for sexual pleasure. Critics of conservative pornography legislation have compared criminal snuff films to lawful commercial films. Protected films may first graphically depict sex and then graphically depict murder. Murder is not explicitly eroticized. Obscene depictions of rape, for example, those produced by Robert and Janet Zicari, and mutilation have been prosecuted because they appeal to prurient interests. It has been argued that rated-R films may depict sex, rape, and murder in a manner that may arouse viewers. Yet, pornographic films are singled out because sex scenes are more explicit, not because of the violence depicted. The same problem arises in other fetishistic films, like stump porn. If actually performed, stump porn, in which an appendage is removed from a victim, would violate health codes and likely result in aggravated battery or attempted murder charges (Larsen & Haller, 2002). Snuff, rape, and mutilation films are a paradoxical affront to conventional understandings of sexuality. Some members of society may be entertained by sexually violent depictions, but traditional attitudes dominate interpretations of the Constitution and impede challenges to restraints against depictions of simulated sexual violence.

U.S. v. Extreme Associates considered the legality of extremely violent depictions (Cusack, 2013; *U.S. v. Extreme Associates, Inc.*, 2005). Pornography film producer Robert Zicari produced several other hard-core films, including *Forced Entry* featuring his wife Janet Zicari as Lizzie Borden. The federal government in Pennsylvania prosecuted him for films depicting rape, gang rape, excrement, sacrilege, murder, and other hard-core themes. Using strict scrutiny, a federal district court handed down a landmark decision protecting the material. The judge cited numerous legal theories and precedents, including excessive burdens on speech, the right to privacy, and weak state power to regulate morality. The federal district court dismissed the charges. However, the appellate court disagreed that the government could not proscribe the material and overturned the district court by reinstating the charges. Zicari, who was also charged, was not convicted at trial but pleaded to the charges and served time in federal prison.

Robert Zicari, also known as Rob Black, is the son of a pornographer who owned an adult film store (Abowitz, 2013). His father was allegedly hassled by authorities approximately 160 times for selling adult toys; his mother was also arrested at his father's store for selling vibrators. This may be one reason why Zicari was willing to knowingly push the envelope with his films. He compares boundary-breaking in pornography that simulates violence to boundary-breaking in interracial, transsexual, and gay pornography. He claims that others in the industry have produced authentically violent films that are indefensible. Zicari differentiates his work from films that inflict violence on actors.

> They pushed it to a point where you can't defend it. Because what I did was a fantasy. I was able to preach it is a movie. It is a guy in a costume. Now you have companies that do it in the guise of BDSM [bondage sadomasochism].

> You put a girl on a dog chain and chain her to a wall and then keep her there for two days and take a cattle prod and electrocute her and do all this under the guise of a documentary. You are taking the element of the movie out. Now, you are doing torture. You are taking the fantasy out. Now all of the sudden it's, "Let's really do this under the guise of BDSM." (Abowitz, 2013)

The line between actual violence and simulated violence is not clear in some films. Zicari's case and other cases suggest that such distinctions are irrelevant in obscenity prosecutions. In *People v. Samuels* (1967), a defendant was charged with conspiracy to produce and distribute obscenity because he spliced film rolls containing images of bondage, simple and aggravated assault, and sodomy. At trial, the defendant testified that he had self-diagnosed his urges as sadomasochistic. He alleged that he began depicting homosexual sadomasochism to manage his violent desires in a consensual, "harmless" environment. The defendant claimed that aggravated assault was not committed because whipping and markings were simulated. The defendant pleaded not guilty to the charges. Only his conviction for aggravated assault was upheld on appeal. Depictions served as evidence of harm, which satisfies an analysis under the Harm Principle, discussed in Chapter 1. However, obscenity analyses rely on *Miller v. California* (1973), not the Harm Principle.

"Scat" and "Piss" Films

Pornographic depictions of feces and urine will likely be treated as obscenity under federal and state law. One section of the federal code defines obscenity specifically to include excrement. This definition applies to material shown to children, but not to material seen by adults (Prosecutorial Remedies and Other Tools to End the Exploitation of Children Today Act of 2003 [PROTECT Act] §§2252B, 2003). Many state laws articulate similar proscriptions against pornographic depictions of excretory functions (Va. Code Ann. § 18.2-372, 2008; Wyo. Stat. Ann. § 6-4-301(a)(iii), 2005). A few courts have found that certain material depicting excrement, when taken as a whole, is artistic and nonobscene; courts are more likely to find depictions of excrement to be nonobscene when that material is literary and only involves words. This was discussed in more detail in Chapter 3.

Pornographers have attempted to defend scat and piss works from prosecution under *Miller* (*Miller v. California*, 1973). They have argued that their work did not violate obscenity statutes because they used props (e.g., water hoses or chocolate ice cream) rather than actual excrement. However, obscenity laws clearly include depictions that are not limited to memorializations of sexual activity involving actual feces and urine. Unprotected depictions include drawings, literature, and other works that do not utilize actual excrement.

Another argument is that pornographers who depict excrement create shock art, not pornography. For example, Marco Fiorito is a Brazilian pornography film director. Fiorito simulated coprophagia (i.e., consumption of feces) in the well-known film reel "2 Girls 1 Cup." He became the subject of a federal forfeiture case, and he became involved in the federal indictment of his U.S. business agent, Daniel Croce. Fiorito was never prosecuted. The disposition of this case was discussed in greater detail in Chapter 4. "2 Girls 1 Cup" was a free pornographic film reel available online to advertise a fetish movie *Hungry Bitches* (MFX Video, 2007). In *Hungry Bitches*, actors allegedly consumed revolting bodily substances (e.g., vomit and feces). The trailer "2 Girls 1 Cups" went viral on the Internet (Cusack, 2012). In a statement to the U.S. government, Fiorito stated that he is a fetishist. His statement may be taken to mean that fetishistic films like "2 Girls 1 Cup" are not criminal within the meaning of *Miller* because they are shocking not prurient or offensive. His film may have been designed as a form of shock art, but not to arouse prurient interests. Arguably, the film attempts to arouse shameful or morbid interests in sexuality because the actors are nude, they share an open-mouth kiss, and a third nude person defecates into the cup. On one hand, the film does not seem to violate community standards under the *Miller* test because numerous people in various communities voluntarily watched the film for humor and revolt and then recorded "reaction videos" on Youtube.com. On another hand, the reaction videos may illustrate that the film reel offended average members of their communities. Shortly after Croce's prosecution and forfeiture of Fiorito's business assets, pornography film director Ira Isaacs attempted to use the shock art defense. He distributed *Mako's First Time Scat*, *Hollywood Scat Amateurs No. 7*, and *BAE 20/Avantgarde Extreme* (USA vs. Ira Isaacs Video Images, n.d.). He was also found guilty of distributing obscenity.

In his statement, Fiorito claimed that his films were lawful in his native country, Brazil. On many occasions, the court has rejected expansion of *Miller* to consider online community standards or international values. In *U.S. v. Thomas* (1996), a U.S. Postal Inspection Service agent had conducted an undercover sting of a pornography distributor. The agent in Tennessee received sexually explicit films depicting bestiality, sodomy, child sex acts, sadomasochism, incest, and urination. The defendant in *Thomas* argued that online pornography transmission requires the court to consider online communities not geographic communities, but that argument was rejected because online pornography dealers know or should know in which jurisdictions they are transmitting pornography. Similarly, international pornographers cannot substitute local standards in the United States for foreign standards simply because works are produced outside the United States. However, reaction videos produced throughout the country attest to the widespread acceptance of Fiorito's film reel by members of different communities.

Simulated Depictions Possessed by Minors

Transmitting nude drawings or other simulated depictions to children is not per se illegal. Sex educators may lawfully give to children depictions of genitals for educational and scientific purposes. Educational materials depicting nudity or sex may be alleged to be pornographic. For some adolescents, pornography is a form of sex education (Ekstrand, Tydén, Darj, & Larsson, 2007; Flood, 2009). Ekstrand et al. (2007) found that teens believe sex education provided by schools is more legitimate than education achieved by viewing pornography (Ekstrand et al., 2007). When minors possess simulated nude images of adults, the means by which they acquired the depictions or the intentions with which the depictions were produced could factor into determinations of whether a crime has been committed under the PROTECT Act. Transmitting scientific drawings to children as pornography may be illegal if the depictions are corruptive or obscene. Excessively graphic sex education websites depicting intercourse or aroused genitals may be illegal under the PROTECT Act. Explicit figures or models may also violate the PROTECT Act.

The *Miller* test is built into the PROTECT Act. Material that is legal for adults may be obscene for children because erotic material may corrupt youth (Salmon & Diamond, 2012). Under *Miller*, depictions are nonobscene if they possess serious scientific (Figure 16.2) or artistic value. However, there is no possible finding of "educational value" under *Miller*. Educational depictions

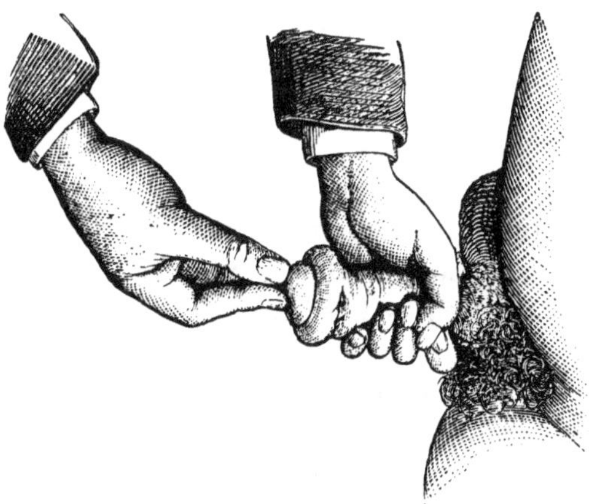

Figure 16.2 Explicit drawing of paraphimosis reduction.

would need to possess serious scientific value, but serious scientific value does not necessarily equate with serious educational value. Simulations graphically depicting minors engaging in sexual conduct are likely unprotected. Any educational, artistic, or scientific value is likely to be *de minimis*, which is insufficient. Simulated depictions that are not specified to be of adults may appear to be depictions of minors. This may make them illegal depictions under the PROTECT Act and *Miller*, but not under child pornography statutes.

To an extent, teachers are responsible, as *loco parentis*, to protect children's well-being (Nunziato, 2007). Parents have a broad and fundamental right to raise their children (*Pierce v. Society of the Sisters*, 1925). Laws that prohibit children from accessing pornography do not infringe on parental rights or teachers' roles. In *Ginsberg v. New York* (1968), the U.S. Supreme Court separated adults' freedom of speech from minors' access to pornography. The state's interest in keeping children from harm is a compelling interest that may impinge parents' rights in the least restrictive way to protect children. By limiting minors' access to pornography, they assist parents and teachers in protecting children (Saunders, 2007). However, depictions of simple nudity given by parents to children are not likely to be corruptive because they are nonobscene, and some jurisdictions permit parents to give pornography to minors.

The government may or may not have the power to impinge on minors' speech rights to access material possessing serious literary, scientific, political, or artistic value. Purveyors of erotic material and educators must be able to gauge age-appropriate content before it is distributed to minors. This legal requirement attests to the importance of understanding social norms, which are embedded into the law. Individuals who produce and transmit materials with sexual themes must recognize norms. Social norms must not be violated at the local level under *Miller*. Norms were discussed in Chapter 1.

Conclusion

Under obscenity statutes, simulations are not legally distinguishable from actual depictions. In most legal contexts, explicit content is prosecuted, and the medium in which content is depicted is irrelevant. Thus, drawings, photographs, and films would receive similar treatment. Simulations are distinguishable from actual depictions under child pornography statutes. Child pornography laws can only be used to prosecute sexually explicit or harmful depictions of actual children. However, obscenity laws may be used to prosecute simulated depictions of children. In a few jurisdictions, specific adults may be permitted to transmit adult material to children. However, adults are proscribed from (1) transmitting obscenity in every jurisdiction, (2) using simulated depictions to solicit children, and (3) transmitting simulations if they believe that they are actual depictions of children.

References

Abowitz, R. (2013, April 21). Rob Black, porn's dirty whistlebower, spills trade secrets. *The Daily Beast.* Retrieved from http://www.thedailybeast.com/articles/2013/04/21/rob-black-porn-s-dirty-whistlebower-spills-trade-secrets.html

April, K. (2012). Cartoons aren't real people, too: Does the regulation of virtual child pornography violate the First Amendment and criminalize subversive thought? *Cardozo Journal of Law and Gender, 19*, 241–271.

Cusack, C. M. (2011). Busting patriarchal booby traps: Why feminists fear minor distinctions in child porn cases, an analysis of social deviance with in gender, family, or the home (etudes 4), *Southern University Law Review, 39*, 43–70.

Cusack, C. M. (2012). Two films, one law. *Entertainment, Art, and Sports Law Journal, 23*(3), 62.

Cusack, C. M. (2013). Obscene squirting: If the government thinks it's urine, then they've got another thing coming. *Texas Journal of Women and the Law, 22*, 45–69.

Cusack, C. M. (in press). *Animals in the criminal justice system.* Piscataway Township, NJ: Transaction Publishers.

Ekstrand, M., Tydén, T., Darj, E., & Larsson, M. (2007). Preventing pregnancy: A girls' issue. Seventeen-year-old Swedish boys' perceptions on abortion, reproduction and use of contraception. *The European Journal of Contraception and Reproductive Health Care, 12*(2), 111–118.

Flood, M. (2009). The harms of pornography exposure among children and young people. *Child Abuse Review, 18*(6), 384–400.

Friedman, M. L. (1996). Keeping sex safe on the information superhighway: Computer pornography and the First Amendment. *New York Law School Law Review, 40*, 1025.

Ginsberg v. New York, 390 U.S. 629 (1968).

Hungry Bitches (MFX Video 2007).

Larsen, R., & Haller, B. A. (2002). The case of "Freaks": Public reception of real disability. *Journal of Popular Film and Television, 29*(4), 164.

Little, B. (2014, January 17). Child porn charges net Voorhees man 7 years in state prison. *Gloucester Township Patch.* Retrieved from http://gloucestertownship.patch.com/groups/police-and-fire/p/child-porn-charges-net-voorhees-man-7-years-in-state-prison

Miller v. California, 413 U.S. 15 (1973).

New York v. Ferber, 458 U.S. 747 (1982).

Nunziato, D. C. (2007). Technology and pornography. *Brigham Young University Law Review, 2007*(6), 1535–1584.

Paris Adult Theatre I v. Slaton, 413 U.S. 49, 56 n. 6 (1973).

Pinkus v. U.S., 436 U.S. 293 (1978).

People v. Cochran, 28 Cal 4th 396 (2002).

People v. Kirkpatrick, 316 N.Y.S.2d 37 (Crim. Ct. 1970).

People v. Samuels, 250 Cal. App. 2d 501 (1967).

Pierce, Governor of Oregon, et al. v. Society of the Sisters of the Holy Names of Jesus and Mary, 268 U.S. 510 (1925).

Prosecutorial Remedies and Other Tools to End the Exploitation of Children Today Act of 2003 (PROTECT Act) §§2252B (2003).

Rhode Island v. Coriander, 2010 R.I. Super. LEXIS 79; N2-2008-0278A (R.I. 2010).

R.I. Gen. Laws § 11-9-1.3 (2010).

Salmon, C., & Diamond, A. (2012). Evolutionary perspectives on the content analysis of heterosexual and homosexual pornography. *Journal of Social, Evolutionary, and Cultural Psychology*, *6*(2), 193–202.

Saunders, K. W. (2007). www.Sam's_Stationery_and_Luncheonette.com: Bringing Ginsberg v. New York into the Internet Age. *Brigham Young University Law Review*, *2007*(6), 1661–1690.

Stanley v. Georgia, 394 U.S. 557 (1969).

The average female porn star? A California-born brunette with a size 34B bra named Nikki. (2013, February 19). *Daily Mail Online UK*. Retrieved from http://www.dailymail.co.uk/femail/article-2280750/The-average-female-porn-star-A-California-born-brunette-size-34B-bra-named-Nikki.html

The ten-year-old girl called "Sweetie" who has caught more than a thousand sexual predators including 110 Britons. (2013, November 4). *Daily Mail Online UK*. Retrieved from http://www.dailymail.co.uk/news/article-2487397/Terre-des-Hommes-creates-CGI-girl-called-Sweetie-entice-child-porn-predators.html#ixzz2rXQa6WKk

United States Sentencing Commission. (2012). Victims of child pornography. Retrieved from http://www.ussc.gov/Legislative_and_Public_Affairs/Congressional_Testimony_and_Reports/Sex_Offense_Topics/201212_Federal_Child_Pornography_Offenses/

U.S. v. Extreme Associates, Inc., 2005 WL 121749 (W.D.Pa. Jan 20, 2005) (NO. CRIM.03-0203); 431 F.3d 150 (3d Cir. 2005).

U.S. v. Handley, 564 F.Supp.2d 996, 999 (S.D. Iowa, 2008).

U.S. v. Hotaling, 634 F.3d 730 (2011).

U.S. v. Kutzner, Rule 11 Plea Agreement (D. Idaho, 2010). Retrieved from http://reason.com/assets/db/12876937541067.pdf

U.S. v. Thomas, 74 F.3d 701 (1996).

U.S. v. Whorley, 550 F.3d 326, 330 (C.A. 4 12/18/08).

U.S. v. Williams, 553 U.S. 285 (2008).

USA vs. Ira Isaacs Video Images: Criminally obscene or art? (n.d.). Celebrity Justice. Retrieved January 31, 2012, from http://www.uslaw.com/pop/ira_isaacs_scat_videos/

Va. Code Ann. § 18.2-372 (2008).

Virtual sex. (1995, February 9). *The Harvard Crimson*. Retrieved from http://www.thecrimson.com/article/1995/2/9/virtual-sex-pthe-internet-is-a/?print=1#

Wyo. Stat. Ann. § 6-4-301(a)(iii) (2005).

Fantasies and Free Speech

17

Overview

Attempted criminalization or prosecution of impure thoughts is antithetical to a free society. However, communication of certain impure thoughts may amount to conspiracy when fantasies are described as plans. This is an unsettled area of law, because regulation of pornographic fantasies online seems to challenge long-standing principles of constitutional law and criminal law.

Internet and Fantasies

The First Amendment protects freedom of thought and freedom to engage in the most prurient, offensive, and depraved fantasies (*Stanley v. Georgia*, 1969; *Wooley v. Maynard*, 1977). The government has no right to protect adults' minds from the effect of obscenity. In *Stanley v. Georgia* (1969), the government argued the traditional and persistent argument that viewing obscenity may lead to sexual deviance, antisocial conduct, and sexual violence. The Court held that viewing obscenity in private and indulging in thoughts or ideas, no matter how aberrant, is a right enjoyed by free people in the United States. Education and punishment are means at the government's disposal for controlling crime. Government-sponsored thought control to suppress emotional and intellectual needs is an inappropriate method for deterring deviant behavior. The Court in *Stanley* held that the government would not achieve its aim of controlling crime or antisocial behavior by banning fantasies. Proscribing possession of obscenity to control sex crimes would be like controlling books about vegetables because people could use them to produce moonshine.

The Court held that the "state has no business telling a man, sitting alone in his own house, what books he may read or what films he may watch. Our whole constitutional heritage rebels at the thought of giving government the power to control men's minds" (*Stanley v. Georgia*, 1969). This premise has been adopted by some courts when considering whether literary characters' fantasies are obscene (*Commonwealth v. Gordon et al.*, 1949). However, other courts have challenged the idea that obscenity may be distributed to explain and promote a fictional character's fantasies when an actual person's fantasies may not be written and distributed if they are obscene. Sometimes, explicit sexual fantasies are essential to characters' development. This was discussed in Chapter 3. The *Miller* test is used to determine whether works depicting literary character's sexual fantasies possess serious literary value and may be distributed (*Miller v. California*, 1973). Nevertheless, such debates reflect cultural and jurisprudential perception that some humans, thus some literary characters, engage in explicitly sexual fantasies.

Protection of fantasies extends to a person's home, but may not extend over the Internet. "Whatever the power of the state to control public dissemination of ideas inimical to the public morality, it cannot constitutionally premise legislation on the desirability of controlling a person's private thoughts" (*Stanley v. Georgia*, 1969). Possessing pornographic objects, files, and literature in one's home is legal. Some means for possessing pornography that involve the public (e.g., buying, downloading, or trading) are not legal. Articulating fantasies on the Internet may not be illegal unless the words used amount to obscenity. Transmitting obscene fantasies over the Internet (e.g., chatting with others) extends beyond the home.

Criminal allegations resulting from posting sexual fantasies online are not uncommon. Online child pornography offenders may be preoccupied with mental fantasies (Elliott, Beech, & Mandeville-Norden, 2013). Child sex offenders who use pornography are more prone than hands-on offenders to endorse or read deeply emotional fiction stories that emphasize character-based narratives. Offenders' endorsement of fantasy may correlate with use of child pornography because actual victims appear to be like fictional characters. One reason may be that many child pornography depictions are designed to communicate fantasies (e.g., children's delight).

The government cannot solely punish fantasies about children. For example, some nonobscene sexual stories about children may be legal. However, the government may attempt to demonstrate criminal intent to abuse children. Criminal intent is wholly distinguishable from fantasy and thought (*Ex parte Nyabwa*, 2012). Fantasy is not a crime, but communicating obscene fantasies and soliciting minors is criminal. Solicitation offenses often involve grooming and describing sexually explicit conduct to a minor in graphic detail to create sexual arousal. Children who solicit pornography from anyone or who solicit johns by graphically depicting themselves may also fall within statutes that suppress speech acts and actions (*U.S. v. Williams*, 2007). Offenders may claim that allegedly solicitous communications were legal because communications (1) were fantasies, and (2) fantasies were inexplicit. They may claim that titillating talk is fantasy, not obscenity. Their arguments may fail if offenders possessed the requisite mental state.

Conversations about sadomasochistic sex may not be lawful. Online conversations about violence, whether self-inflicted or inflicted on others, need not explicitly depict sex acts as long as they explicitly depict violence and appeal to prurient interests in violation of applicable statutes and average sensitivities in the community. The *Miller* test is not limited to depictions that describe genitals, penetration, ejaculation, or other forms of sexual contact. Graphic descriptions of sadomasochistic abuse may meet *Miller*'s prongs (Or. Rev. Stat. § 167.062, 2009). Fantasies about abuse cannot be proscribed, but depictions of sexual violence are not immunized because graphic aspects are fetishistic rather than traditionally sexual.

Conspiracy

Recent cases have demonstrated that the government is interested in prosecuting violent fantasies as conspiracies. Conspiracy is an agreement between two or more people to commit a crime at some point in the future. Conspiracies are inchoate crimes that do not require attempts to complete crimes, but do require that at least one overt step be taken in furtherance of a crime. Because the government cannot prosecute thoughts, proving that a step has occurred is essential to successful prosecution of conspiracy. Government agents enter Internet chat rooms and bulletin boards to gather evidence that sexual discussions are part of conspiracies to commit violent acts.

In 1990, a defendant was tried for conspiring to kidnap and conspiring to commit sexual exploitation of a child (*U.S. v. Depew*, 1990). Court records describe the facts of the case as "a tale of unspeakable evil and tragedy narrowly averted" (*U.S. v. Depew*, 1990). Two undercover law enforcement agents conspired with the defendant to kidnap, sexually abuse, and murder a boy; film the abuse; and sell the pornography. The parties met online through a bulletin board for sexual deviants that served to connect users. Agents posed as homosexual pedophiles and met in person with the defendant. They recorded their meeting with him and recorded phone conversations detailing their conspiracy. The parties discussed that the defendant could kidnap a boy riding a skateboard. The boy could be placed into a waiting van. The defendant wanted to tie, hang, strangulate, suffocate using a bag, drown, and beat the boy. He desired to have sex with the boy while he was bound, struggling, and suffocating. The defendant offered to castrate the child and suffocate the boy with his severed testicles if the co-conspirators preferred that the boy bled to death. The defendant considered using ether to subdue the boy and using muriatic acid on the boy's corpse to disfigure and dispose of it. He also considered using paint remover to dissolve evidence and dumping the corpse in a swamp. During conversations with agents, the defendant discussed past attempts to molest and murder other male teens. In this crime, the defendant wanted to abuse a young teen because he theorized that teen boys can sustain physical abuse better than younger boys. The defendant was uncertain about his plans and discussed many fantasies. He believed that his discussions failed to constitute conduct. He argued that he did not intend to commit crimes. However, the jury believed that he wanted to and intended to torture, sexually abuse, and murder the boy.

Operation Sunflower, discussed in Chapter 9, spawned major online investigation efforts to aid child targets of sexual exploitation. That case began with conversations posted to an online bulletin board. The offender, a teen boy, sought advice about how to sexually exploit a young child. International law enforcement agents believed that those conversations indicated the offender's intent to engage in conduct. Because conspiracy is completed when any overt step is taken in furtherance of the crime, fantasies may evidence conspiracy when the first meeting is held to discuss the crime or when advice is first sought about how to complete the crime.

Conclusion

Increased candor online, increased predators online, and increased fervor within the criminal justice system may create new intersections between criminal law and constitutional law. Legislatures could redraft laws to clarify and define differences between fantasies and conspiracies. Greater education among Internet users may be necessary. Nevertheless, steps taken in furtherance of crime will inevitably escalate fantasies to conspiracies.

References

Commonwealth v. Gordon et al., 66 Pa. D. & C. 101 (1949).

Elliott, I. A., Beech, A. R., & Mandeville-Norden, R. (2013). The psychological profiles of Internet, contact, and mixed Internet/contact sex offenders. *Sex Abuse*, *25*(1), 3–20.

Ex parte Nyabwa, 366 S.W.3d 710 (Tex. Crim. App. 2012).

Miller v. California, 413 U.S. 15 (1973).

Or. Rev. Stat. § 167.062 (2009).

Stanley v. Georgia, 394 U.S. 557 (1969).

U.S. v. Depew, 751 F. Supp. 1195 (1990).

U.S. v. Williams, 553 U.S. 285 (2007).

Wooley v. Maynard, 430 U.S. 705 (1977).

Punishments for Pornography

18

Overview

Federal and state penological theories and policies differ. Some scholars and members of the criminal justice system perceive federal punishments as being more severe than state punishments. One reason is that state-level offenders may receive increased probation, whereas federal offenders may receive harsher prison sentences. Pornography offenders are punished by various statutory schemes, and child pornography offenders may incur abuse from corrections inmates. Lax governmental sanctions and nongovernmental repercussions challenge traditional retributive notions and rehabilitative possibilities. Rehabilitative responses are discussed further in Chapter 21.

Statutes of Limitations

Statutes of limitations delimit the amount of time within which the government may prosecute a crime. Policy rationales are that (1) offenders should not spend their entire lifetime worried about a haunted past; (2) remorse and reform may be demonstrated if offenders fail to recidivate; (3) evidence becomes stale, unreliable, or nonexistent after a period of time; and (4) the government should not be interested in crimes that pose no threat and can no longer be proved. Though jurisdictional requirements vary, in general, probable cause must arise before the statute has run. Statutes may run at different times depending on the level of crime. Prosecution of more serious crimes is generally delimited by longer statutes of limitations. Jurisdictions group crimes into levels. Usually, jurisdictions specify time limits for prosecution of pornography offenses in accordance with their severity. Misdemeanors may run after a few months or years, but felonies typically allot a few years or decades (La. Crim. Proc. Art. 571.1, 2014). For example, simple possession of obscenity or production involving animal cruelty may be unprosecutable after two years, but commercial production offenses against children may run after 10 years or 30 years, depending on the severity of abuse (Cal. Pen. Code § 801.2, 2014; La. Crim. Proc. Art. 571.1, 2014). Statutes of limitations for crimes involving children may be a few years but may also extend until after the child has turned 18 years old (720 ILC § 5/36, 2014). These statutes of limitations are designed to give victims time to prosecute after reaching the age of majority. A few felonies may not be subject to any statute of limitations. For example, production of snuff films is likely to be prosecutable at any time because many jurisdictions fail to impose any statute of limitation on prosecution of murder.

Federal Punishments for Obscenity

Chapter 71 of the U.S. Code criminalizes obscenity. Under federal law, obscenity is punished using sentencing ranges depending on the seriousness and frequency of crimes. Transferring obscenity to a minor through interstate or foreign commerce is punishable under federal law only if the minor is 16 years old or younger. In general, possession, receipt, transport, and distribution of synthetic child pornography are punished by identical penalties under Section 1466A. The number of depictions, recidivism, and the content of depictions may affect sentencing. Following release from incarceration, child pornography offenders may be ordered to abstain from viewing any pornography or from using the Internet for a certain period of time.

Obscenity offenses under Chapter 71 require no sentencing mandatory minimum. Producing, selling, distributing, transporting, and receiving obscenity that depicts adult actors carries a statutory maximum prison sentence of 5 to 10 years. Transporting two or more issues or copies of the same publication or depiction or more than five obscene depictions creates a rebuttable presumption that depictions are for sale or are intended for distribution. Section 1464 punishes uttering obscenity, indecent speech, or profanity on the radio or cable television with a fine or a prison term of fewer than 24 months, or both. Residents or undocumented aliens convicted of obscenity charges likely face deportation following the completion of their sentences. Offenders convicted of obscenity must forfeit obscene materials, any property, and all gross profits earned from obscenity. Criminal forfeiture may include profits from acting in films if actors are charged with producing, transporting, mailing, receiving, or shipping pornography. Civil forfeiture may also result when criminal forfeiture is required. Supervised release or suspended sentences may be imposed for obscenity offenders.

Federal Punishments for Child Pornography

Federal sentences are guided by Federal Sentencing Guidelines. Federal sentences can range from light punishments to life imprisonment for various types of offenses. A single action can result in numerous charges at the federal level or charges at both federal and state levels. Often, offenders who commit crimes using the Internet are charged with state and federal crimes because their violations traverse state or national boundaries. When federal guidelines recommend fewer years than statutory minimums, statutory ranges prevail. The great majority of Department of Justice (DOJ) respondents, 86%, reported that they have observed disparities between state and federal sentences for child pornography offenses. Eighty percent of respondents described lower sentences among state offenders as being substantially different from federal sentences (DOJ, 2010). One-fifth of federal agents surveyed reported that sentencing is dependent on the exact offense committed, offender's history, and accompanying offenses (DOJ, 2010). Downward departures from guideline ranges may result from plea bargaining, substantial assistance to the government, defense motions, or other reasons.

The federal government provides sentencing guidelines for production offenses. Under sentencing guidelines, production offenders face a mandatory sentence minimum of 15 years with a maximum of 30 years (United States Sentencing Commission [USSC], 2012). Predicate offenses shift mandatory sentence ranges upward to between 25 years and 50 years for one prior sex offense and 35 years to life in prison for an offender's third conviction. If a victim is 16 years old or younger in both prior offenses, then the mandatory sentence is life imprisonment. Beginning in 1992, 90% of production offenders received prison, and the remaining offender, 1 of 10 offenders, received probation (USSC, 2012). In 2010, all federal production offenders were sentenced to prison, and none were granted probationary leniency. The Prosecutorial Remedies and Other Tools to End the Exploitation of Children Today Act of 2003 (PROTECT Act) requires any convicted child pornography offender to serve a mandatory probationary term of five years to lifetime supervision. Currently, guidelines call for judges to impose the minimum as a policy statement. In 2010, the average probation term was 323 months for federal offenders convicted of production offenses. Receipt, delivery, and traffic convictions carried average probationary terms of 274 months. On average, possession offenders were sentenced to 220 months of supervision. Offenders charged with crimes involving obscenity and children were sentenced to an average of 43 months of supervision (USSC, 2012).

Nonproduction offenses include (1) distribution (e.g., peer-to-peer (P2P) file sharing), (2) transportation (e.g., shipping and mailing), (3) receipt, and (4) possession of child pornography. Sentences for nonproduction offenses may be enhanced if nonproduction offenders have a history of criminal sexually dangerous behavior demonstrating a pattern of behavior (*Booker v. U.S.*, 2005; USSC, 2012). Under sentencing guidelines, the minimum penalty advised for advertising child pornography is 15 years imprisonment, which is raised to 25 years and 35 years for second and third offenses, respectively. There are no federal sentencing minimums for possession of child pornography. The maximum term of imprisonment is 10 years for depictions of children over the age of 12 years, and 20 years for depictions of children younger than 12 years. The minimum is 10 years in incarceration for prior offenses, but the maximum does not exceed 20 years in incarceration for a depiction of any child. Receipt, distribution, and possession with the intent to distribute or sell may require a five-year minimum sentence and a maximum sentence of 20 years. Prior state or federal charges shift the range upward to between 15 years and 40 years. When mandatory minimums are not imposed, probation is unavailable for offenders who committed Class A or B felonies (18 U.S.C. § 3561(a)(1), 2014).

In 2012, 30% of convicted nonproduction offenders had a history of sexually dangerous behavior, including nonproduction, contact, and noncontact offenses (USSC, 2012). Histories were established by allegations, prior convictions, and judicial findings. Only those histories admitted by defendants or proved by the government can be considered during sentencing (*Booker v. U.S.*, 2005). The government reported to the USSC that of 1,654 nonproduction offenders, 41% had received enhanced sentences for distributing child pornography (18 U.S.C. § 2G2.2(b)(3), 2014; USSC, 2012). Of 683 enhanced sentences, 38% had previously committed criminal sexually dangerous behavior (USSC, 2012). Of 971 offenders whose sentences did not include enhancements, 34% had previously committed criminal sexually dangerous behavior. Enhancements did not reflect the rate of criminal sexually dangerous behavior committed by offenders in the past. Sentencing for 518 offenders previously convicted of criminal sexually dangerous behavior averaged 138 months, which is longer than the average sentences of 1,043 offenders, who had not engaged in sexually dangerous crimes. Sentence enhancement may vary depending on whether a pattern of behavior is established by previous convictions or presentence reports. The average sentence for 236 offenders with prior convictions was 160 months, but the average sentence was 120 months for 282 offenders whose patterns were established only by presentence reports. The average sentence was 102 months for 288 offenders who either had a pattern of activity or committed a predicate sex offense but did not receive enhancements for either. Among 230 offenders whose sentences were enhanced statutorily or under the guidelines, or both, the average sentence was 186 months. When history of offenses included contact offenses, the average sentence was 157 months. Noncontact recidivists were sentenced on average to 107 months of incarceration. Forty-four percent of DOJ (2010) agents reported that, on average, offenders are incarcerated for 10 to 15 years. Intrastate, interstate, and international solicitations are encountered; however, not all offenders are charged with state and federal charges because the majority of violations occur intrastate.

The deterrence theory of crime states that severe, swift, and certain punishments deter crime. Severe penalties are designed to deter child pornography. However, adversarial proceedings and advancements in technology have thwarted the federal government's ability to swiftly and certainly punish pornographers (*Osborne v. Ohio*, 1990). Adversarial proceedings ensure justice for defendants, but create lengthy gaps between perpetration and punishment that may disassociate offenses from punishments. The USSC analyzed federal child pornography cases in 2010. Most offenders who trafficked in materials involving sexual exploitation of minors did so without any financial incentive. They trafficked using P2P, which allowed them to download freely and directly. Punishment is not certain because use of P2P may result in a range of crimes and penalties. The government has been unable to produce or rely on research demonstrating that harsh punishments affect P2P file sharing (USSC, 2012). Considering that these offenses often occur in global forums and networks, succinct research would likely be impossible.

In 2014, the Department of Homeland Security and Immigration and Customs Enforcement (ICE) shut down a major online solicitation operation involving mostly teen boys in Britain, Canada, New Zealand, Australia, and Belgium (Chiacu, 2014). Of 251 victims, it is believed that 244 were from the United States. Offenders sometimes posed as females online to solicit pornography from boys through social network sites. A few victims were as young as toddlers. ICE reported that this bust yielded more victims than any other single operation. Over 27,000 subscribers were under investigation or charged. Offenders used The Onion Network (TOR) to share images over the Dark Net. The network was discovered only after an offender used the federal mail to contact a child. Use of sophisticated technology, international networks, and fake identities online make offenders difficult to locate, investigate, arrest, try, and sentence in the United States. ICE said, "We cannot arrest our way out of this problem: education is the key to prevention. … The fact is that many other children are still in danger" (Chiacu, 2014). Greater research is needed about appropriate and effective education methods and whether education would sufficiently lessen the threat of predators and technology. Further studies are needed to determine to what extent sentencing guidelines or threat of harsh sentences deter domestic or international offenders.

State-Level Punishments for Obscenity

State-level punishments for obscenity vary. Fines, jail, prison, innovative court orders, probation, and other remedies may depend on the offense, the offender's age, the offender's history, municipal laws, and other factors. California is the pornography capital of the United States because it is one of the few jurisdictions that regulates pornography production and will not prosecute it. People who deal in obscenity in California for the first time are guilty of committing a misdemeanor, but recidivists may be fined up to $50,000 (Cal. Pen. Code § 311.2, 2014). Dealing in obscenity, uttering obscenity, drawing obscenity, indirectly or directly informing minors about where to obtain obscenity, bringing obscenity into a prison, committing child and adult production offenses, and failing to label explicit material are all first-degree misdemeanors in California. Recidivists face third-degree felony charges. Offenders also are guilty of third-degree felonies if they disseminate material to minors that is harmful and partially depicts nudity, sadomasochism, or sexual conduct, or they permit minors to view live sexual performances that are harmful. However, no felony is committed for allowing minors to view or attend sexual depictions if a child's parent accompanies the child. Recidivists are guilty of second-degree felonies. In California, like other jurisdictions, there is no requirement for offenders convicted of obscenity to register locally as sex offenders (*Barrows v. Municipal Court of Los Angeles Judicial Dist.*, 1970).

Texas' obscenity statute mirrors the facts and reasoning behind *Miller v. California* (1973) by making it a Class C misdemeanor to knowingly or intentionally distribute or display obscenity in reckless disregard for the offense or alarm that it may cause to others (Tex. Stat. § 43.22, 2014). Punishable by a fine of less than $500, this sanction enforces the government's interest in keeping private material out of the public eye where it may offend average members of the community. This principle is exhibited in many state statutes, which make it a misdemeanor to display obscenity (18 Pa.C.S. § 5903, 2013). Classifying this crime as a misdemeanor suggests that displaying obscenity may disturb public life but does not necessarily injure others.

Some jurisdictions participate in creative remedies. In Kansas, obscenity offenders may be penalized with fines or imprisonment and may be required to pay collateral of up to $50,000 to ensure compliance with the law for up to two years at the risk of forfeiture (K.S.A. § 21-6401, 2012). In New York and other jurisdictions, the court may condition probation on an offender's termination of employment where the offender sold obscenity, for example, in an adult store (*People v. Johnson*, 1983).

Ranges for State Punishments for Child Pornography

State-level punishments for child pornography production vary widely depending on whether offenders (1) demonstrate a pattern, (2) were involved commercially, (3) targeted prepubescent or postpubescent minors, and (4) depicted minors or promoted pornography to minors, or both. In addition to federal punishments, convicted sex offenders may need to register in state registries and comply with local restrictions against sex offenders.

Production and commercial offenses may carry more severe penalties than nonproduction and noncommercial offenses. For example, production offenses in Ohio are second-degree felonies punishable by a prison term of two years to eight years (Or. Rev. Stat. Ann. 2919.229(B)(5), 2013). Commercially dealing in child pornography in California incurs a possible fine of up to $100,000, and conviction includes the possibility of imprisonment for between two years and six years (Cal. Pen. Code § 311.2, 2014). Commercially advertising obscenity featuring children is a felony punishable with two to four years in prison or up to one year in county jail. It is also punishable by a fine up to $50,000 (Cal. Pen. Code § 311.10, 2014). Noncommercial trading of child pornography between adults is punishable by up to one year in county jail or a fine of up to $2,000, or both, or a term in state prison or a fine of up to $10,000, or both. Recidivists are guilty of a felony (Cal. Pen. Code § 311.1, 2014).

In Massachusetts, purposefully disseminating harmful material to minors is punishable with a term of up to five years in state prison or two and a half years in a house of correction or jail (Mass. Gen. Laws Ann. 272, § 28, 2013). Stand-alone fines or fines coupled with prison sentences may be between $1,000 and $10,000 for the first offense; between $5,000 and $20,000 for the second offense; and between $10,000 and $30,000 for any subsequent offenses. This statute does not create strict liability. A minor's age must have been reasonably ascertainable or known. Disseminating child pornography in Massachusetts is punishable by a term in state prison between 10 years and 20 years or a fine of $10,000 to $50,000, or both (Mass. Gen. Laws Ann. 272, § 29, 2013). The court may order the offender to pay 300% of the monetary value derived from disseminating the material if it is greater than the fine. Many states' statutes harshly punish exploitation, but may punish exposing minors to pornography more leniently. For example, in some states, parents may be exempted from prosecution for distributing nonobscene adult material to their children (La. Rev. Stat. Ann. 14 §92, 2014).

Most solicitation offenses are punished under state law. Among National Drug Intelligence Center (NDIC) interviewees, 84% reported that most online solicitors reside in the same area or state as the victim (DOJ, 2010). In Illinois, solicitation and production offenses, including engaging or soliciting a child or depicting or posing a child in sexual or sadomasochistic conduct, are a felony punishable with mandatory fines between $1,000 and $100,000 (720 ILCS 5/11-20.1, 2014). Sex offenders who commit pornography or solicitation offenses and have previous convictions for criminal sexually dangerous conduct in any jurisdiction must serve a mandatory minimum sentence of nine years and pay a mandatory fine between $2,000 and $100,000. Online solicitation offenses often involve prostitution. Approximately one-quarter of NDIC interviewees reported that they perceive child prostitution sentences to be less severe at the state level than at the federal level and that state sentences should be more extensive (DOJ, 2010). Approximately as many respondents reported that there are no differences between state sentences and federal sentences. However, 78% reported that they are unable to support any perceptions about sentencing disparities with current research because it is insufficient.

Plea bargaining may result in suspended sentences and imposition of probation. Probation is not a legal right possessed by offenders (*Sachs v. State*, 2013). It is leniency offered by the court. Sentences for child pornography or solicitation may be suspended and probation may be granted on the conditions that offenders (1) refrain from possessing child pornography or sexually stimulating material and (2) submit to home visits. Some probation terms prohibit offenders from engaging in any paraphilic behaviors, including transvestism or sadomasochism. Probation may be revoked if the terms of the plea agreement are violated. Certain people may be statutorily barred from receiving probation (La. Rev. Stat. Ann. 14 §92, 2014). For example, parents who contribute to the delinquency of a minor may be restricted from some or all sentence suspension and probation.

A risk determination may be made when the court weighs a pornography offender's eligibility for probation, suspended sentencing, or immunity (NRS 176A.110, 2014). Production offenders, promoters, and disseminators may be eligible depending on their risks of recidivism. An expert may be required to certify that a psychosexual evaluation was administered to determine that an offender does not pose a high risk. State and federal courts may restrict solicitation offenders' or child pornography offenders' use of the Internet or other electronics as long as restrictions are tailored to rehabilitative and supervisory rationales (NRS 176A.413, 2014; USSC, 2012). Courts may prohibit offenders from owning computers, checking e-mail, or using chat rooms. Exceptions to the use of electronics may be granted for offenders who aid or train law enforcement or use specialized equipment for work.

Offenders may be given probation in lieu of serving time. Some critics believe that this remedy may be inappropriate because it is too lenient or harsh depending on the crime. This argument played out in a case involving a priest who was charged with possession of a few pornographic images of children (Murray, 2013). The government argued that the defendant should be sentenced to prison because paying for child pornography is a serious crime that creates demand for child exploitation and production. The defense argued that the priest had no prior criminal records and cooperated with authorities, thus imposition of a long probationary term would be too severe. The defendant pleaded. Because of his plea, he could have faced deportation, but prior to sentencing, the defendant attempted to flee to the Philippines.

Thus, the threat of deportation did not seem like a serious punishment. The priest was sentenced to two and a half years in a house of corrections. These facilities may not have perimeter walls or guard towers to guard misdemeanants and low-risk offenders. The defendant's sentence was suspended, and a term of probation was imposed for five years.

One-fifth of NDIC interviewees reported that state offenses typically receive probation, but the same number of respondents reported that in their experiences, state offenses receive one year to five years of incarceration (DOJ, 2010). Solicitation is usually a state-level or local offense. Approximately one-sixth of NDIC experts stated that the average state-level online solicitor only received probation. Many first-time solicitors may receive probation terms that limit access to computers or use of technology. Concurrent offenses influence the possibility of probation at the state level.

Inmate Codes

In prison, any kind of sex offender may be the most loathed inmate (Garrison, 2011; Hensley, Wright, Tewksbury, & Castle, 2003). Inmates who have committed sex offenses against children may be called "Chesters" or "Chomos" by fellow inmates. Chomos may be people who trafficked in children or abused children during pornography production offenses. They are the lowest and least respected inmates in the prison hierarchy. Sex offenders, especially Chomos, may be robbed, raped, battered, or murdered by individual inmates or groups of inmates (Anderson, 2013). Some inmates who are unfairly labeled as Chomos may suffer identical repercussions to those who are guilty of sex offenses (Goad, n.d.).

Undeterred by incarceration, inmates may inflict violence on behalf of society, to avenge innocent children, to express their opinions about an abuser's behavior, to enforce inmates' prison codes, to punish abusers, to deter recidivism, to incapacitate, to sympathize with their own children, to equalize power, to achieve status, to demonstrate prowess, to achieve social justice, and for other reasons (Sex Offenders in Prison, 2013). Public awareness that Chomos are targeted in incarceration may effectively deter some prospective sex offenders who fear violent reprisal in prison.

Child sex offenders in prison are targeted because they are usually loners. They may not form deep friendships and intimacy because of fear of exposure. Child sex offenders are unable to become fully insulated by gangs. Prison gangs, which offer protection to members, require vetting. Gangs that become aware of Chomos may commit violent offenses against them even if they are members or friends of the gang. Being a loner and evading conversations about criminal history may cue other offenders about a Chomo's crime. To compensate for their vulnerability, Chomos may practice religion in prison; religion offers them penance and group membership. Sex offenders may be forced to group together in prison, share bunks, or be housed in the same dorm. This grouping together for safety by sex offenders may further reinforce inmates' control over them.

Conclusion

Inside and outside prison, members of society who participate in the criminal justice system seem highly committed to punishing sex offenses and harms against children. However, some pornography offenses, like file sharing, may not be met with harsh sentences. One penological approach is to ramp up all sentencing to deter crimes and incapacitate offenders. Another approach is to continue to focus governmental resources on more serious crimes. Depending on probationary term, supervised release may complement stiff sentences, help to reform inmates, or pose an insignificant threat to offenders.

References

18 Pa.C.S. § 5903 (2013).

18 U.S.C. § 2G2.2(b)(3) (2104).

18 U.S.C. § 3561(a)(1) (2014).

720 ILCS 5/3-6 (2014).

720 ILCS 5/11-20.1 (2014).

Anderson, N. (2013, August 18). Taking down "the largest child pornography conspiracy ever prosecuted." Ars Technica. Retrieved from http://arstechnica.com/tech-policy/2013/08/operation-joint-hammer-taking-down-the-largest-child-pornography-conspiracy-ever-prosecuted/

Barrows v. Municipal Court of Los Angeles Judicial Dist. (1970) 1 Cal 3d 821, 83 Cal Rptr 819, 464 P2d 483, 1970 Cal LEXIS 352.

Booker v. U.S., 543 U.S. 220 (2005).

Cal. Pen. Code § 311 (2014).

Cal. Pen. Code § 801.2 (2014).

Chiacu, D. (2014, March 18). U.S. authorities arrest 14 in porn website involving 251 children. MSN. Retrieved from http://news.msn.com/crime-justice/us-authorities-arrest-14-in-porn-website-involving-251-children

Department of Justice. (2010, August). The national strategy for child exploitation prevention and interdiction. Retrieved from http://www.justice.gov/psc/docs/natstrategyreport.pdf

Garrison, C. (2011, May 12). Inmates like Michael Devlin on bottom of prison pecking order. *River Front Times*. Retrieved from http://blogs.riverfronttimes.com/dailyrft/2011/05/michael_devlin_stabbed_prison_hierarchies.php

Goad, J. (n.d.). Jim Goad's guide to prison slang of the Pacific Northwest. JimGoad.net. Retrieved from http://www.jimgoad.net/prisonslang.html

Hensley, C., Wright, J., Tewksbury, R., & Castle, C. (2003). The evolving nature of prison argot and sexual hierarchies. *The Prison Journal*, *83*(3), 289–300.

K.S.A. § 21-6401 (2012).

La. Crim. Proc. Art. 571.1 (2014).

La. Rev. Stat. Ann. 14 §92 (2014).
Mass. Gen. Laws Ann. 272, § 28 (2013).
Mass. Gen. Laws Ann. 272, § 29 (2013).
Miller v. California, 413 U.S. 15 (1973).
Murray, G. V. (2013, February 27). Fitchburg priest gets suspended sentence for child porn, thefts. Telegram. Retrieved from http://www.telegram.com/article/20130227/NEWS/130229686/1116
NRS 176A.110 (2014).
NRS 176A.413 (2014).
Or. Rev. Stat. Ann. 2919.229(B)(5) (2013).
Osborne v. Ohio, 495 U.S. 103 (1990).
People v. Johnson (1983, Crim) 118 Misc 2d 983, 462 NYS2d 549.
Sachs v. State, 985 N.E.2d 374 (2013).
Sex offenders in prison. (2013, March 11). X-con. Retrieved from http://x-con.hubpages.com/hub/The-Road-to-Ruin-Pt-14-Child-Offenders-in-Prison
Tex. Stat. Ann. § 43.22 (2014).
United States Sentencing Commission. (2012). Report to the Congress: Federal child pornography offenses. Retrieved from http://www.ussc.gov/Legislative_and_Public_Affairs/Congressional_Testimony_and_Reports/Sex_Offense_Topics/201212_Federal_Child_Pornography_Offenses/

Crooked Members of the Criminal Justice System

19

Overview

Members of the criminal justice system have been arrested for child pornography, obscenity, and crimes involving fantasy. Quite often, public figures are shamed by the media. Their statuses within the justice system are discussed by the public to highlight their moral hypocrisy and the gravity of their breaches.

Officers

Some law enforcement and corrections officers commit pornography offenses. Officers may also access evidence depicting child abuse, obscenity, or child pornography. They may be knowledgeable about how to contact child prostitutes online. In areas with higher incidents of child trafficking, officers may be more likely to solicit children online, and they may attempt to groom children using child pornography obtained through the course of employment. For example, Texas is a region known for human trafficking and child prostitution. Many examples of Texas law enforcement and corrections officers becoming involved with online solicitation have come to the public's attention (Two Charged in Sexual Assault, 2014). One man was hired as a county detention officer in Texas, but lost his job before he began working in corrections (Ortiz, 2014). The weekend before he was to begin, he was arrested for attempting to solicit online an undercover agent whom the officer believed to be a minor. In another case, a police officer attempted to groom a child online for approximately one year (Colagiovanni, 2012). His conversations were sexual, and he engaged in some allegedly inappropriate activity in person with a child.

Numerous cases of law enforcement being arrested for child pornography have shocked public conscience in recent years. A police chief in Mount Pleasant, New York, was arrested in 2014 for possessing child pornography (Remizowski & Brown, 2014). Department of Homeland Security investigated the captain, who used peer-to-peer file sharing to obtain more than 100 photos and videos of child pornography. The chief allegedly began downloading images of exploitation to research sexual abuse. He taught sex abuse awareness through a religious program to young children. The police chief claimed that he wanted to become informed about sex abuse, at first, but then he continued to view pornography for more than a year. In Washington, D.C., an on-duty police officer entered the bedroom of a teen who returned to her home after being reported missing; the officer ordered her to remove her clothing (Segraves, 2013). He told the victim that he needed to photograph injuries that she sustained while she was missing. The officer took one dozen nude photos of the victim. Police searched his camera and recovered other images believed to be of minors. D.C. Police Chief Cathy Lanier said,

> We invest a great amount of time and effort to ensure that we are hiring the right people and we continue to proactively monitor integrity across the department … but to learn of an allegation of this kind against a person who is sworn to protect our children, it is both shocking and disturbing. (Segraves, 2013)

The police chief's statement aptly expresses society's sentiments toward officers who sexually exploit children or abuse their authority to commit sex crimes.

A highly publicized case in New York demonstrated that some police access criminal records to produce obscenity (Feyerick, Levitt, Kessler, & Hanna, 2012). Abuse of sex offender registries was discussed in Chapter 5. In 2012, a New York police officer illegally accessed a national crime database. The officer selected approximately 100 ideal female victims from a crime database, downloaded the women's pictures and contact information, and began to surveil them. He conspired online to abduct, rape, torture, cook, and eat female victims. Co-conspirators may merely have been fantasizing about anthropophagy (Cusack, 2011). The gray area spanning between obscenity, fantasy, and conspiracy is discussed in Chapter 17. In this case, the police officer may have gone beyond obscenity or fantasy. He wrote a "blueprint" of how to commit crimes against a particular victim (Feyerick et al., 2012). In his blueprint, the officer listed materials that he needed to commit crimes, as well as details about the victim (e.g., height and bra size). The police officer allegedly negotiated online with a co-conspirator who wished to pay the officer to abduct an alternate victim. The police officer maintains that he was fantasizing, but U.S. Attorney Preet Bharara summarized what is likely a common response to the officer's actions. Bharara said, "This case is all the more disturbing when you consider [the defendant]'s position as a New York City police officer and his sworn duty to serve and protect" (Feyerick et al., 2012).

Judges, Prosecutors, and Public Defenders

Judges, prosecutors, and public defenders may participate in pornography crimes (Judge Charged, 2003). Sometimes, officers of the court may seem to be held to higher standards, but at other times, their knowledge or power indirectly creates an advantage or may result in leniency. A British judge was charged with buying child pornography from a U.S. website (Leapman, 2008). He also was charged with production offenses. He retired six days prior to being charged, which entitled him to keep his full pension even though he downloaded child pornography while serving as a judge. Though he cited poor health as the reason for his retirement, it is possible that he was aware of the government's investigation against him. In California, a judge, who served as a Little League umpire, pleaded to four counts of child pornography, though he allegedly possessed thousands of sexually explicit depictions of young boys and molested at least one child (Welborn, 2013). In his personal journal, he described frequenting public showers and areas where he could be around children, and he discussed his desire to commit hands-on offenses. The state considered him to be a serious threat, but after six years of house arrest, he was sentenced to only 27 months in federal prison for possession. On the basis of a victim's testimony, the judge was originally charged in state court with molestation, but the statute of limitations had run on the charge.

An assistant attorney general in Maine, who was a top prosecutor for drug offenses, was convicted by the federal government of 13 counts of possession and transmission of child pornography (Russell, 2013). The presence of child pornography in the attorney's wife's e-mail account was reported by Yahoo.com to the National Center for Missing and Exploited Children. Seven of his charges were vacated, but while out on bail, the offender participated in several violations. He sold counterfeit watches, violated a court order by removing an ankle monitoring device, printed and used fraudulent checks, and fled the jurisdiction. He was arrested by federal marshals within one month, but his attorneys argued that he should not be sentenced for fleeing or for contempt of court. The offender's actions may be related to mental illness, co-morbidities, or other factors, but his behavior seemed to demonstrate blatant disregard for law, which he swore to uphold for nearly two decades.

A federal prosecutor in Gulf Breeze, Florida, coached girls softball and basketball and was married to a popular schoolteacher (Burns, 2010; Goodnough, 2007). The prosecutor was arrested during an online solicitation sting. The prosecutor believed that he traveled to Detroit with a doll and Vaseline to have sex with a five-year-old female. He told undercover agents that he had raped numerous children. Though he was not charged with obscenity, his requests for child sex allegedly explicitly referenced sodomy and vaginal intercourse. Objects in his possession (e.g., dresses and underwear) supported an inference that he participated in grooming victims. Before he was arrested and committed suicide, he requested from the Department of Justice (DOJ) an opportunity to receive training about child molestation even though he worked on federal civil property and forfeiture cases. The DOJ denied his request but did not flag it as suspicious. In retrospect, it seems that the offender may have been trying to seek help or use government resources to learn how to improve his strategies. Following prosecution, the local sheriff said, "The fact that an Internet child sex suspect is a law enforcement official shouldn't be unexpected. ... The people who are doing it come from all walks of life. ... It doesn't surprise us anymore" (U.S. Prosecutor Accused, 2007).

A prosecutor in Atlanta was criticized, but not prosecuted, for distributing video evidence of minors performing oral sex; the depictions were distributed pursuant to media requests under the Freedom of Information Act (Prosecutor under Fire, 2007). The minor victims were the subject of a criminal case, and their faces were fully visible in the depictions. The depictions constituted child pornography under federal law, but federal prosecutors asked the Atlanta prosecutor to stop distributing the videos, but did not enjoin the prosecutor or charge him with distribution and other crimes. Reporters and others who requested approximately one dozen copies were not prosecuted for receipt. This case seemed to fly in the face of policies designed to protect minors and laws prohibiting transmission of child pornography. It also challenges federal law enforcement's self-perception of being tough on nonproduction child pornography crimes (United States Sentencing Commission [USSC], 2012).

A public defender in Pittsburgh was arrested for raping young girls and possessing 400 depictions of child pornography (Ex-public Defender Guilty, 2008). In a flagrant breach of his professional and ethical duties, the offender downloaded pornography onto his county-issued laptop computer. A public defender in Ohio was convicted of possessing, distributing, and receiving hard-core images of young children and infants being abused and raped (Miller, 2010). He expressed deep emotional pain about losing his family, behaving dishonorably, and providing images to others who may have become addicted to the same material that possessed him psychologically. He faced up to 20 years in federal prison, but committed suicide in his cell. Of his suicide, his attorney remarked, "He must have felt the sentence was so severe, so steep that he had nowhere to go and took his own life" (Miller, 2010). This analysis may reflect natural human sympathy toward the prospect of a long prison term, or it may articulate a view that members of the justice system anticipate to be treated more leniently than other offenders.

Child Welfare

Local commercial abuse operations may be thinly veiled within the child welfare system (Commercially Sexually Exploited Children, 2013). Gerald Sandusky, who founded The Second Mile charity for troubled youth, was convicted of abusing numerous children over the span of 15 years. In 1998, protective services in Sandusky's jurisdiction were provided by Children and Youth Services (CYS) and the Pennsylvania Department of Public Welfare (DPW) (Cosentino, 2013). Debra Long, the mother of Matt Sandusky, an 11-year-old child fostered by Sandusky, alleged that Sandusky had an inappropriate relationship with her son. This claim was not sufficiently substantiated by the state, even though the state investigated Sandusky for engaging in naked full body contact with a young boy, Victim #6, while in a shower (Cosentino, 2013; Morgan, 2013). Chapter 9 discusses investigation and substantiation of abuse reports. Investigators and prosecutors determined that Sandusky did not inappropriately touch the boy by embracing and lifting him under the shower water (Cosentino, 2013).

DPW failed to comply with Pennsylvania law by privately investigating the allegations instead of informing Sandusky's employer (Cosentino, 2013). Sandusky worked for The Second Mile, a child care agency. DPW also failed to notify the courts of its investigation of Sandusky, a foster parent. During the investigation, which lasted several weeks, DPW and the state's attorney did not determine that Sandusky was not an abuser. Penn State police failed to disclose to DPW that the state's evaluating psychologist believed that Sandusky was a predator who was grooming children. The psychologist did not rigorously attempt to initiate any intervention through CYS or Centre County Courts (Morgan, 2013). The police and the assistant district attorney accepted the evaluation, but a Penn State detective authorized a second evaluation to be conducted by John Seasock, an unlicensed individual, who described Sandusky's actions as falling in a gray area (Cosentino, 2013). As an independent contractor, that evaluator was commercially contracted to CYS, which also held several contracts with The Second Mile; the independent contractor was later contracted by Penn State (Cosentino, 2013). The state college police, who believed that Sandusky's behavior demonstrated a lapse in boundary judgments, never followed up with the campus police about the results of the investigation (Schweber, 2011). When the CEO of The Second Mile was made aware of the investigation, he further supported the characterization of abuse as a gray area by asking Sandusky to wear swimming trunks in the future while showering with children (Morgan, 2013).

Because of these failures, Sandusky continued to participate in a child pornography ring, molest children, and traffic children to coaches, wealthy boosters, and others (Freeh, Sporkin, & Sullivann, 2012; Jerry Sandusky Was Part of Child Porn Ring, 2012; Perel, 2012). In 2008, the attorney general's office in Pennsylvania was notified that a child claimed to have been molested by Sandusky (Curry, 2013). Under Tom Corbett, who was the attorney general at that time, investigators looked into the allegations for three years. Meanwhile, Sandusky was permitted to continue working with children at The Second Mile. Though Corbett convened a grand jury in 2008, charges were not filed until 2011. Corbett later became the governor of Pennsylvania and was investigated for his role in the Sandusky debacle by the Pennsylvania attorney general, Kathleen Kane. Kane suggested that Corbett remained complicit to maintain donations and solidify power leading up to his 2009 gubernatorial run. Corbett permitted organized access to children in exchange for donations, salary, and power. Decades after Sandusky abused Victim #6, he was convicted of unlawful contact with minors, corruption of minors, and endangering the welfare of children (Associated Press, 2013). In total, he was convicted of 45 counts of sex abuse (Curry, 2013). Complicit university administrators were charged with perjury, obstruction of justice, and other related offenses (Associated Press, 2013). In response to protective services failures, the state reformed laws and protocol (Scolforo, 2012).

Foster care homes are routinely targeted by traffickers for recruitment (Smith, Vardaman, & Snow, 2009). In Boston, Massachusetts, a study demonstrated that 95% of female minors had been solicited by a pimp for recruitment while living in a foster care group home. In-person and online recruitment of local children in foster care may lead children to become delinquent (Smith, Vavdaman, & Snow, 2009). Traffickers, pedophiles, complicit authority figures, or conspirators know that delinquency is often a symptom of commercial sexual exploitation. Control exerted by pimps, trauma, and learned hostility cause youth to cycle through the justice system as sex offenders, addicts, violent offenders, or nonviolent offenders.

Prospective foster parents with felony child pornography or abuse offenses will often be precluded from fostering children (Arkansas Department of Human Services, Division of Children and Family Services, 2013). Offenders are typically not allowed to foster children if they have committed production offenses against children or have been convicted of possessing child pornography. However, in many jurisdictions, prospective foster parents may request an alternative compliance that permits them to participate in the child welfare system even though they have been convicted of pornography production offenses, promotion of obscene materials, permitting a child to be abused, or public display of obscenity. Misdemeanor crimes of moral turpitude or contributing to a minor's delinquency may also qualify under alternative compliance provisions. In some jurisdictions, the law excuses pornography possession for bona fide purposes (*Fraser v. Sleeper*, 2007). This exception makes possession by pedophiles working within the system virtually unstoppable. For example, several child psychologists and psychiatrists have been charged and convicted of possessing child pornography (Kalinowski, 2011; McFall, 2013; Vargas, 2011; Waldron, 2013). Some have been convicted of downloading child pornography to hospital or state computers. These professionals often work with children involved in child welfare, family cases, and sex abuse. In states that do not exempt such behavior, offenders may escape stigmatization of registering in a sex offense registry by moving to a state that recognizes these exceptions after conviction. In the new state, offenders may not be guilty of the crime for which they were convicted; they may not need to register. Thus, the criminal justice system may fail on all counts once pornographers and abusers are exempted from the law. Chapter 5 further discusses exemption from sex offender registry requirements.

Political Leaders

Political leaders have been publicly shamed by pornography offenses. Pornography offenses may render some politicians hypocrites in their communities. Some of these leaders have taken public positions against premarital sex or pornography; others have built reputations on being law-abiding and honest.

One possibly hypocritical political leader was Osama Bin Laden. Western pornography was discovered at his compound in Pakistan. Bin Laden, who abhorred Western pornography, morals, and society, once said of Western society, "You plaster your naked daughters across billboards in order to sell a product without any shame. You have brainwashed your daughters into believing they are liberated by wearing revealing clothes, yet in reality all they have liberated is your sexual desire" (Shane, 2011). When U.S. forces invaded his compound, they discovered many pornographic films on hard drives and jump drives, but reports do not claim that Bin Laden downloaded or viewed pornography. Nevertheless, the existence of American pornography within his compound demonstrates that Bin Laden, an antipornography leader, may have viewed pornography or been aided by people who view pornography.

Politicians charged with pornography offenses may exhibit hypocrisy and betray their communities. Maryland has often been the federal district to most aggressively pursue production offenses (USSC, 2012). A former aide for a U.S. senator in Maryland hanged himself after he was charged with attempted distribution and possession of child pornography (Dishneau, 2014). His suicide may demonstrate the immense pressure faced by politicians who betray their communities and politicians' unwillingness to submit to the criminal justice system. A former Democratic U.S. Senate candidate in South Carolina won the primaries and then was charged with felony and misdemeanor obscenity charges (Clark, 2010). He allegedly disseminated, procured, and promoted obscenity to a college student. Even after he was arrested, one of his political platforms was "accountability." Several city mayors have been charged with possession of child pornography in the past few years (Pa. Mayor Faces Child-Porn Charges, 2011; Rosen, 2012). In one case, a former Alaskan mayor was charged with possession and production offenses. He possessed numerous depictions of child pornography and videos of himself engaging in sexual activity with minors (Rosen, 2012). The former mayor, who served on the city council and the school board, was once given a "Citizen of the Year" award. He pleaded guilty to seven counts.

Some conservative activists and fundraisers have been prosecuted for possession of child pornography despite party lines that tend to oppose premarital sex, pornography, adultery, and other immorality (Cataldo, 2001). One highly publicized example is of a very well-known Republican fundraiser who paid two teenage females to pose for pornography in a hotel room. During his arrest, he was in possession of schoolgirl costumes and photography equipment, and albums of pornography were in his car (Conservative Fund-raiser on Probation for Child Porn, 2003). He was charged with production and possession. The albums in his car were excluded from evidence, and he was sentenced only to probation. Critics claimed that he was given a light sentence because of his powerful political connections.

Conclusion

Political leaders, judges, prosecutors, public defenders, officers, and child care workers may intentionally infiltrate the system to obtain access to victims and images of abuse. They may also believe that they will evade justice if they serve as public figures. At times, offenders may manipulate the system, but they cannot escape it. Public shaming and reputational damage may impose severe consequences, in addition to penological responses.

References

Arkansas Department of Human Services, Division of Children and Family Services. (2013, August). Publication 22: Standards of approval for foster and adoptive homes. Retrieved from http://humanservices.arkansas.gov/dcfs/DCFSpublications/PUB-022.pdf

Associated Press. (2013, January 22). Victim 6 sues Penn State, Sandusky, Second Mile charity. *Fox News*. Retrieved from http://www.foxnews.com/us/2013/01/22/victim-6-sues-penn-state-sandusky-second-mile-charity/#ixzz2PpG04Xn1

Burns, M. (2010, September 9). Roy Atchison on the paper trail of a pedophile part 1. Retrieved from http://www.margieburns.com/2010/09/roy-atchison-on-the-paper-trail-of-a-pedophile-part-1/

Cataldo, A. L. (2001, June 23). Man gets federal term for child porn. *Inquirer Suburban*. Retrieved from http://articles.philly.com/2001-06-23/news/25323661_1_child-pornography-abortion-doctor-nicholas-morency

Clark, S. (2010, August 13). South Carolina senate candidate Alvin Greene indicted on obscenity charge. *Fox News*. Retrieved from http://www.foxnews.com/politics/2010/08/13/grand-jury-indicts-senate-candidate-alvin-greene-obscenity-charge/

Colagiovanni, L. (2012, April 11). Corpus Christi police officer arrested for soliciting a 15-year-old girl online. Examiner.com. Retrieved from http://www.examiner.com/article/corpus-christi-police-officer-arrested-for-soliciting-a-15-year-old-girl-online

Commercially Sexually Exploited Children. (2013). Report problem statement: California Health and Human Services Agency. Retrieved from www.chhs.ca.gov/Documents/CSEC_Report-Problem_Statement.docx

Conservative fundraiser on probation for child porn. (2003, April 23). WBALTV. Retrieved from http://www.wbaltv.com/Conservative-Fund-Raiser-On-Probation-For-Child-Porn/8935158

Cosentino, D. (2013). Reminder: Pennsylvania's Child Protective Services failed to stop Jerry Sandusky, too. DeadSpin. Retrieved from http://deadspin.com/5946359/reminder-pennsylvanias-child-protective-services-failed-to-stop-jerry-sandusky-too

Curry, C. (2013, February 1). Governor's handling of Jerry Sandusky case under investigation. *ABC News*. Retrieved from http://abcnews.go.com/US/pennsylvania-governors-handling-jerry-sandusky-case-investigation/story?id=18378718#.UWHocxzvun8

Cusack, C. M. (2011). Placentophagy and embryophagy: An analysis of social deviance within gender, family, or the home (etude 1). *Journal of Law and Social Deviance*, *1*, 112–168.

Dishneau, D. (2014, January 14). Deputies: Former aide to senator found dead in Md. MSN. Retrieved from http://news.msn.com/us/deputies-former-aide-to-senator-found-dead-in-md

Ex-public defender guilty of child rape, child pornography. (2008, March 7). *Pittsburgh Post Gazette*. Retrieved from http://www.post-gazette.com/local/breaking/2008/03/07/Ex-public-defender-guilty-of-child-rape-child-pornography/stories/200803070141#ixzz2usdawcyo

Feyerick, D., Levitt, R., Kessler, J., & Hanna, J. (2012, October 25). Prosecutors: NYPD officer conspired to kidnap, cook, eat women. CNN. Retrieved from http://www.cnn.com/2012/10/25/us/new-york-officer-cannibalism/

Fraser v. Sleeper, 2007 VT 78 (2007).

Freeh, Sporkin, & Sullivann, LLP (2012, July 12). Report of the special investigative counsel regarding the actions of the Pennsylvania State University related to the child sexual abuse committed by Gerald A. Sandusky (The Freeh Report). Retrieved from http://progress.psu.edu/assets/content/REPORT_FINAL_071212.pdf

Goodnough, A. (2007, September 29). Town is shaken after prosecutor's arrest in a child-sex sting. *The New York Times*. Retrieved from http://www.nytimes.com/2007/09/29/us/29florida.html?pagewanted=all

Jerry Sandusky was part of child porn ring, Greg Bucceroni, former "child prostitute" claims. (2012, September 20). *Huffington Post*. Retrieved from http://www.huffingtonpost.com/2012/09/20/jerry-sandusky-child-porn-ring_n_1900800.html

Judge charged with child pornography possession. (2003, January 15). *RTE News*. Retrieved from http://www.rte.ie/news/2003/0115/34080-porn/

Kalinowski, B. (2011, September 7). Child psychiatrist arrested on child pornography charges. *Citizen's Voice*. Retrieved from http://citizensvoice.com/child-psychiatrist-arrested-on-child-pornography-charges-1.1199085

Leapman, B. (2008, June 8). Retired judge charged over child porn. *London Evening Standard*. Retrieved from http://www.standard.co.uk/news/retired-judge-charged-over-child-porn-6959631.html

McFall, M. (2013, September 9). Utah psychiatrist David F. Wilson arrested for child porn. *The Salt Lake Tribune*. Retrieved from http://www.psychsearch.net/utah-psychiatrist-david-f-wilson-arrested-for-child-porn/

Miller, D. J. (2010, January 18). Former Medina County assistant public defender is found dead in his jail cell after child porn conviction. Cleveland.com. Retrieved from http://blog.cleveland.com/metro/2010/01/former_medina_county_public_de.html

Morgan, E. (2013, April 6). To tell the truth: Would the real Mark Emmert please stand up? Voice of the FREEHdom Fighters. Retrieved from http://notpsu.blogspot.com/2013_04_01_archive.html

Ortiz, I. (2014, February 2). Sheriff's jailer arrested on online solicitation of a minor charges. *The Monitor*. Retrieved from http://www.themonitor.com/news/local/article_9360c6ac-902d-11e3-9c60-001a4bcf6878.html

Pa. mayor faces child-porn charges. (2011, July 14). Vindy.com. The Valley's Homepage. Retrieved from http://www.vindy.com/news/2011/jul/14/pa-mayor-faces-child-porn-charges/

Perel, D. (2012, August 13). Witness: I saw Sandusky and Penn State booster abuse boys on private plane. RadarOnline. Retrieved from http://radaronline.com/exclusives/2012/08/sandusky-penn-state-investigation-booster-abused-boys-private-plane/

Prosecutor under fire in teen sex case. (2007, July 13). *USA Today*. Retrieved from http://usatoday30.usatoday.com/news/nation/2007-07-13-teen-sex-tape_N.htm

Remizowski, L., & Brown, P. (2014, January 24). Police chief of New York town arrested on child pornography charges. CNN. Retrieved from http://www.cnn.com/2014/01/23/justice/new-york-police-chief-arrested/

Rosen, Y. (2012, May 1). Jack Shay, former Alaska mayor, pleads guilty to child porn charges. *Huffington Post*. Retrieved from http://www.huffingtonpost.com/2012/04/30/jack-shay-child-porn-_n_1466368.html

Russell, E. (2013, March 1). Ex-prosecutor who fled Maine printed fake checks. *Kennebec Journal*. Retrieved from http://www.kjonline.com/news/Ex-prosecutor-who-fled-Maine-tried-to-print-phony-checks-to-finance-trip-.html

Schweber, N. (2011, November 9). Investigation of Sandusky in 1998 raises questions. *The New York Times*. Retrieved from http://www.nytimes.com/2011/11/10/sports/ncaafootball/aftermath-of-1998-sandusky-investigation-raises-additional-questions.html

Scolforo, M. (2012, November 27). Pennsylvania task force on child protection may seek law changes in wake of Jerry Sandusky case. *Huffington Post*. Retrieved from http://www.huffingtonpost.com/2012/11/27/pennsylvania-task-force-on-child-protection-jerry-sandusky_n_2197298.html

Segraves, M. (2013, December 4). D.C. police officer arrested for production of child pornography. *NBC Washington*. Retrieved from http://www.nbcwashington.com/news/local/DC-Police-Officer-Arrested-for-Production-of-Child-Pornography-234261121.html

Shane, S. (2011, May 13). Pornography is found in Bin Laden compound files, U.S. officials say. *The New York Times*. Retrieved from http://www.nytimes.com/2011/05/14/world/asia/14binladen.html?_r=0

Smith, L. A., Vardaman, S. H., & Snow, M. A. (2009). The national report on domestic minor sex trafficking: America's prostituted children. Shared Hope International. Retrieved from http://sharedhope.org/wp-content/uploads/2012/09/SHI_National_Report_on_DMST_2009.pdf

Tilley, J. L. (2011, November 9). Sandusky case shows where Pa. Child Protective Services law fails. *The Patriot News*. Retrieved from http://www.pennlive.com/editorials/index.ssf/2011/11/where_pa_child_protective_serv.html

Two charged in sexual assault of child investigation. (2014, February 14). Houston, Texas *ABC News*. Retrieved from http://abclocal.go.com/ktrk/story?section=news/local&id=9432645

United States Sentencing Commission. (2012). Report to the Congress: Federal child pornography offenses. Retrieved from http://www.ussc.gov/Legislative_and_Public_Affairs/Congressional_Testimony_and_Reports/Sex_Offense_Topics/201212_Federal_Child_Pornography_Offenses/

U.S. prosecutor accused of seeking sex with girl, 5. (2007, September 18). *Fox News*. Retrieved from http://www.foxnews.com/story/2007/09/18/us-prosecutor-accused-seeking-sex-with-girl-5/

Vargas, R. A. (2011, April 13). Retired Covington psychiatrist pleads guilty to attempted possession of child pornography. *The Times Picayune*. Retrieved from http://www.nola.com/crime/index.ssf/2011/04/retired_covington_psychiatrist.html

Waldron, M. (2013, January 31). Nye Co. school psychologist arrested on child pornography charges. KTNV. Retrieved from http://www.jrn.com/ktnv/news/189297991.html

Welborn, L. (2013, August 21). Ex-judge Kline gets prison. *Orange County Register*. Retrieved from http://www.ocregister.com/articles/kline-59382-court-computer.html?page=1

Evidence

20

Overview

This chapter discusses evidentiary standards, chain of custody, recantation, and child witnesses. Evidentiary standards protect defendants and permit the government to prove cases beyond a reasonable doubt. Chain of custody is an evidentiary requirement that has become more technical in recent years because of hashing systems, temporary caches, and file corruption. Child pornography production offenses may be tried in court. Trials may involve child witnesses. Child witnesses are vulnerable and sensitive and may be traumatized. They may be affected by the process of being confronted by defendants during their testimony, and yet they may be unreliable because they are highly suggestible and have weaker memories. Suggestibility and memory were discussed in Chapter 9.

Evidentiary Standards

The use of technology, for example, Photoshop®, online bulletin boards, and peer-to-peer file sharing, facilitates pornography transmission, but it also records evidence (*Sable Communications of Cal., Inc. v. F.C.C.*, 1989; *U.S. v. Thomas*, 1996). Some offenders redact images of child pornography (*U.S. v. Grimes*, 2001). They may pixelate or place black boxes over children's genitals or faces. Using the *Dost* (*U.S. v. Dost*, 1986) factors discussed in Chapter 5, courts may find that inexplicit sexual images that are redacted constitute child pornography. The presence of black boxes or pixelization on a victim's face does not present an insurmountable evidentiary challenge. Pixelization of faces may make identifying child witnesses more difficult, but experts may be called on to establish a child's age if the child cannot be identified. Experts may examine the depicted subject's pubescence, body structure, environment, and other details to determine whether a depicted subject is a child victim.

Evidence collected from computers may be used to demonstrate that offenders who possess obscenity attempted to distribute or receive images or succeeded in doing so. In spite of the legality of possessing obscenity in private, it is illegal to transmit or deal in obscenity (e.g., trading or selling obscenity). Possession of more than a few obscene depictions of actual or synthetic pornography may be evidence of receipt or attempt to distribute (*U.S. v. Kutzner*, 2010). A variety of depictions or multiple copies of the same image may violate obscenity statutes. Some statutes articulate this standard, and many courts have applied this reasoning.

In addition to other information, forensic reviews can discover deleted data, how frequently files were downloaded, Internet search key words, which searches were conducted before or after illegal material was sought online, metadata that identifies when a file was created and last opened, and the days and times that files were downloaded (Luehr, 2005). This evidence may be direct or circumstantial. The United States Sentencing Commission (USSC) reported to Congress that 23% of experts found that child pornography offenders use cleaning programs to hide child pornography downloads (USSC, 2012). The presence of programs like "History Kill" and "Window Washer" that clear deleted files may serve as circumstantial evidence (*U.S. v. Bass*, 2005). Any forensic data could provide circumstantial evidence about which member of a household may have conducted Internet searches for pornography. Data could also be used to demonstrate that a suspect was home and had access to a particular computer at a specified date and time.

Though many offenders claim not to know that pornography was downloaded onto their computers, the government is rarely convinced by this argument (USSC, 2012). Offenders have argued that they accidentally encountered child pornography in the course of viewing adult pornography. Most offenders are arrested after numerous and persistent downloads, not a single download or a couple of scattered accidents (USSC, 2012). A review of more than 2,600 presentence reports demonstrates that federal child pornography offenders download hundreds or thousands of images throughout weeks, months, or years of file sharing. Because knowledge of possession is an element that the government must prove, offenders' downloading habits may be used to support the inference that downloading was not accidental. Offenders often categorize depictions according to fetishes and victims' genders and ages. Series of depictions contain a common theme or element. Organization demonstrates knowledge of the files. A typical collection may be subdivided into specific series (e.g., "boys posing soft" and "erect teens"). Organized series may also be used to demonstrate intent to engage in file sharing, even though not all images in a series depict abuse or nudity.

Bulletin boards like Reddit and file-sharing programs like LimeWire allow anonymous users to post and share files. Bulletin boards experience high amounts of traffic for child pornography. Membership is necessary to join some bulletin boards and participate in some file-sharing programs. Direct evidence that these sorts of programs or bulletin boards were used to download any obscenity or child pornography may also serve as circumstantial evidence that other illegal depictions present on the same computer were knowingly transmitted using the same program or bulletin board.

Temporary Internet files that are not organized or saved may not evidence a defendant's knowledge beyond a reasonable doubt (*U.S. v. Dobbs*, 2011). In one case, a defendant possessed 150 child pornography images in his cache. A forensic expert testified that the defendant had searched online for "very young sex," "erotic preteen," "youngest porn," "pedo pics," and "preteen Lolita"" (*U.S. v. Dobbs*, 2011). The user conducted the searches methodically by advancing pages dozens of times, but the user exercised no control over the images. While the searches indicated an attempt to view child pornography, and the defendant visited websites associated with child pornography, the defendant may not have knowingly viewed images or possessed images. Files in his cache, however, bore no evidence that the defendant downloaded files or had viewed that material. It could not be proved that the defendant had viewed images in the cache because invisible temporary Internet files, not displayed on a computer's monitor, can download automatically from sites without users' knowledge. Evidence must be viewed in a light most favorable to the government, but, in that case, the government's evidence did not overcome a reasonable doubt that the images were voluntarily and knowingly received into the defendant's cache. The defendant was not guilty of an attempt offense because there was no evidence that he committed any overt act to take a substantial step toward downloading the images in his cache.

Evidence of sex tourism may be difficult to obtain, especially when offenders travel to foreign jurisdictions (USSC, 2012). Tourists may travel unaccompanied to secretly produce pornography, which eliminates potential witnesses. Evidence collection may burden investigators in some cases. Time and financial expense involved in international investigations may be substantial (Department of Justice [DOJ], 2010). Extradition of foreign witnesses presents a considerable obstacle for prosecutors. Sending agents abroad and paying for witnesses to travel to the United States may be cost prohibitive for local and state agencies. These difficulties may deter the government from investigating or pursuing some cases.

Evidentiary and procedural standards may prevent international investigations. When offenders arrive in foreign nations, they may use cell phones to make minimal contacts with foreign targets. Conflicts of law may impede U.S. authorities' ability to investigate and collect evidence using wiretaps, recordings, and video surveillance. U.S. authorities may be unable to engage in typical evidence-gathering strategies because of the effect of these restrictions on the admissibility of evidence in U.S. courts. If U.S. authorities fail to comply with foreign laws or U.S. laws while in other countries, then evidence could be considered to be inadmissible depending on how laws are violated and which laws are violated.

Wiretaps or recordings that are unwarranted or lack prior judicial approval are per se inadmissible (*Katz v. U.S.*, 1967). Under The Federal Wiretap Act,

Title III, individuals may challenge probable cause or appropriate constitutional safeguards required to minimize intrusion into privacy (18 U.S.C. § 2510, 2006). However, Title III's power does not extend extraterritorially (Nelson, 2009). When foreign officials obtain evidence through means that would violate the U.S. Constitution, U.S. courts are not bound to follow the exclusionary rule. When U.S. officials participate in a joint venture with a foreign government to obtain evidence, a three-pronged test is used to determine whether evidence is admissible: "(1) Is the participation of agents of the United States so substantial as to constitute a joint venture? (2) if so, was foreign law complied with? and, (3) if it was not, did U.S. agents act on a 'reasonable belief that the foreign search complied with the foreign country's law'?" (Nelson, 2009, p. 345). If U.S. agents substantially participated or if foreign officials served as U.S. agents, then illegally obtained evidence may be excluded. Courts may also exclude evidence if the manner in which a foreign government collected the evidence shocks judicial conscience. This exception is rare. The Chinese government, for example, allegedly routinely intercepts phone calls and e-mails. Thus, their evidence could be inadmissible in U.S. courts. However, this characterization seems to contradict the PATRIOT Act (Uniting and Strengthening America by Providing Appropriate Tools Required to Intercept and Obstruct Terrorism), which has been used to conduct indiscriminate phone taps on all U.S. citizens. So, interpretation of which surveillance methods shock judicial conscience may be open for political debate.

The rules of evidence are not always applicable. Any party may present evidence that is inadmissible during trial at sentencing hearings if it is probative to the issue of sentencing. Admissible evidence may include circumstances or nature of a crime, a party's character history and background, mental and physical illnesses, financial losses suffered by the victim, gains made by the defendant, and other mitigating or aggravating factors.

Chain of Custody

The government must demonstrate that a chain of custody exists for evidence to be admissible (Luehr, 2005). Proving chain of custody involves showing that evidence has been in the government's control and preserved in its original form from the moment it was first obtained by the government. Establishment of chain of custody requires (1) testimony verifying that evidence introduced is, in fact, the evidence that prosecutors claim to have introduced; (2) testimony demonstrating a chain of continuous possession by persons handling the evidence from the moment it was seized to the moment the evidence arrived in court; and (3) testimony verifying that evidence remained substantially the same to be presented by each person who handled the evidence.

To prove chain of custody, the government relies on forensic experts. Forensic experts must handle evidence at every step of an investigation to ensure that data are preserved (Luehr, 2005). Investigations often begin with e-mail messages or Internet service provider account information that is traced to a residence. Then, a warrant is obtained to seize technological devices. When a computer or technological device is seized, an expert must handle it to avoid contamination or loss of evidence. For example, turning on a computer may erase temporary files, overwrite deleted data, reset the dates on evidence, and have other corruptive effects on evidence. Metadata that recorded when files were created, downloaded, and last accessed could be corrupted or changed. Following seizure, a mirror image of the computer must be created. Experts create and store an identical "sacred" copy of the original. Latent and visible data are copied into a bit-stream format. Original data are blocked so that no new data can be produced on the original computer. This preserves the original data and allows experts an opportunity to create additional mirrors if necessary. Records are kept that detail when the first drive is removed from its secure location, when it is examined, the purpose of the examination, and the identity of the examiner.

Data are authenticated and cataloged using a hashing system that assigns a unique series of numbers and letters to each piece of data. The hash system satisfies chain of custody requirements by allowing experts to match their data to the original hard drive. One of the most popular hash systems used is MD5. Experts search for evidence about victims using the hash system. Some images located within computers may previously have been assigned a hash value during other cases. Experts may rapidly search for and sort identifiable hashes present in computers. In addition to searching hash values, a forensic examiner may also search e-mail files or temporary buddy files from chats to locate information about victims. Experts will examine terms searched for online using temporary Internet files. These files are also cataloged using the hash system.

When the DOJ raids a home believed to be a hub for an online child pornography community, agents may wish to obtain members' user information as quickly as possible (Anderson, 2013). Seizing computers and searching data at a lab may not be feasible. Any time lapse between the raid and the search may tip off community members, who will change their usernames or delete their accounts. Onscene triage allows law enforcement to quickly examine data for information about other users, passwords, and time-sensitive leads or evidence. Site administrators may spread data across dozens of encrypted hard drives to prevent onsite searches. However, authorities can pressure suspects to divulge password information. Police may video record the raid to overcome Fourth Amendment challenges. At the scene, authorities will immediately respond to the evidence and then seize the remaining evidence to undergo lengthier forensics and hashing.

The chain of custody may become irrelevant under specific circumstances. For example, when the court takes judicial notice of common knowledge, then it may not need to be proved in court. An example would occur when a defendant is charged with possessing material harmful to a minor (Miller, 2012). If the defendant admits that he possessed *Playboy* magazines, then the actual, original magazine that was seized may not need to be submitted into evidence in court to demonstrate that it contains nudity because it is widely recognized that all *Playboy* magazines depict partial nudity. The issue to be proved is whether that material is harmful to minors.

Child Testimony

Defendants possess a constitutional right to confront an accuser under the Sixth Amendment. This right guarantees that defendants will meet face-to-face with witnesses at trial and have an opportunity to cross-examine witnesses. Defendants may confront witnesses by objecting to portions of witnesses' direct testimony. Child victims could suffer psychological harm when confronted by defendants in the courtroom. Past trauma may be enflamed, and children may experience shame, anxiety, panic, and other negative psychological effects. In many jurisdictions, child witnesses are heard using closed-circuit one-way or two-way cameras. The child may be examined and cross-examined in a room with a prosecutor and defense counsel. The court is able to see and hear the child; however, the child may be unable to see or hear the defendant. The defense has an opportunity to confront the child, but the child is not emotionally damaged by being in the same room as the abuser. Avoiding psychologically harming children is a compelling state interest. In *Maryland v. Craig* (1990), the Court held that this narrowly tailored procedure permitting child victims to testify outside the courtroom is the least restrictive means for achieving that governmental purpose. The Court's analysis was mixed between intermediate and strict scrutiny. Thus, the Court also held that the government's interest in protecting child victims and public policies undergirding the law only needed to be important, not compelling.

In general, testimony given by victims of sexual abuse need not be corroborated by other witnesses, because sexual abuse in usually committed in private. Direct and circumstantial evidence may be presented to persuade a jury beyond a reasonable doubt, but additional evidence may not be necessary. Often, the testimony of child witnesses may be the only evidence available (Mass. Gen. Laws Ann. 272, § 29, 29B, 2013). Critics claim that false allegations have led to convictions because child witnesses tug at juries' heartstrings, and the law does not require more evidence than a child's testimony. However, if the law were to require greater evidence, guilty defendants could go free. Balancing these interests is difficult, yet justice prevails because it is twice as likely that cases will not be charged if a second piece of evidence does not corroborate a victim's disclosure of abuse (Walsh, Jones, Cross, & Lippert, 2008).

Sometimes a child's testimony can be compelled. In some jurisdictions victims may want to recant their accusations but will still be required to participate (Long, 2007). For example, a victim may have participated willingly in an alleged crime (e.g., production offense), but later discloses the crime to authorities. When the government intervenes, the victim may recant or may wish to terminate the proceedings. In many jurisdictions, the victim may be required to participate. Jury members may view recantation unfavorably, signaling to them that the witness lied. Recantation may be used to impeach the witness. If the witness surprises the prosecution by failing to appear for trial, then previous out-of-court statements made by the victim may be entered into evidence. However, in other cases, victim-centered participation is important to the government (State of New Hampshire Office of the Attorney General, 2012). Prosecutors may make attempts to understand why child witnesses may change their minds and choose not to participate. In these instances, victims who realize that they created an undesired course of action may discontinue their involvement in legal proceedings.

Conclusion

The criminal justice system is composed of some procedural requirements and some discretionary procedures that reflect society's most important values. Constitutional requirements must be followed to ensure justice and preserve free society. Justice may require victims to be compelled to participate. Certain harms are of sufficient magnitude to require the government to proceed irrespective of victims' willingness. However, society also recognizes that the state does not necessarily have an independent interest in prosecuting all defendants. Victims who have not suffered harm may prefer to become disentangled from the justice system. During proceedings, they may distance themselves from defendants by testifying outside the courtroom. When defendants are prosecuted, the government must meet evidentiary standards and constitutional requirements to preserve fairness.

References

18 U.S.C. § 2510 (2006).

Anderson, N. (2013, August 18). Taking down "the largest child pornography conspiracy ever prosecuted." Ars Technica. Retrieved from http://arstechnica.com/tech-policy/2013/08/operation-joint-hammer-taking-down-the-largest-child-pornography-conspiracy-ever-prosecuted/

Department of Justice. (2010, August). The national strategy for child exploitation prevention and interdiction. Retrieved from http://www.justice.gov/psc/docs/natstrategyreport.pdf

Katz v. U.S., 389 U.S. 347 (1967).

Long, J. G. (2007). Introducing expert testimony to explain victim behavior in sexual and domestic violence prosecutions. American Prosecutors Research Institute. Retrieved from http://www.ndaa.org/pdf/pub_introducing_expert_testimony.pdf

Luehr, P. H. (2005). Real evidence, virtual crimes the role of computer forensic experts. *Criminal Justice, 20*(3), 14–23.

Maryland v. Craig, 497 U.S. 836 (1990).

Mass. Gen. Laws Ann. 272 § 29, 29B (2013).

Miller, C. (2012). *Evidence: Best evidence rule.* CALI eLangdell Press. See http://www.cali.org/sites/default/files/BestEvidenceRuleMiller07292013.docx

Nelson, K. A. (2009). Transnational wiretaps and the Fourth Amendment. *Hastings Constitutional Law Quarterly, 36*(2), 329–352.

Sable Communications of Cal., Inc. v. F.C.C., 492 U.S. 115 (1989).

State of New Hampshire Office of the Attorney General. (2012). A model protocol for response to adult sexual assault cases. Governor's Commission on Domestic and Sexual Violence. Retrieved from http://doj.nh.gov/criminal/victim-assistance/documents/sexual-assault-protocol.pdf

United States Sentencing Commission. (2012). Report to the Congress: Federal child pornography offenses. Retrieved from http://www.ussc.gov/Legislative_and_Public_Affairs/Congressional_Testimony_and_Reports/Sex_Offense_Topics/201212_Federal_Child_Pornography_Offenses/

U.S. v. Bass, 411 F.3d 1198 (10th Cir. 2005).

U.S. v. Dobbs, No. 09-5025 (10th Jan. 5, 2011).

U.S. v. Dost, 636 F.Supp. 828 (S.D.Cal. 1986).

U.S. v. Grimes, 244 F.3d 375 (2001).

U.S. v. Kutzner, Rule 11 Plea Agreement (D. Idaho, 2010). Retrieved from http://reason.com/assets/db/12876937541067.pdf

U.S. v. Thomas, 74 F.3d 701 (6th Cir. 1996).

Walsh, W. A., Jones, L. M., Cross, T. P., & Lippert, T. (2008). Prosecuting child sexual abuse: The importance of evidence type. *Crime and Delinquency, 56*(3), 436–454.

Pornography Addiction, Retribution, and Rehabilitation

21

Overview

A variety of interventions have been proved to be successful as well as unsuccessful. Treatment for pornography addiction, pedophilia, and other paraphilia may involve clinical therapy, institutionalization, outpatient therapy and family therapy, lie detection, drug treatment, supervised release, and prison. Ultimately, no single response from the criminal justice system has effectively deterred or reformed all pornography offenders. Even some incapacitated offenders continue to commit pornography offenses.

Incapacitation and Rehabilitation

Risk of recidivism is the basis for incapacitation and rehabilitation of offenders. Prison is a form of incapacitation that meets penological aims by preventing offenders from inflicting future harms on society; rehabilitation seeks to reform prisoners before they reenter society. Yet, neither approach is completely effective. National Drug Intelligence Center (NDIC) experts reported that recidivism among child pornographers is high (United States Sentencing Commission [USSC], 2012). However, 82% said that they were unaware of any definitive statistics describing recidivism rates among child pornography offenders. Incapacitation and rehabilitation responses each require greater research.

The main goal for offering treatment to sex offenders is prevention of recidivism. Some important reasons for providing treatment are addressing criminogenic needs, satisfying community needs, increasing morality, exercising authority over abnormal and deviant forms of sexuality, developing social responsibility, and increasing empathy for victims among offenders. Ideally, generalized treatment may reduce recidivism, but individualized treatment targets specific risks and addresses comorbidities. Individualized treatment of online pornography offenders should address not only sex abuse but also addictions and problematic Internet use. Problematic Internet use may include addiction, deviance, and antisocial behavior related to participation in online communities. Addressing addiction and problematic Internet use may educate offenders about how to create situational changes. Society may benefit when rehabilitated offenders make positive changes and become more productive.

Incapacitation is necessary in some cases. One reason that society may respond with incapacitation is the possibility that offenders will resist rehabilitation. Not all offenders are amenable to treatment, and offenders cannot be compelled to change. Increased sentences incapacitate offenders who may resist treatment, recidivate, and commit sexually dangerous crimes. One of the most common recommendations made by experts in the federal government is to increase mandatory minimum sentences for child pornographers (USSC, 2012). The USSC reported that in 2002, 51% of child pornography producers received upward adjustments in their sentences because they preyed on children younger than 12 years of age (USSC, 2012). Six years later, 47% of sentences had upward adjustments. In the years between, percentages of upward adjustments fluctuated between 39% and 69% (USSC, 2012). USSC data demonstrate that 42% of child pornography trafficking sentences in 2002 received upward adjustments because depictions included sadomasochistic abuse (USSC, 2012). Six years later, 70% of trafficking sentences received the same upward adjustment (USSC, 2012).

The USSC reported that 56% of experts believe that child pornography offenders would best be deterred by longer sentences, stricter probation or parole conditions, and increased fines (USSC, 2012). Almost half of experts believe that prohibiting convicts' use of computers, wireless devices, and the Internet would effectively deter recidivism because it would eliminate inappropriate sexual outlets (USSC, 2012). They also believe that recidivism was somewhat situational and triggered by access to online pornography. Experts reported their belief that federal law should require Internet service providers to filter child pornography, maintain regulated records, and report suspected offenses, which would aid in rehabilitation processes, like probation (USSC, 2012).

The court may incapacitate offenders with consecutive rather than concurrent sentences. For example, a court in Iowa imposed two consecutive sentences for two sex abuse violations resulting from a single incident in which the defendant video recorded sex with his girlfriend (*State v. O'Toole*, 2005). The court found that multiple factors indicated that the defendant suffered from sexual compulsion. The defendant's sexual compulsion posed a sufficient threat to society to merit consecutive sentences. Consecutive sentences were retributive, and consecutive sentences would incapacitate the offender for a longer period of time. Factors considered by the court to determine that the defendant suffered from sexual compulsion included his possession of commercial pornography, viewing pornography online, and use of adult devices. These factors alone may not seem to amount to evidence of sexual compulsion; however, the offender failed probation for a prior conviction on indecent exposure charges. The court felt that a harsher sentence was necessary to stop the defendant from compulsively sexually victimizing others.

In addition to increased sentences and increased restrictions on parole or probation, incapacitation may include chemical castration. Chemical castration has correlated with reduced recidivism or reduced urges more than surgical castration (Laws & O'Donohue, 2008). Some experts claimed that chemical castration is ineffective, but just as many, 14%, reported that increased sentencing would be effective (USSC, 2012). However, 67% of experts claimed that the effect of any incapacitation on recidivism is unknown (USSC, 2012).

Jails

Most correctional facilities prohibit violent and sexual media. Correctional facilities attempt to optimize safety within the prison and maximize inmates' potential to reform. Thus, prisons may forbid inmates from viewing R-rated films depicting sex or violence (*Avila v. Cate*, 2011; Calvert & Murrhee, 2012). For these reasons, pornography and masturbation are forbidden in most jails. Since prison offers little, if any, privacy, viewing pornography and masturbating in prison are likely to be public acts, which is one important reason for proscribing them (Cusack, 2014). Restrictions against pornography and masturbation meet retributive and rehabilitative aims. Inmates, especially sex offenders, ought to learn self-control while in prison, improve their coping skills, learn to follow rules, and behave in conformity with society.

Avoiding public indecency lowers risk for sex crimes in prison, especially among males (Cusack, 2014). Masturbation is linked with sexual assault and turning out male inmates. When inmates masturbate in bunks, showers, or secluded areas of prison that offer more privacy, it increases their chances for being sexually assaulted in prison. Gunning (i.e., public masturbation by males in prison) may be performed intentionally to intimidate female guards; gunning may also relate to sexual compulsion or mental illness.

If offenders engage in public pornography viewing and masturbation in prison, then their risks for recidivism upon reentry may increase because they fail to conform to normative public behavior, fail to respect authority, and fail to develop sexual self-control (Cusack, 2014). Proscriptions against pornography and masturbation in incarceration prepare inmates for reentry, allow inmates to focus on rehabilitative forms of coping, reduce access to addictive materials and opportunities to engage in compulsive behaviors, and serve retributive goals.

Inpatient Programs

In institutional settings, such as commitment facilities and houses of correction, inmates may be ordered to undergo standard or individualized treatment plans. Meaningful participation is voluntary and requires willingness to change. Individualized and standard treatment plans often include group treatment. For the most part, group therapy aids offenders' self-esteem, coping skills, and socialization. One possible counterproductive consequence of group treatment is that sex offenders may form sexually aberrant social networks within prisons. Despite that possibility, sex offenders may make healthy alliances, request to bunk or dorm with each other, and benefit from safety in numbers.

Some sex offenders may be institutionalized. Courts may sentence offenders possessing serious mental defects to correctional facilities that specialize in mental health treatment. When offenders are so mentally ill that they are incompetent, they may be institutionalized until they are well enough to stand trial. Sex offenders may receive inpatient treatment until they are able to appreciate the charges against them or meaningfully participate in proceedings. Sometimes, sex offenders are subject to civil commitment indefinitely after their sentences have been served. They may be civilly committed after their sentences are completed. In *Kansas v. Hendricks* (1997), the Court held that mental abnormalities in some sex offenders create uncontrollable compulsivity. They continue to be dangerous to society after they have served their sentences. In *Hendricks*, the Court was asked to decide whether civil commitment following completion of a prison term constitutes double jeopardy. The answer was no. It does not. Civil commitment of child pornography offenders is lawful as long as offenders continue to present danger to society. Civil commitment may result when any person presents a danger to him- or herself or others; it occurs after the sentence is completed because offenders continue to be dangerous. Civil commitment is not a term of the original sentence, and it is not a second sentence. It is a civil measure that does not impose a second criminal punishment for the same crime on an offender. Therefore, it does not create double jeopardy.

To initiate civil commitment proceedings, the Bureau of Prisons or the attorney general (USSC, 2012) first certifies sexually dangerous persons. Release from civil commitment is stayed until a legal determination is made by the court. If the federal government carries its burden by clear and convincing evidence, then the court may commit a sexually dangerous person to remain in the attorney general's custody until the offender is successfully treated. To carry its burden, the government must demonstrate that an offender suffers from a mental disorder, whether congenital or developed. The government must demonstrate that because of a mental disorder, the offender will likely be unable to refrain from other sexually dangerous behavior in society. Sexually dangerous behavior is not limited to hands-on production offenses and may include other pornography offenses. Sexually dangerous offenders may also be civilly committed by the state (720 ILCS 5/11-20.1, 2014). However, state procedures may vary. For example, a state may require the government to prove its case beyond a reasonable doubt, which is a higher burden than at the federal level (*In Re Commitment of Charles Steven Chapman*, 2013).

Major goals of inpatient therapy are to develop understandings of a pornography offender's risk for contact offenses, an offender's motivations and victim demographic, an offender's fetishistic interests, and an offender's involvement in online community activity (USSC, 2012). A full psychosexual evaluation must be conducted using actuarial instruments and clinical evaluations to make risk assessments. During a risk assessment, an offender's sexual history and interests will be documented and evaluated. Information that may be recorded includes mental abnormalities, behaviors, substance abuse, crimes, history of sexual and physical abuse, mental illness, childhood experiences, medical history, family history, and sexual partners. Clinicians may give offenders personality assessments to develop appropriate treatment plans. Clinicians will assess cognitive distortions and deviant attitudes toward children, which often play a role in pornography and contact offenses. Offenders often attempt to hide or deny deviant attitudes or desires. Objective physical evaluations may be used to determine whether offenders are pedophiles or hebephiles or suffer from other nonspecified paraphilia. Penile phallometric tests measure physical responses created in an offender's genitals when aroused. Visual response time tests determine an offender's specific interests in age groups and genders. To determine whether offenders are still aroused by child pornography, clinicians may expose them to depictions of different genders, ages, and fetishes (e.g., hard-core pornography of young boys and nude images of teen females). Therapists may examine an offender's pornography collection or detailed records of collections. Image cataloging was discussed in Chapter 19. Clinicians must be knowledgeable about common classifications of pornography, for example, fetishes, ages, states of arousal, sex acts, and victim demographics (Burgess, Carretta, & Burgess, 2012).

The routine activity theory holds that situational crimes occur because of an absence of effective controls and presence of attractive targets. The routine activity theory may apply to online offenders who are addicted to the Internet or become heavily involved in online communities (Babchishin, Hanson, & Hermann, 2011). The presence of suitable targets in unprotected environments (e.g., the Internet) permits predators to anonymously prey undeterred. Offenders who are motivated by fantasy, desire, or peer acceptance may access images or solicit victims online. Internet regulation could make online offending activity riskier or more difficult and thus less desirable. An institution may directly impose control during inpatient therapy, but development of internal control, environmental control, and sexual control are also important goals for inpatient therapy.

Once an offender is evaluated, cognitive behavioral therapy (CBT) can be customized to treat offenders behaviorally and cognitively (Babchishin et al., 2011). This approach aims to rewire offenders' actions and thoughts, and it may involve prescription medications, like selective serotonin reuptake inhibitors. CBT or portions of this approach may be maintained after offenders complete their sentences or are released from civil commitment. Polygraph testing may be used after reentry to ensure CBT's effectiveness.

Outpatient Programs

Therapeutic responses within the community are available for offenders and members of the community, including offenders' families. Outpatient treatment may be available to self-identified pornography addicts, probationers, and parolees. A few jurisdictions preemptively offer services to people who fear that pornography addiction is increasing their risks to commit crimes. Many private groups, such as churches or Sexaholics Anonymous, offer counseling and support for pornography addiction. Little is known about pathological pornography use (Ley, Prause, & Finn, 2014). Thus, treatment for pathological pornography use may not be successful. Yet, outpatient programs may include monitoring of home-life activities or involvement in extracurricular activities to replace poor coping skills and problematic Internet use.

Men were surveyed who (1) were not involved in corrections, (2) lived within their communities, (3) had not been convicted of sex offenses, and (4) felt sexually attracted to minors (Neutze, Seto, Schaefer, Mundt, & Beier, 2011). A sample of 155 men who met the *Diagnostic and Statistical Manual of Mental Disorders* (American Psychiatric Association, 2000) criteria for pedophilia or paraphilic attraction to pubescent children indicated that their sexual behavior over the past six months, including viewing child pornography and hands-on offenses, was not very different than lifetime behavior. This may indicate that without intervention, behavior is likely to remain unchanged.

Excessive sexual behaviors may be treated as disorders (Schneider, 2004). To treat disorders, clinicians may tease behaviors apart into three categories. In the first level, behaviors are classified as normal. This level includes tolerable masturbation and pornography viewing. Level two classifies illegal behavior, like voyeurism, exhibitionism, and obscene phone calls. Behaviors are classified in this category because they victimize others. Level three behaviors result in severe consequences for victims. The third level includes hands-on offenses and production offenses. Clinicians may determine whether behavior at a particular level results from stimulus and opportunities in a deviant's environment or whether behavior is part of a pattern. Repeated offenses may relate to mental illness or compulsive behavior. If behavior appears to relate to sex addiction, then clinicians determine the level of intervention.

Deviants are treated in three stages. The first stage should be designed to disrupt delusions about sex addition and create realizations about the need for change. This requires intervention, confrontation of denial, and education. Online child pornography offenders are as educated as the general population, but they are 200% more likely to be unemployed (Babchishin et al., 2011). Employment and constructive occupations detract attention from and opportunity for deviance. Maintaining employment may result in overall self-improvement. Thus, in the second stage, planning to practice abstinence and designing a course for self-improvement are essential. During the second stage, partners and family are involved. Shame is reduced by family members' participation in and attendance to group therapy. Their attendance may also strengthen commitment to rehabilitation through planning. At this stage, multiple addictions may be treated. The third stage flows from the second stage because underlying issues are explored with the help of family members. Memories, traumas, and other contributing factors may be discussed and treated.

Almost all NDIC experts reported that child pornographers may receive available treatment, yet slightly more than half doubted the effectiveness of treatment, and more than one-third believed that treatment was ineffective (USSC, 2012). Effectiveness of treatment may be influenced by an offender's age, the duration of treatment, the kind of treatment, an offender's self-control, and an offender's access to supervisory or support networks. Polygraph testing is often used to guide treatment programs and validate their effectiveness.

The federal government uses several therapeutic approaches that are considered to be best practices in the field. The Bureau of Prisons attempts to manage child pornography sex offenders using specialized regional sex offender management programs that include residential and nonresidential levels of treatment intensity. Under the "containment model" of treatment, offenders are treated following reentry into the community using community-based supervision and other services, including polygraph testing (USSC, 2012). Offenders on probation or supervised release work closely with a supervising officer, therapist, and polygraph expert. Community collaboration, multiagency networking, risk assessment, therapeutic intervention, and concentrated community supervision increase safety for the community. Community members participate because they directly benefit.

Addressing noncompliance with treatment is important in state-level and federal-level programs. Implementation of and adherence to specific policies are vital for offenders. Ideally, offenders should understand possible consequences that will result from noncompliance at multiple levels and through multiple agencies. They must view distinct steps of rehabilitation and distinct agency participants as being aligned albeit separate forms of authority. The Adult Sex Offender Program (ASOP) in Cook County, Illinois, reported positive results by developing best practices (Illinois Criminal Justice Information Authority, 2001). Offenders' treatment included polygraph testing, objective personality testing, and objective sexual preferences testing. Group therapy was required weekly for 90 minutes. Individual therapy sessions were required twice each month. Therapists reported that offenders made positive changes in their lifestyles, social relationships, employment status, and sobriety. ASOP offenders were arrested sooner than those in control groups, and they also were less likely to commit new sex crimes. This demonstrates the effectiveness of the program, as does the fact that ASOP offenders had probation revoked at higher rates. Strict probation conditions proved to tolerate less noncompliance. However, it does not attest to the effectiveness of therapeutic interventions. Furthermore, strict programs require specific financial resources. Jurisdictions implementing special treatment programs may require increased law enforcement training and personnel to focus on investigation. Rehabilitating child pornography offenders consumes an extraordinary amount of resources even though they are a small percentage of total offenders. Thus, management, oversight, and enforcement may be deficient. Outpatient rehabilitation programs should not be idealized. Inadequate resources sometimes limit the quality of professional participation, amount and rigor of training, and consistency of policy implementation.

Pedophilia

Treatment for child pornography is often unsuccessful. This failure may relate to low success rates for treating pedophilia. One reason for a low success rate is that no single cause for pedophilia has been discovered (Khol, 2013). Pedophilia has been treated as a sexual orientation, a disease, a disorder, an antisocial behavior, and a deviant lifestyle. Researchers point to the fact that some pedophiles are repulsed by incest with children to demonstrate that pedophilia is a sexual orientation. Yet, many pedophiles are attracted to and victimize relatives (USSC, 2012). Other researchers commonly suggest that pedophilia results from trauma, mental deformities, and other abnormalities because of its comorbid relationships with other illnesses. Antisocial behavior is present in many criminal behaviors. Described by some researchers as the most predictive factor in pedophilia and fetishistic pornography addiction, antisocial behavior may relate to frontal lobe abnormalities or trauma, and it usually onsets or manifests in childhood. Some researchers suggest that interest in prurient material may progress to where it causes users to drift from normal sexual interests into deviance.

There is a well-established relationship between antisocial behavior and sexual deviance in some offenders. Offenders may be indiscriminately attracted to deviant sexual stimulation or continuously crave new and more depraved experiences. Desensitization to child pornography may lower resistances to other aberrant forms of child sexual exploitation, which supports the idea that pedophilia is a social disease or a deviant lifestyle. Under the rational choice theory, child pornography users choose to view pornography. Thus, relationships between deviance, lifestyle, and antisocial behavior may not be unidirectional.

Motivations vary among offenders, which further complicates the establishment of causality. For example, sometimes offenders may use child pornography to validate pedophilia, while at other times, offenders may use pornography to groom victims. Some offenders adhere to specific *modi operandi*, while others engage in a combination of activities. Lack of understanding about what causes pedophilia makes treating the use of child pornography more difficult. However, overlapping understandings may be synergized under a biopsychosocial treatment model. Biopsychosocial approaches may consider offenders' proclivities, trauma, exposure to pornography at young ages, genetic tendencies for low impulse control, substance use, predatory behavior, poor coping skills, and other factors (Grigorenko, 2012).

Significant portions of child pornographers have engaged in sexually dangerous behavior and are pedophiles. Pedophiles may not be forthcoming about their desires and, thus, may downplay their risk for recidivism. Actuarial instruments may be administered to objectively assess risk of recidivism. Many actuarial instruments are checklists that score factors to assess the likelihood of risk. Some instruments may consider offenders' criminal and personal histories. Other instruments (e.g., Static-99) focus on victims' demographics and offenders' violence. However, no actuarial instruments have been designed to measure the future risk of child pornography offenses for pedophiles who have no history of criminal sexually dangerous behavior (USSC, 2012). In general, actuarial instruments possess about 50% accuracy for predicting recidivism. Use of actuarial instruments is important, but it must be supplemented by expert evaluation. Actuarial instruments should be administered by clinicians who can evaluate offenders.

Conclusion

Incapacitation and rehabilitative notions of justice seem to countervail each other at times; however, penological aims have been satisfied by both approaches. Oftentimes, success of incapacitation, supervision, and treatment depend on an offender's individual motivation and biopsychosocial factors and a jurisdiction's resources.

References

720 ILCS 5/11-20.1 (2014).

American Psychiatric Association. (2000). *Diagnostic and statistical manual of mental disorders* (4th ed., text rev.). Washington, D.C.: APA.

Avila v. Cate, No. 1:10-cv-01208, 2011 U.S. Dist. LEXIS 73809 (E.D. Cal. July 8, 2011).

Babchishin, K. M., Hanson, R. K., & Hermann, C. A. (2011). The characteristics of online sex offenders: A meta-analysis. *Sex Abuse, 23*(1), 92–123.

Burgess, A. W., Carretta, C. M., & Burgess, A. G. (2012). Patterns of federal Internet offenders: A pilot study. *Journal of Forensic Nursing, 8*(3), 112–121.

Calvert, C., & Murrhee, K. C. (2012). Big censorship in the big house—a quarter-century after *Turner v. Safley*: Muting movies, music and books behind bars. *Northwestern Journal of Law and Social Policy, 7*(2), 257–300.

Cusack, C. M. (2014). No stroking in the pokey: Promulgating penological policies prohibiting masturbation among inmate populations. *Journal of Law and Social Deviance, 7*, 80–124.

Grigorenko, E. L. (Ed.). (2012). *Handbook of juvenile forensic psychology and psychiatry.* New York: Springer.

Illinois Criminal Justice Information Authority. (2001). Specialized sex offender probation in Cook County links supervision, treatment was reported to have a "vibrant" sex offender treatment program. *On Good Authority, 4*, 7.

In Re Commitment of Charles Steven Chapman, 2013 Tex. App. LEXIS 11404 (2013).

Kansas v. Hendricks, 521 U.S. 346 (1997).

Khol, J. V. (2013, December 22). Compelling evidence: How much is enough? Pheromones.com. Retrieved from http://pheromones.com/compelling-evidence-much-enough/

Laws, D. R., & O'Donohue, W. T. (2008). *Sexual deviance.* New York: Guilford Press.

Ley, D., Prause, N., & Finn, P. (2014). The emperor has no clothes: A review of the "pornography addiction" model. *Current Sexual Health Reports, 6*(20), 1–12. doi:10.1007/s11930-014-0016-8

Neutze, J., Seto, M. C., Schaefer, G. A., Mundt, I. A., & Beier, K. M. (2011). Predictors of child pornography offenses and child sexual abuse in a community sample of pedophiles and hebephiles. *Sexual Abuse, 23*(2), 212–242.

Schneider, J. P. (2004). *Understanding and diagnosing sex addiction.* Hoboken, NJ: John Wiley & Sons.

State v. O'Toole, 2005 Iowa App. LEXIS 1251 (Iowa Ct. App. Oct. 26 2005).

United States Sentencing Commission. (2012). Report to the Congress: Federal child pornography offenses. Retrieved from http://www.ussc.gov/Legislative_and_Public_Affairs/Congressional_Testimony_and_Reports/Sex_Offense_Topics/201212_Federal_Child_Pornography_Offenses/

International and Comparative 22

Overview

International policies and perspectives on pornography may be analyzed comparatively. Foreign nations' policies may reflect ethnic and cultural understandings, thus those policies should not be judged (Cusack, 2014). Cultural homogenization is not a legitimate goal of the criminal justice system and is antithetical to the mission of a free society. Nevertheless, concerns about policies that fail to end abuse and international human rights violations are relevant, especially when international or foreign crimes affect American society.

Europe

European laws regulating and criminalizing pornography vary widely. For example, for many years, Denmark had no child pornography laws, while the United Kingdom has maintained strict obscenity laws. Under Danish law §235, Article 3, children who are 15 years old may consent for others to possess nude depictions of them, but under Article 2, Danes may not distribute or deal in pornography of any person under the age of 18 years. Thus, it seems that Danish laws are guided by underlying concerns about protecting children from exploitation. Denmark's approach contrasts with England's historical prosecution of obscenity and explicit materials enforced by the Obscene Publications Squad (British Library, n.d.). Enforcement of traditional morality has long seemed to be the focus of the United Kingdom's laws and enforcement policies. For example, at the beginning of the 20th century's sexual revolution, two magazines, *IT* and *Oz*, were searched and inventory was temporarily seized by the Obscene Publications Squad because the magazines published gay materials. Like U.S. policies at that time, homosexual content was considered to be an affront to public morality in the United Kingdom. Despite public scrutiny, *Oz* magazine later invited minors to guest edit the magazine. Children between 14 years old and 18 years old edited a special edition discussing minors' views of sexual freedom, drugs, corporal punishment, and other implicitly devious themes. The government charged the magazine's editors with obscenity and conspiracy to corrupt minors.

Figure 22.1 *Oz* magazine cover, 1971.

Student editors testified on behalf of the magazine that the kinds of comic strips and ideas depicted in the magazine were no more immoral or obscene than drawings shared between youth at school. The United Kingdom did not consider minors' intellectual freedom to be more important than public morality. Thus, the students' testimony failed to convince the jury that *Oz* editors were not guilty. The editors were convicted by the lower court under the Obscene Publications Act (Figure 22.1).

The International Centre for Missing and Exploited Children (ICMEC) reported in 2012 that many European nations provide legal definitions of child pornography and criminalize it (ICMEC, 2013). Definitions of *child pornography* may include depictions of partially clothed children, drawings, and explicit conduct. These nations may also criminalize simple possession and distribution. Several nations require Internet service providers (ISPs) to report child pornography. The following nations have implemented at least four kinds of legal protections for children: Belgium, Denmark, Estonia, Finland, France, Georgia, Germany, Greece, Hungary, Ireland, Italy, Kosovo, Latvia, Liechtenstein, Macedonia, Malta, Moldova, Monaco, the Netherlands, Norway, Romania, Slovak Republic, Sweden, Switzerland, and the United Kingdom.

The U.S. government has viewed Eastern European countries very suspiciously because of sex trafficking and child pornography activity. Eastern European nations have participated in global networks peddling child pornography. Some of these nations have accepted payments online from Americans. Many U.S. agencies have reported that Russians play the greatest role in organized transnational child pornography crime (United States Sentencing Commission [USSC], 2012). Russia is considered to be a No. 1

nation for production offenses (Newton, 2011). Children in Russia suffer from sexual abuse at alarming rates. Though much of the abuse is unreported, hundreds of reports are filed each month. Russian authorities may remove thousands of Russian websites featuring child pornography each month, but they are unable to stop the problem.

European pornographers have been nabbed in some of the largest U.S. and international stings (Anderson, 2013). These investigations may be very difficult because foreign governments often ignore child pornography. Sixty-eight percent of National Drug Intelligence Center (NDIC) experts reported that foreign governments are uncooperative with child pornography investigations. One major international investigation was successful in 2008 when a massive pornography network, The Cache, was raided in Baltimore, Maryland. The investigation began in 2006, when an incest video seized in Australia depicted a victim in Belgium. While under investigation, a Flemish father who molested his daughter tipped off police about an Italian photographer who produced child pornography in Ukraine. The Italian photographer produced and sold more than 100 child pornography videos through a password-protected section of a child modeling website. Italian police seized 50,000 electronic messages from interested customers in 28 countries; 11,000 of those e-mails came from the United States. In response, Europol planned Operation Koala at The Hague. European police identified 2,500 suspects in 19 countries. Hundreds were arrested. The Federal Bureau of Investigation (FBI) investigated 700 leads and arrested 60 U.S. residents through Operation Joint Hammer. Joint Hammer was ongoing, but in 2008, it led to the dismantling of The Cache after the site's administrators were discovered and raided, though The Cache warned users that child pornography was forbidden, The Cache was a renowned trading site where child pornography was somewhat encouraged by administrators. Arrest of the first administrator led to Operation Nest Egg. Operation Nest Egg yielded information from throughout the United States and led authorities to 22 top users. All the top users pleaded guilty to possessing hundreds of thousands of images and to hands-on offenses. Plea bargains signed by offenders in Operation Nest Egg provided authorities with information for Operation Delego, which took down Dreamboard. Dreamboard used The Onion Router (TOR), but authorities were able to convert screen names into real names. The majority of offenders arrested were in the United States, but several were arrested in European countries, like Denmark. These operations involved nearly two dozen European police agencies, the FBI, Immigration and Customs Enforcement, the U.S. Postal Inspection Service, the Department of Justice, and Europol. These offender, victim, interagency, and operational linkages support law enforcement's perception that child pornography is a globalized epidemic with a significant portion of activity occurring between the United States and Europe.

Latin America

Aruba, Bahamas, Barbados, Bolivia, Brazil, Chile, Colombia, Costa Rica, Dominican Republic, El Salvador, Honduras, Jamaica, Mexico, Nicaragua, Panama, Paraguay, St. Vincent and the Grenadines, and Trinidad and Tobago at a minimum have laws that do four of the following: (1) define child pornography, (2) criminalize child pornography, (3) criminalize simple possession, (4) require ISPs to report suspected child pornography, and (5) criminalize distribution (ICMEC, 2013). In the past seven years, Argentina, Belize, Cuba, Ecuador, Guatemala, St. Kitts and Nevis, Suriname, and Uruguay have adopted at least one new child pornography law.

Antipornography laws may not reflect stringency or cultural attitudes toward pornography. For example, in Cuba, computers per capita are the lowest in Latin America. Thus, online child pornography offenses would be statistically lower. Yet, all pornographic material is prohibited in Cuba. No pornographic material is manufactured in Cuba, and none may enter through customs. Illegal pornography may be traded in person, but speculation about black markets or networks lacks scientific research. The same is true in Guyana, where viewing, possessing, or dealing any pornography is illegal.

Child pornography offenses in Cuba may be punished by fines and prison. Serious offenses may be punished by long prison sentences or capital punishment. In the United States, capital punishment for brutal rape was previously constitutional, though now only Uniform Code of Military Justice permits capital punishment for rape (10 U.S.C. § 920 Art. 120, 2013; *Coker v. Georgia*, 1977). Capital punishment for rape reflects traditional values about the gravity of rape and society's condemnation of it. However, there is no contemporary evidence of capital punishment sentences for child pornography in Cuba. Severe prison sentences for serious crimes in Cuba and the United States are similar.

Cuban and Guyanan laws stand in stark contrast to Mexican and Brazilian attitudes about pornography and their pornography industries. Erotic depictions are openly sold at newsstands in Mexico. Depictions of soft-core pornography and erotic nudity are socially acceptable. Mexico is the world's second-largest producer of child pornography (McLaughlin, 2012). Lawmakers have attempted to combat the problem, but like the War on Drugs, their efforts are failing. Like Mexico, Brazil attempts to crack down on child pornography. Anecdotally, Brazil has been described as very liberal toward pornography. Films produced in Brazil have allegedly depicted hard-core themes without prosecution. Under Brazil's Penal Code Articles 233 and 234, statutory language regarding obscene acts and depictions is vague. However, statutes seem inclusive by banning obscene drawings, paintings, and writings. In one case, child pornography was distributed to Brazilians from a network hub in Argentina. Brazilian authorities worked to bring down an international network transmitting child pornography files over the Internet to Argentina, Chile, Colombia, Costa Rica, Ecuador, Spain, Uruguay, and Venezuela (Xinhua, 2013). Operation International Purity 2 resulted in 19 raids and 30 arrests in Argentina after police discovered a production studio hidden in a secret room above a false ceiling (Depsky, 2013).

Africa

African nations tend to be some of the most traditional or least progressive nations throughout the world. Human rights violations toward homosexuals, females, and other political minorities have allegedly been inflicted by governments and cultures abiding by patriarchal norms. Norms were discussed in Chapter 1. Critics of morality-based restrictions sometimes raise human rights violations allegations. Critics allege that pornography content bans go hand in hand with political oppression of homosexual and female sexual empowerment. Relationships between morality, pornography bans, and sexual oppression of racial minorities, women, and children were discussed in greater detail in Chapter 2 and Chapter 5. Bans allegedly strengthen oppressive or religious regimes that marginalize political minorities, and suppression of nontraditional speech may validate social ostracization of certain groups. In the majority of African countries, same-sex relationships are illegal, and homosexuals are reportedly politically oppressed (Gander, 2014). Homosexuals have been physically attacked and killed. Uganda passed an antigay bill around the same time that an antipornography bill was passed. The government seems to have announced that deviance and immorality will be punished. The antipornography bill not only targeted lewd public displays but banned women from wearing miniskirts and displaying their thighs in public. At first, enforcement was abusive, and police mobbed and manhandled women wearing miniskirts. The timing of these two laws and their underlying social policies may demonstrate connections between suppression of female and homosexual sexuality, obscenity, and legislated morality.

Antipornography feminist theory could provide an alternate viewpoint to critics' contentions. Strict proscriptions against pornography may eliminate some exploitation and trafficking associated with pornography. Elimination of some exploitation to an extent may justify infringements on rights or freedoms. However, politically oppressed individuals who attempt to flee their nations may become involved in human trafficking, which undermines the antipornography argument to some extent. Human trafficking may originally be entered into voluntarily, but some victims are abducted, sold, or forced. Human trafficking could lead victims into international sexual slavery, including pornography production in the United States. For example, Asian women are reportedly tricked, abducted, and trafficked into South Africa for prostitution (Porn, Sex Trafficking, and Jacob's Story, 2012). After they have been abused, drugged, and emotionally broken, they may be relocated temporarily to California to produce pornography in low-budget productions. Thus, trafficking and human rights issues in Africa may be relevant to pornography issues in the U.S. criminal justice system.

Over the past couple of years, a battle over morality and the legality of pornography in Egypt has played out in Egyptian courts. Antipornography proponents have argued that Egyptians' consumption of pornography may corrupt public morals and detract viewers from other decent pursuits. Attempts to ban pornography or lift bans on pornography may relate to relatively high rates of online pornography consumption in Egypt (Porn Websites Among Most Visited, 2012). One study showed that pornography websites are Among the most visited sites in the country. Controversy over pornography and pornography bans in Egypt may persist in the coming years as the nation's leadership and youth explore conservative and liberal policies. One unchanging element of Egyptian law has been Egypt's opposition to child pornography (U.S. State Department, 2013). Child pornography websites are censored in Egypt. Dealing in child pornography carries a minimum sentence of five years and fines of US$29,000. Egypt is distinct from other African nations because numerous African countries have no laws against child pornography. However, absent legislation does not necessarily indicate that production or online offenses are common in the following nations: Algeria, Angola, Benin, Burkina Faso, Central African Republic, Chad, Comoros, Congo, Côte d'Ivoire, Equatorial Guinea, Eritrea, Ethiopia, Gabon, Ghana, Guinea, Guinea-Bissau, Lesotho, Libya, Mozambique, Namibia, Niger, São Tomé and Príncipe, Somalia, Swaziland, and Zimbabwe (ICMEC, 2013).

Asia

Regions in Asia include Russia, the Middle East, South Asia, Southeast Asia, and East Asia. Each of these regions responds to pornography differently. Russia is discussed further in this chapter's section about Europe. In the Middle East, pornography may incur severe punishments. For example, one Persian man designed photo-uploading software that was used by pornography websites (Dehghan, 2012). Islamic Republic of Iran claimed that the offender designed and moderated a pornography website, but his family maintained that pornographic websites nonconsensually used his software. He allegedly confessed under pain and duress and was sentenced to death for "insulting the sanctity of Islam," which "[spread] corruption on Earth."

Western media outlets claimed that the charges were vague and that a death sentence was inappropriate. Morality seems to be the basis for the charges and the sentence. Though capital punishment is not imposed on pornographers in the United States, life sentences may be. Those sentences may also be based on morality.

In Islamic Republic of Pakistan, pornographic productions are exhibited publicly (Sex, Drugs and Beards, 2013). Young men attend X-rated film showings and smoke hashish and cannabis. X-rated films are covertly played at mainstream theaters. Patrons must be in the know, because films are not advertised. Films' plots sometimes surround moral dilemmas, like which marriage arrangement would better suit the protagonist—an arranged marriage to a cousin or true love. The protagonist must engage in hours of explicit sex with each potential bride to arrive at the correct answer. Exhibition of these films highlights relationships between private morality, public morality, tradition, sex, and pornography; these relationships are also relevant in the United States. Yet, one reason that film showings have remained successful is that films are locally produced, not Western made. Theaters are promoted by powerful individuals, but criticized by politically powerful groups. A controversial theater in Peshawar, Pakistan, has shown films for more than 30 years in a district that borders areas occupied by Taliban and Al-Qaeda militants. One theater was attacked and burned down, but it reopened soon after the attack. Pakistani mainstream films are forbidden from depicting kissing, and the presence of pornographic film theaters in the region continues to break moral tradition.

ISPs block dozens of websites in India that have permitted obscene content (Press Trust of India, 2013). The Department of Telecommunications, the Ministry of Communications and Information Technology, the Ministry of Information and Broadcasting, the Ministry of Home Affairs, the Internet Service Providers Association of India, the court, and the advocacy group Kamlesh Vaswani worked together to obstruct access to obscenity online. Obscenity was labeled a major cause of crime against females. Without laws against obscenity, these agencies argued that public demand would go unchecked and production offenses would rise.

In Southeast Asia, governmental and social approaches vary. Republic of the Philippines is the largest producer of child pornography in the world. Children in the Philippines are commonly exploited by production offenses and solicitation offenses (PH among Top 10 Child Porno Producers, 2014). Many online offenders exploit Filipino children for pornography, and solicitors may visit the Philippines to commit hands-on offenses. Sex tourists choose countries in which they can produce pornography and engage in sex tourism. Commercial sex enterprises are criminalized, but commonly tolerated in the Philippines. Some scholars argue that sex enterprises should be regulated rather than criminalized because victims would be better protected. Proponents argue that decriminalization of pornography (e.g., manga) and regulation other sexual industries has decreased sexual victimization in Japan (April, 2012). Yet, according to NDIC experts, U.S. citizens and residents traveling to Asia do not choose Japan as often as they choose the Philippines, Thailand, and other third-world and impoverished countries.

Foreign child sex enterprises are industrialized, mechanized, and insulated from U.S. law enforcement to an extent (Jeffreys, 2009). Use of the Internet by foreign child prostitutes means that many children no longer work at the street level. They may conduct business exclusively online (The Ten-Year-Old Girl Called 'Sweetie,' 2013). Sex tourism may begin with online solicitation of minors and result in child pornography production. Among NDIC respondents, 100% reported that tourists produce images in foreign countries and transport them into the United States (USSC, 2012). More than half reported that locating and extraditing victims is impractical. Almost half reported that collecting evidence is too difficult, and one-third attributed stymied investigations to policy conflicts with foreign governments.

Many U.S. states specifically criminalize participation in sex tourism. For example, in the state of Washington, residents are forbidden from participating in businesses that promote or facilitate sex tourism (Wash. Rev. Code § 9A.88.085, 2013). Washington's legislature defined *sex tourism* to include pornography. Foreign women and girls are often targeted by anti-sex-tourism laws in their home nations because sex tourism is important to some foreign economies. American johns may not be subject to discipline abroad for their actions. Washington's legislature rationalized that johns should neither be permitted to travel from the United States to engage in sex tourism nor be permitted to transport pornography into Washington.

Over the past 10 years, People's Republic of China has distinguished itself from other East Asian nations by regulating online speech, deanonymizing Internet login, blocking some social media, and banning pornography (McDonald, 2012). In 2009, more than 5,000 people were arrested for pornography offenses in China. In a country of 1.5 billion people with 350 million Internet users, this figure is low compared to arrest rates for pornography offenses in the United States. In the United States, thousands of offenders are convicted and sentenced in federal court alone each year (USSC, 2012). The Chinese government has allegedly shut down only approximately 10,000 websites featuring pornographic content. China is looking to increase enforcement against all Internet crimes, so the government offers \$1,000 rewards for information about pornographic websites. It also promotes installation of computer censorship programs (i.e., Green Dam Youth Escort). Chinese in the United States have attempted to request asylum for pornography offenses because of the allegedly stern punishments for pornography crimes in China (*Liu v. U.S.*, 2007). The Chinese have sentenced pornographers to death, for example, in a case in which an offender produced 440,000 pornography books (Death Sentence, 1994). However, capital sentences for pornography offenses seem to be infrequent. China has been a world leader in its response to Internet addiction (Vincent, 2014). It was the first to treat Internet addiction as a mental illness. China's Communist Youth League alleges that 17% of postpubescent minors are addicted to the Internet in China. Since 2004, the government has opened 400 institutions to treat 24 million youth. South Korea also has experienced alarming Internet addiction, and Japan now treats Internet-addicted schoolchildren. Children who spend more time unmonitored online may be at greater risk for encountering pornography and obscenity, sharing child pornography, and being victimized by pornography solicitors.

Republic of Singapore is a nation known for strict laws regulating public comportment. *Obscenity* is defined by materials that tend to deprave or corrupt people who witness it; material must be taken as a whole. This definition is similar to *Miller v. California*'s (1973) definition of *obscenity*, which requires material to be taken as a whole. *Miller* was developed from *Roth v. U.S.* (1957), and *Roth* related to *Regina v. Hicklin*, an English case from 1868 (Goodroad, 1998). *Regina v. Hicklin* defined *obscenity* based on audiences' moral corruption and depravity. Singapore also defines *obscenity* as corruptive. *Miller* does not require obscenity to possess a tendency to corrupt or deprave audiences. It only requires that depictions appeal to prurient interests and offend the community.

Obscene publications in Singapore carry sentences of up to two years and much heavier fines. Possessing obscene films makes offenders strictly liable under Singapore's Film Act 107 § 30. Simple possession is punishable by up to six months in prison. Knowing possession is punishable by up to one year in prison for the first offense. Child pornography offenses are punishable by up to five years in prison. However, in Singapore, publicly displaying obscenity carries only a $100 fine or less than one month in prison.

Canada and Australia

Australian and Canadian authorities have played important roles in international investigations and sting operations. One reason is that offenders in Australia and Canada sometimes work together in illegal pornography operations. It seems likely that Australians and Canadians may volunteer their computers to serve as relays for The Onion Router, and offenders in each country use The Onion Router to transmit obscenity and child pornography (Maley, 2012). Australian and Canadian authorities have worked closely with U.S. and foreign authorities to bring down networks and share evidence.

Project Spade started in Canada with a sting of a massive website offering child pornography (Levy, 2013). The sting, which lasted three years, was the largest ever in Canada. In Canada, 108 offenders were arrested, 76 American offenders were arrested, and 164 offenders in Spain, Mexico, South Africa, and other countries were arrested. Law enforcement in 30 nations, including Ireland, China, Greece, and Norway, rescued 386 sexually abused young children, including 6 Australian children. Worldwide, between 300 and 400 offenders were arrested for producing and trading 350,000 child abuse images and 9,000 videos. Offenders included 40 schoolteachers, 32 child services volunteers, 6 law enforcement employees, 9 medical workers, 9 clergy, and 3 foster parents. Sixty-five offenders were arrested in Australia even though child pornography is not criminalized in nearby nations, that is, Kiribati, Marshall Islands, Micronesia, Nauru, Palau, São Tomé and Príncipe, Solomon Islands, and Tuvalu (ICMEC, 2013; Arts Law Center of Australia, 2014). Despite lacking child pornography laws, these small nations play almost no part in international trafficking of child pornography.

The Australian government criminalizes all obscenity using a standard that is similar to *Regina v. Hicklin* (1868). Australian states also criminalize indecency, which seems to require higher moral standards than criminalization of obscenity. The Australian Film Commission, Screen Australia, is a federally funded agency created by the Screen Australia Act 2008 (Arts Law Center of Australia, 2014). Screen Australia was designed to replace the Film Finance Corporation Australia, the Australian Film Commission, and Film Australia Limited. Screen Australia does not classify obscenity. Unclassified films are contraband. Exhibiting and possessing unclassified films are crimes. Controversially, Screen Australia has refused to classify films that depict female ejaculation (Cusack, 2013). Screen Australia classifies films individually and does not outright ban depictions of female ejaculation; however, it will not classify offensive fetish films. Prurient interest in urine is an example of an offensive fetish. Critics, free speech advocates, and pornographers have argued that the government's conflation of urine with female ejaculation is sexist and impinges on lawful speech. Though at least one pornographer allegedly attempted to scientifically prove to the film board that female ejaculate differs from urine, depictions of squirting may continue to be unclassified in the future because films are reviewed on a case-by-case basis. The argument that female ejaculation is nonobscene has been made in the United States, and it was discussed in greater detail in Chapter 4. Australia's film classification board will not classify sexually violent films. In one case, *LA Zombie*, an unclassified Film, was shown at an underground screening in Australia (Zombie Porn, 2010). *LA Zombie* is a pornography film about zombies, which allegedly features depictions of sadomasochistic bondage. The film, directed by a Canadian, Bruce LaBruce, was screened by Richard Wolstencroft at his house. Wolstencroft's house was raided by Australian law enforcement. He was charged with "exhibiting and possessing an unclassified film."

Canadian obscenity standards are somewhat different than U.S. and Australian standards. Canada's interpretation of obscenity mainly relies on the Harm Principle (*R. v. Butler*, 1992). Films are analyzed according to the degree of harm that they pose. Obscenity includes explicit sexual films that are violent or use threats of violence. Pornography that is not violent but degrading or dehumanizes actors or poses a substantial risk of harm may be obscene. Artistic films are nonobscene; however, realistic gore movies have been alleged to corrupt morals and have been prosecuted (Detective at Obscenity Trial Testifies, 2012). Critics have called Canada's standards sexist because they tend to protect women. However, obscenity laws focus on harm to all participants, including male participants (e.g., bottoms, slaves, and submissives). U.S. obscenity laws focus on prurient interests and offense to the community. U.S. child pornography laws focus on harm caused to child victims (*New York v. Ferber*, 1982; *U.S. v. Williams*, 2008). In the United States, adult actors may pose as children, and these depictions may be distributed, as long as subjective and objective beliefs are not held that depictions are authentic child pornography (Cusack, 2011). In Canada, depictions of minors are classified as child pornography, irrespective of whether actors are adults (Canada Code 163.1(a)(i), 2014). However, it is an affirmative defense that the offense did "not pose an undue risk of harm" to minors (Canada Code 163(6)(b), 2014). Australians and Canadians prosecute synthetic pornography (i.e., obscene cartoons and Japanese manga).

Conclusion

Sex trafficking, production offenses, and pornography crimes are abundant on each continent. Technology has permitted members of foreign jurisdictions to share pornography and moral values. Cultural interpretations of morality and sexuality vary laws and enforcement. This complicates attempts to enforce U.S. laws, and it hinders institutionalization of predominant cultural attitudes (Cusack, 2014). Despite cultural and moral differences among nations, in recent years, a majority of nations have become aware of child pornography offenses, and they have attempted to intervene using law and police powers. Yet, some efforts have been limited. International and interagency collaboration has been insufficient to surmount international crime circuits. Policy and political conflicts sometimes impede investigations and prosecutions, and at other times, technology, secrecy, and online communities facilitate evasion.

References

10 U.S.C. § 920 Art. 120 (2013).

Anderson, N. (2013, August 18). Taking down "the largest child pornography conspiracy ever prosecuted." Ars Technica. Retrieved from http://arstechnica.com/tech-policy/2013/08/operation-joint-hammer-taking-down-the-largest-child-pornography-conspiracy-ever-prosecuted/

April, K. (2012). Cartoons aren't real people, too: Does the regulation of virtual child pornography violate the First Amendment and criminalize subversive thought? *Cardozo Journal of Law and Gender, 19*, 241–271.

Arts Law Center of Australia. (2014). Arts Law Information Sheet: Classification and Censorship. Retrieved from http://www.artslaw.com.au/info-sheets/info-sheet/classification-and-censorship/

British Library. (n.d.). Corrupters of public morals. Retrieved from http://www.bl.uk/learning/histcitizen/21cc/counterculture/undergroundpress/publicmorals/corrupters.html

Canada Code 163 (2014).

Coker v. Georgia, 433 U.S. 584 (1977).

Cusack, C. M. (2011). Busting patriarchal booby traps: Why feminists fear minor distinctions in child porn cases, an analysis of social deviance with in gender, family, or the home (etudes 4). *Southern University Law Review, 39*, 43–70.

Cusack, C. M. (2013). Obscene squirting: If the government thinks it's urine, then they've got another thing coming. *Texas Journal of Women and the Law, 22*, 45–69.

Cusack, C. M. (2014). In opposition of cultural institutionalization of speech following U.S. intervention into foreign governments. *Barry Law Review* (19)2 (in press Spring 2014).

Death sentence for printing porn. (1994, September 20). *Chicago Tribune*. Retrieved from http://articles.chicagotribune.com/1994-09-20/news/9409210199_1_sentenced-hebei-printing

Dehghan, S. K. (2012, January 18). Iran confirms death sentence for "porn site" web programmer. *The Guardian UK*. Retrieved from http://www.theguardian.com/world/2012/jan/18/iran-death-sentence-porn-programmer

Depsky, A. (2013, August 13). Thirty arrested in child pornography ring. *Argentina Independent*. Retrieved from http://www.argentinaindependent.com/currentaffairs/thirty-arrested-in-child-pornography-ring/

Detective at obscenity trial testifies gory images looked fake. (2012, December 11). *CBC News*. Retrieved from http://www.cbc.ca/news/canada/montreal/detective-at-obscenity-trial-testifies-gory-images-looked-fake-1.1164679

Gander, K. (2014, February 27). Uganda mini-skirt ban: Protests after women are assaulted and forced to undress in public. Retrieved from http://www.independent.co.uk/news/world/africa/uganda-miniskirt-ban-protests-after-women-are-assaulted-and-forced-to-undress-in-public-9155773.html

Goodroad, S. L. (1998). The challenge of free speech: *Asian Values v. Unfettered Free Speech*, an analysis of Singapore and Malaysia in the new global order. *Indiana International and Comparative Law Review, 9*, 259–318.

International Centre for Missing and Exploited Children. (2013, March 26). Despite increase in global child protection laws many countries still do not consider child pornography a crime. Retrieved from http://www.icmec.org/missingkids/servlet/NewsEventServlet?LanguageCountry=en_X1&PageId=4877

Jeffreys, S. (2009). *The industrial vagina: The political economy of the global sex trade*. New York: Routledge/Taylor & Francis Group.

Levy, M. (2013, November 15). 348 arrested in global child porn investigation. *The Sydney Morning Herald*. Retrieved from http://www.smh.com.au/national/348-arrested-in-global-child-porn-investigation-20131115-2xke5.html#ixzz2vsSdbmwq

Liu v. U.S., 231 Fed. Appx. 195 (2007).

Maley, P. (2012, May 22). Abusers run for "dark net" cover. *The Australian*. Retrieved from http://www.theaustralian.com.au/technology/abusers-run-for-dark-net-cover/story-e6frgakx-1226362847245#

McDonald, J. (2012, December 28). China real-name registration is now law in country. *Huffington Post*. Retrieved from http://www.huffingtonpost.com/2012/12/28/china-real-name-registration_n_2373808.html

McLaughlin, K. A. (2012). Securing the U.S. Mexico border: Case of child pornography. *Women Lawyers Journal*, *97*(1–2), 31–32.

Miller v. California, 413 U.S. 15 (1973).

New York v. Ferber, 458 U.S. 747 (1982).

Newton, P. (2011, June 2). Russia: Where keeping child porn is legal. CNN. Retrieved from http://www.cnn.com/2011/WORLD/europe/06/02/russia.child.porn/

PH among top 10 child porno producers—PNP. (2014, January 18). Yahoo! Retrieved from http://ph.news.yahoo.com/ph-among-top-10-child-porno-producers-pnp-191833212.html

Porn, sex trafficking, and Jacob's story. (2012, March 25). Pure Hope. Retrieved from http://purehope.net/porn-sex-trafficking-and-jacobs-story/

Porn websites among most visited in Islamic countries. (2012, November 14). *Huffington Post*. Retrieved from http://www.huffingtonpost.com/2012/11/14/porn-websites-among-most-viewed-islamic_n_2130317.html

Press Trust of India. (2013, June 27). Government orders ISPs to block 39 websites hosting obscene content. Gadgets: NDTV. Retrieved from http://gadgets.ndtv.com/internet/news/government-orders-isps-to-block-39-websites-hosting-obscene-content-384808

R. v. Butler, 1 S.C.R. 452 (1992).

Regina v. Hicklin, LR 3 QB 360 (1868).

Roth v. U.S., 354 U.S. 476 (1957).

Sex, drugs and beards: An afternoon in a Pakistani porn cinema. (2013, December 23). Channel 24. Retrieved from http://www.channel24.co.za/Movies/News/Sex-drugs-and-beards-an-afternoon-in-a-Pakistani-porn-cinema-20131223

The ten-year-old girl called "Sweetie" who has caught more than a thousand sexual predators including 110 Britons. (2013, November 4). *Daily Mail UK Online*. Retrieved from http://www.dailymail.co.uk/news/article-2487397/Terre-des-Hommes-creates-CGI-girl-called-Sweetie-entice-child-porn-predators.html#ixzz2rXQa6WKk

United States Sentencing Commission. (2012). Report to the Congress: Federal child pornography offenses. Retrieved from http://www.ussc.gov/Legislative_and_Public_Affairs/Congressional_Testimony_and_Reports/Sex_Offense_Topics/201212_Federal_Child_Pornography_Offenses/

U.S. State Department. (2013). Egypt 2013 human rights report. Retrieved from http://www.state.gov/documents/organization/220562.pdf

U.S. v. Williams, 553 U.S. 285 (2008).

Vincent, A. (2014, January 23). China's Internet rehabs highlighted by Web Junkie documentary. *The Telegraph UK*. Retrieved from http://www.telegraph.co.uk/culture/film/film-news/10591750/Chinas-internet-rehabs-highlighted-by-Web-Junkie-documentary.html

Wash. Rev. Code § 9A.88.085 (2013).

Xinhua. (2013, August 10). Brazil arrests 4 in bust against child pornography. *Global Times*. Retrieved from http://www.globaltimes.cn/content/802936.shtml#.Ux6e1j9dUwo

Zombie porn screening leads to police raid. (2010, November 12). *ABC News*. Retrieved from http://www.abc.net.au/news/2010-11-11/zombie-porn-screening-leads-to-police-raid/2333196

The Future 23

Overview

Contemporary understandings of pornography and use of the criminal justice system to regulate pornography relate to historical perspectives and policies. This was discussed in Chapter 3. Future understandings are likely to be relevant to historical and traditional understandings. Yet, technological advancements may challenge the criminal justice system in new ways. Sexting, online viewing of child pornography, and emerging thought-control technologies may require new analyses and responses from the criminal justice system. Traditional attitudes may continue to inform new policies and limit new technologies, but traditional attitudes may be reformed by new understandings. The criminal justice system may revise approaches to classifying offenders and offenses.

Sexting

Sexting is transmission of nude or seminude photos of minors voluntarily distributed by minors to romantic targets. Minors use cell phones to transmit photos through text messages. Depending on the depiction, sexts may fall under child pornography, harmful materials, and obscenity statutes. Sexting differs from solicitation offenses because recipients are often in the same age cohort as distributors. Proponents of sex-positive attitudes, discussed in Chapter 1, argue that teens should not be penalized for sharing and receiving depictions (Reddington & Kreisel, 2009). Critics of sexting laws argue that voluntary sexting should not be analogized to predatory behavior. Laws denying teens the right to consent to sex and sexting may idealize teens' sexual purity. The law should be shaped to address reality, as it develops over time, to best protect children. Childhood sexuality was discussed in Chapter 1 and Chapter 5.

Arguments in support of laws penalizing youth are that child pornography laws must require strict liability. Sext images may exist in perpetuity even after distributors and possessors are adults. Thus, adults may possess or distribute the depictions. Even though the subject of the photo ages with time, the subject depicted in the photo does not. The depiction of child pornography is preserved. Children who sext may not attempt to produce child pornography, but their images may always serve as child pornography. Sexted images have been collected by pornographers and exhibited as child pornography (Fields, 2014).

The government acknowledges the difference between production offenses and "youth-only experimental" pornography production (United States Sentencing Commission [USSC], 2012). Even though teens have heard that the government prosecutes children, USSC reports that children are not regularly prosecuted in relation to sexting offenses (USSC, 2012). Offenses do not typically come to the attention of law enforcement, and when they do, police rarely arrest teens for sexting offenses. In 2010, no minors were sentenced for "youth-only experimental" pornography offenses. There is no reason to believe that the criminal justice system will take an increasingly prosecutorial position against child sexting. For example, in Florida, sexting is prohibited by statute (Fla. Stat. § 847.0141, 2012). Minors are forbidden from transmitting to other minors any nude depiction that constitutes material harmful to minors. Mere possession is criminal, but not if the minor (1) did not solicit the photos, (2) reported the transmission to guardians or school authorities, and (3) did not forward the depiction. Multiple transmissions qualify as a single offense if they are transmitted within the same 24-hour period. Florida does not criminalize the first violation. Thus, two images sent more than 24 hours apart would result in criminal charges. For the first offense, the state requires eight hours of community service, participation in a suitable training course, or payment of a $60 fine. A subsequent offense is treated as a first-degree misdemeanor. After a minor has been found to commit a prior misdemeanor offense, a third offense is a third-degree felony. Minors may be additionally charged with transmitting obscenity or with lewd and lascivious exhibition if sexts depict sadomasochism, bestiality, masturbation, or other similar acts (Fla. Stat. § 847.0135, 2012). Florida's treatment of sexting rehabilitates first-time offenders rather than punishes them. However, Florida punishes obscenity distribution and recidivism among teens in a fashion that prepares them for entrance into adult citizenship.

Sexting does not seem to be as widespread among teens as it may be among adults. About half of teens engage in sex, and many sext teens (Hilinski-Rosick & Freiburger, 2012). In a study of nearly 1,000 college students, who averaged about 19 years old, approximately one-third had sent nude photos of themselves using text messaging. Two-thirds of respondents were aware that minors had been arrested for sexting. Almost half of those students who had sexted sent multiple photos. Fewer than 10% of students forwarded other teens' private photos to a third party. More than half of students disclosed receiving nude images from other teens. Younger students were more likely to send and forward sext messages. Age was not associated with receiving sext messages, but male gender was associated with receiving sext messages.

Another U.S. study about sexting surveyed 1,560 minors between the ages of 10 and 17 years (Mitchell, Finkelhor, Jones, & Wolak, 2012). That study found that only 2.5% of youth admitted to being the subjects of self-produced pornography, and only 1% appeared in or produced explicit depictions. Fewer than 10% reported receiving nude depictions. These researchers concluded that sexting is not normative behavior. Their findings were low compared to Hilinski-Rosick and Freiburger's (2012) findings. Perhaps this is because children who were called on the phone in Mitchell et al.'s (2012) study feared that their parents would discover their answers; however, students who were surveyed in their college classrooms felt greater confidence to self-report. The first study surveyed adults, whereas the second study included young teens and some prepubescent children. The second study is relevant to child pornography policy because USSC reported that according to 51% of experts, child pornography mostly involves prepubescent children, and 67% reported that victims are younger now than in past years (USSC, 2012). The first study is relevant because more than 80% of experts reported than child pornographers victimize children of all ages. Criminal justice responses may consider minors' ages or other facts to develop future policies.

Diagnostic and Statistical Manual of Mental Disorders

In the near future, definitions and treatment of pedophilia may be revised. Three proposed changes have received some attention: (1) pedophilia that results in harm to children may be differentiated from persistent sexual attraction to children; (2) pedophilia may be defined situationally rather than strictly; and (3) hebephilia may be further distinguished from pedophilic disorder.

It is estimated that half of child pornography offenders are pedophiles (USSC, 2012). Estimates show that only around 10% of pedophiles are exclusively interested sexually in children. Most pedophiles and child pornography offenders are married or engage in sexual activity with adults. Some offenders who experience sexual attraction to child victims of pornography experience no sexual attraction to children who are not depicted in pornography. Many child pornography offenders may not presently meet clinical definitions for having a paraphilic disorder. Some child pornography offenders are curious, deviant, antisocial, or interested in belonging to online communities. However, child pornography recipients and distributors are significantly more likely than producers to be sexually interested in children. Producers often commit hands-on offenses for compensation.

The American Psychiatric Association's (APA's) *Diagnostic and Statistical Manual of Mental Disorders* (*DSM*) is a clinical manual used by mental health professionals to define, evaluate, diagnose, and treat mental disorders. The fifth revision, *DSM-V* (APA, 2013a), is now in print. In the *DSM-V*, pedophilic disorder may be diagnosed if (1) over a six-month period, a person, who is 16 years old, experiences recurrent and intense sexual arousal, fantasies, or behaviors involving a child; (2) the person acted on the urges with a child, or the fantasies caused interpersonal difficulty or personal distress; and (3) objects of the person's fantasies are children younger than 13 years or are prepubescent. The *DSM-V* specifies diagnoses between sexual attraction to males, females, or both; incest and nonrelatives; and exclusive or nonexclusive attraction to children. Other than including damage to interpersonal relationships in the *DSM-V*, the diagnosis criteria for pedophilic paraphilic disorder remained relatively constant between *DSM-IV* and *DSM-V*.

USSC reports that pedophilia is defined by persistent sexual interest in sexually immature victims (USSC, 2012). This definition highlights the problematic nature of pedophilia. Some deviants may not have persistent sexual interest in children, which could mean that their attraction is not problematic. Persistent attraction is defined by USSC to include "thoughts, fantasies, urges, sexual arousal, or behavior" (USSC, 2012). This definition seems to be unspecific insofar as it provides no quantitative guidelines, for example, many thoughts or frequent fantasies during a six-month period.

In forensic contexts, APA's definition of *pedophilia* is like bootstrapping. In the *DSM-V*, pedophilia is classified with transvestism, sadomasochism, frotteurism, and voyeurism (APA, 2013b). The link between these disorders is that a person who suffers from a disorder finds his or her interests to be problematic or the disorder harms others. For pedophilia, harm to others is defined as "desire for sexual behaviors involving unwilling persons or persons unable to give legal consent" (APA, 2013b). In some cases, children may be willing, but unable legally, to give consent. Thus, the only reason that pedophilia is identified as a paraphilia may be because of legal standards. This criterion makes diagnosis of pedophilia similar to definitions of statutory rape. In this situation, the psychological field may seem to exclusively rely on legal definitions to diagnose pedophilic disorder. These issues likely will continue to be at the forefront of APA discussions and continue spurring criticism of the criminal justice system.

Psychiatric diagnosis, sentencing, and treatment for child pornography addiction are impacted by the *DSM-V* (McManus, Hargreaves, Rainbow, & Alison, 2013). The APA's criteria exclude ongoing relationships between minors unless one is 5 years older than the other child. Thus, older teens who date younger teens are not diagnosed as pedophiles. *DSM-V* criteria exclude hebephilia. Hebephilia, that is, sexual interest in sexually mature minors, is not diagnosed as a mental disorder under pedophilia. However, teen pornography is unprotected speech. Some critics fear that the APA may add hebephilia to the *DSM-V* to respond to criminal justice-oriented needs, not mental illness concerns. The government's definition or description of pedophilia may be used in contexts that include or exclude hebephilia. Some sex abuse laws often differentiate between child victims and teen victims, but some laws do not distinguish between groups. For example, some jurisdictions differently classify children 12 years old or younger with prepubescent children, but other jurisdictions do not differentiate children based on sexual maturity. Some jurisdictions may heighten punishments for abuse of younger children, but other jurisdictions do not.

The *DSM-V* classifies pedophilia as a paraphilic disorder and discusses it as a sexual interest. Hebephilia is not included in pedophilia. This may have some bearing on how society will view the use of synthetic child pornography in the future. The government does not prosecute simple possession of synthetic pornography, but critics are skeptical that it relates to exploitation of minors. In general, critics and scholars have argued two points of view about the use of synthetic pornography. The first point of view is that synthetic pornography can soothe desires for actual child pornography. The contrary point of view is that synthetic pornography fuels the desire for actual pornography and, possibly, hands-on offenses. Labeling pedophilia and hebephilia as a paraphilia may support the idea that use of synthetic pornography may impede treatment. However, viewing pedophilia and hebephilia as sexual interests, but not mental disorders per se, could suggest that in some situations the use of synthetic pornography may be reasonable. If attraction to minors is nonthreatening and nonharmful, then perhaps use of synthetic child pornography may serve a legitimate social purpose. Synthetic pornography was discussed further in Chapter 16.

Child Pornography: Online Viewing

Courts have carefully distinguished and analogized cases to decide whether viewing child pornography online is legal. There is no specified speech right or privacy right to search for child pornography or to view child pornography. Jurisdictions have varied and vacillated on whether viewing depictions online amounts to knowing possession and transmission. *Mens rea* and the *actus reus* elements of the crimes of transmitting or possessing may be disputed if images are only viewed online. A few courts have held that statutes that prohibit transmission and possession apply to viewing images online. Yet, the government must prove knowing possession or transmission. Direct and circumstantial evidence must prove beyond a reasonable doubt that pornography was knowingly possessed or transmitted. Thus, the meaning of "knowing possession" and "knowing transmission," and the evidence required for the government to carry its burden, is not uniformly settled law (*U.S. v. Kuchinski*, 2006).

Currently, viewing child pornography online is likely to be illegal when temporary Internet files of child pornography are cached (*U.S. v. Cray*, 2012). Some courts have held that if offenders enlarge thumbnail images on websites, and images automatically download into offender's computer caches, then offenders have sufficiently exercised control over the images to satisfy statutes requiring possession (*U.S. v. Carpegna*, 2013; *U.S. v. Flyer*, 2011; *U.S. v. Romm*, 2006). When offenders click on images online, they could, at that point, print or save the images. Furthermore, images that are automatically stored in caches as temporary Internet files could be printed, saved, or deleted from that location. This level of control may be sufficient. Contingencies and possibilities, for example, the defendant could have saved the images, may be insufficient in some courts. If a defendant clears a cache after viewing child pornography, then the act could be used as circumstantial evidence that a defendant knew that child pornography was in the cache even though clearing a cache may be a common activity (*U.S. v. Cnockaert*, 2013). Courts may find that deleting temporary Internet files may sufficiently exercise control and dominion over files.

If defendants know that images are cached on their computers, then even if defendants do not actively download images, they may exercise sufficient control over the images and possess the requisite intent to be guilty (*U.S. v. Johnson*, 2013). If defendants do not know that images were downloaded in temporary folders or images are not downloaded, then some courts may not find that defendants knowingly possessed or transmitted images (*U.S. v. Johnson*, 2013). When files are in unallocated spaces on defendants' computers, and files cannot be accessed without forensic expertise, then defendants may successfully claim that they had no knowledge of the files, and circumstantial evidence may not be able to overcome a reasonable doubt that defendants did not view, possess, or transmit child pornography. Yet, if Internet histories reveal that defendants visited sites known to distribute child pornography, then the state may meet its evidentiary burden using circumstantial evidence (*U.S. v. Johnson*, 2011). However, if caches do not possess the images, then possession or transmission of particular images cannot be established (*U.S. v. Dobbs*, 2011). Evidence that files were deleted may serve as circumstantial evidence, but alone cannot sustain a conviction (*U.S. v. Carpegna*, 2013). In some jurisdictions, the state may not need to prove that every file in the cache was viewed (*U.S. v. Cnockaert*, 2013). Yet, without any depictions present on the offenders' computer, the act of the crime may not be proved.

Courts have held that only viewing images online does not exercise sufficient control if images cannot be manipulated (*U.S. v. Navrestad*, 2008). In *People v. Kent* (2010), the appellate court held that viewing pornography online did not constitute knowing possession if cached files were not knowingly downloaded. In response to *Kent*'s possible legalization of viewing child pornography online, the state of New York passed a bill to criminalize intentional viewing or accessing of child pornography online (NY B. § 7742, 2012). Purposefully accessing child pornography websites is statutorily classified as a Class E felony in New York.

Georgia v. Stanley: A Brave New World

In the future, devices might allow mind-to-mind transmission of thoughts or cognitive impulses. Would these kinds of transmissions constitute speech? If so, then would distribution of obscene thoughts be regulated, blocked, or criminalized? Would transmissions receive free speech protection? First Amendment protections presently do not reach thoughts and mental fantasies because thoughts and mental fantasies are not speech. They cannot be criminalized, and they need not be analyzed under First Amendment jurisprudence. Enjoyment of fantasies in private using obscenity is protected under *Stanley v. Georgia* (1969), which analyzes private possession of pornography under privacy rights and substantive due process. In that case, the Court discussed possession of obscenity in one's home. The legal issue was simple possession, not regulation of fantasy. If obscene thoughts could be transmitted, then perhaps regulation of mental fantasies would become an issue. Obscene utterances are not protected, even though they have no material substance. Utterances can be analogized to transmitted mental fantasies. Perhaps transmission software should be designed to censor obscene thought transmission. If use of blocking software could not be required, then the government may need to devise another way to constitutionally enforce thought control to protect the community from unsolicited transmission of obscenity.

A world in which technology blurs public and private fantasies may have come one step closer with the invention of Google Glass. Wearable eyeglasses created by Google, called Google Glass, permit users to view pornography without bystanders possibly viewing the material (Abram, 2014). An "x-ray" app could be designed to simulate nudity. Members of the public could be depicted and viewed by Google Glass wearers. Google Glass also can be used to produce point-of-view pornography. Mikandi.com created an application (app) for Google Glass that facilitates viewing pornography in public. The app was demonstrated at a pornography convention even though it violates Google's policy prohibiting depictions of nudity or explicit sexual material on glassware. Consumer demand is anticipated by the industry, but many are skeptical about the practicality of viewing pornography in public. For example, in many jurisdictions, men may be prosecuted for appearing publically in a turgid state of arousal. Evidence recorded by Google showing that pornography was viewed while the wearer was in public could lead to prosecution under a variety of statutes, like corruption of minors, obscenity, and lewdness. If more people continue to view erotic materials in public, then laws may be adopted to address that in the future.

Conclusion

Deviant sexuality has become more mainstream and tolerated in recent years; simultaneously, legal protection for children has reached a fever pitch in comparison to past centuries. Tensions will likely continue to rise between these two social progressions as deviants test legal boundaries and authorities persecute exploitative industries. Future technology will likely be capable of better protecting children while reinventing and better managing deviant speech. Distinct, yet synergistic, uses of technology may satisfy potential conflicts in the future. However, technology could potentially eradicate privacy to an extent that compromises some constitutional protections for viewing pornography, guarantees to be free from invasions of privacy, or implied rights to be free from exposure to pornography.

References

Abram, S. (2014, January 25). Google Glass may be the future of the porn industry. *Los Angeles Daily News.* Retrieved from http://www.huffingtonpost.com/2014/01/25/google-glass-porn_n_4662944.html?ref=topbar

American Psychiatric Association. (2013a). *Diagnostic and statistical manual of mental disorders* (5th ed.). Arlington, VA: American Psychiatric Publishing.

American Psychiatric Association. (2013b). Paraphilic disorders. Retrieved from http://www.dsm5.org/Documents/Paraphilic%20Disorders%20Fact%20Sheet.pdf

Fields, L. (2014, April 5). Police bust Virginia sexting ring involving more than 100 teens. *ABC News.* Retrieved from http://abcnews.go.com/US/police-bust-virginia-sexting-ring-involving-100-teens/story?id=23208357

Fla. Stat. § 847.0135 (2012).

Fla. Stat. § 847.0141 (2012).

Hilinski-Rosick, M. C., & Freiburger, T. L. (2012). An exploratory analysis of the prevalence of teen sexting. *Journal of Law and Social Deviance, 4,* 120–149.

McManus, M. A., Hargreaves, P., Rainbow, L., & Alison, L. J. (2013, September 2). Paraphilias: Definition, diagnosis and treatment. U.S. National Library of Medicine: National Institutes of Health. Retrieved from http://www.ncbi.nlm.nih.gov/pmc/articles/PMC3769077/

Mitchell, K. J., Finkelhor, D., Jones, L. M., & Wolak, J. (2012). Prevalence and characteristics of youth sexting: A national study. *Pediatrics, 129*(1), 13–20.

NY B. § 7742 (2012).

People v. Kent, 910 N.Y.S.2d 78 (2d Dep't 2010).

Reddington, F. P., & Kreisel, B. W. (Eds.). (2009). *Sexual assault.* Durham, NC: Carolina Academic Press.

Stanley v. Georgia, 394 U.S. 557 (1969).

United States Sentencing Commission. (2012). Report to the Congress: Federal child pornography offenses. Retrieved from http://www.ussc.gov/Legislative_and_Public_Affairs/Congressional_Testimony_and_Reports/Sex_Offense_Topics/201212_Federal_Child_Pornography_Offenses/

U.S. v. Carpegna, U.S. Dist. LEXIS 115002 (2013).

U.S. v. Cnockaert, U.S. Dist. LEXIS 11290 (2013).

U.S. v. Cray, 450 Fed. Appx. 923 (2012).

U.S. v. Dobbs, No. 09-5025 (10th Jan. 5, 2011).

U.S. v. Flyer, 633 F.3d 911 (9th Cir. 2011).

U.S. v. Johnson, 523 Fed. Appx. 219 (2013).

U.S. v. Johnson, 652 F.3d 918 (2011).

U.S. v. Kuchinski, 469 F.3d 853, 863 (9th Cir. 2006).

U.S. v. Navrestad, 66 M.J. 262 (C.A.A.F. 2008).

U.S. v. Romm, 455 F.3d 990 (9th Cir. 2006).

Index

D

I

J

K

L

For Product Safety Concerns and Information please contact our EU representative GPSR@taylorandfrancis.com
Taylor & Francis Verlag GmbH, Kaufingerstraße 24, 80331 München, Germany

www.ingramcontent.com/pod-product-compliance
Lightning Source LLC
LaVergne TN
LVHW011118300926
849160LV00008B/428
9781482260014